# The American Frontier

## Inquiries into American History

*Our Colonial Heritage: Plymouth and Jamestown*
by William Gee White

*The Middle Colonies: New York, New Jersey, Pennsylvania*
by James I. Clark

*The American Revolution*
by D. Duane Cummins and William Gee White

*The Federal Period: 1790–1800*
by Lloyd K. Musselman

*Andrew Jackson's America*
by Thomas Koberna and Stanley Garfinkel

*The American Frontier*
by D. Duane Cummins and William Gee White

*The Origins of the Civil War*
by D. Duane Cummins and William Gee White

*Reconstruction: 1865–1877*
by James I. Clark

*Industrialism: The American Experience*
by James E. Bruner, Jr.

*American Foreign Policy: 1789–1980*
by Thomas A. Fitzgerald, Jr.

*Contrasting Decades: The 1920's and 1930's*
by D. Duane Cummins and William Gee White

*Combat and Consensus: The 1940's and 1950's*
by D. Duane Cummins and William Gee White

*Conflict and Compromise: The 1960's and 1970's*
by D. Duane Cummins


*America at War: World War I and World War II*
by Douglas Waitley

*America at War: Korea and Vietnam*
by Douglas Waitley

*Women in American History*
by William Jay Jacobs

# The
# American Frontier

**D. Duane Cummins**
**William Gee White**

Glencoe Publishing Co., Inc.
Encino, California

REVISED EDITION

Copyright © 1980 by Glencoe Publishing Co., Inc.
Copyright © 1972 by Benziger, Inc.
Copyright © 1968 by Benziger Brothers, Inc.

Glencoe Publishing Co., Inc.
17337 Ventura Boulevard
Encino, California 91316

Collier Macmillan Canada, Ltd.

Library of Congress Catalog Card Number: 68–14972

Printed in the United States of America

ISBN 0-02-652700-6

1 2 3 4 5   82 81 80 79

Sincere appreciation to
B. B Beard,
whose love and affection
for the "Old West" have
been a constant inspiration.

# CONTENTS

For many thousands of Americans in the nineteenth century, the wagon wheel symbolized a way to a new beginning, a better life. For us today, the wagon wheel serves as a symbol of those pioneers and of the courage that sustained them on their way west.

# INTRODUCTION

The word *frontier* means, among other things, a place or region that is in the process of being settled. But in American English, the word *frontier* has a very special flavor. It is not a neutral word like "place" or "region." And it is not a negative word, calling up disagreeable images of poverty, exploitation, ignorance, brutality, or greed. Instead, *frontier* is a word that has very strong *positive* connotations—wide-open spaces, adventure, bravery, excitement, true grit, the taming of a wilderness, the passage from the known to the unknown, the shaping of a new and better way of life.

That most Americans should have such warm and positive feelings about the frontier is, in one sense, rather puzzling. In the early 1800's, for example, many educated easterners would have wrinkled their noses in distaste at the very mention of "the frontier." The frontier, in their view and experience, was a sort of vast rural slum attracting the worst elements of society—the shiftless, the foreign-born, the poor, the criminal, and all the rest who had neither the wits nor the means to lead cultivated or even decent lives. Such a view was of course snobbish, but it was also based at least partly on fact. How, in the next hundred and fifty years, such a viewpoint was almost completely supplanted by an idea of the frontier as a place where the best qualities of the American nation expressed themselves in a distinctive or even quintessential form, is one of the most interesting questions in American history.

It is interesting too that by *the* frontier most Americans mean the Great West in the last half of the nineteenth century—specifically, the West in which lonesome cowboys rode herd over great drives of longhorn steers, the blue-coated cavalry charged a swarm of whooping, war-bonneted Indians, the honest sheriff strode into the street to face down the hired gunslinger, and masked bandits dashed, guns ablaze, out of the local bank.

But there were many frontiers. For almost two hundred years, the *East* was the frontier—Massachusetts, Virginia, Vermont, Georgia, Pennsylvania, Tennessee, Kentucky. In the early nineteenth century, "the West" was Ohio, Indiana, Missouri, Illinois, Michigan—the eastern portion of the area we now call "the Midwest."

Furthermore, any frontier must by definition be thinly settled—must be defined as a portion of land that contains only a small, exploratory fraction of the total population. In addition, each region qualifying as a frontier is usually explored and then used by different groups of people for different purposes at different times—the trappers looking for pelts, the miners looking for gold, the cattlemen looking for rangeland, the farmers looking for tillable acreage.

How then did the popular notion of *the* frontier as a particular place in a particular historical time come about? Since the frontier experience had to be one shared by a relatively small proportion of the total population, how did the notion arise that this experience was the most typically *American* of all, an experience that shaped or otherwise profoundly influenced the formation of the national character? And to what extent *was* the frontier a stage or setting for much that is praiseworthy in men and women—for courage, endurance, ingenuity of thought, and strength of will? These are some of the questions that this book will seek to raise and explore.

# THE FRONTIER

# HYPOTHESIS

Frederick Jackson Turner is regarded as one of America's greatest and most influential historians. Writing during the last decade of the nineteenth century and the early years of the twentieth century, this historian from Wisconsin developed and advanced a new interpretation of American history which has become known as the "frontier hypothesis" or the Turner thesis. Turner has ceased to be the *last* word in frontier history, but it is most appropriate that he have the *first* word in a study concerned with the western experience.

The world of the youthful Turner was a frontier world. He was born during the early months of the Civil War, on November 14, 1861, in Portage, Wisconsin—a small frontier community. Turner commented on his birthplace in a lecture to the students of the Harvard History Club in 1923:

> My birthplace was at the portage where Father Marquette crossed from the Fox [River] to the Wisconsin [River] on his journey down the Mississippi, and which was the highway of many another explorer, but I am forced to admit that this made no impression upon my mind.[1]

[1]Frederick Jackson Turner, *Frederick Jackson Turner's Legacy: Unpublished Writings in American History,* edited by Wilbur Jacobs (San Marino, Calif.: Huntington Library, 1965), pp. 4–5.

The wilderness scene on the opposite page was painted by a German immigrant, Paul Weber, in 1858.

13

Turner was impressed, however, with the variety of cultural elements in the town of Portage. He described the village as a "frontier melting-pot" where one frequently encountered Winnebago Indians as well as a wide range of European immigrants including German merchants, Scottish farmers, Irish raftsmen of the river, and numerous Norwegian, English, and Swiss settlers. The curious thing to Turner was the manner in which these people of divergent cultural and national backgrounds were capable of merging together into a single community.

The historian's father, Andrew Jackson Turner, had migrated from Plattsburg, New York, to Portage, where he became a journalist, Republican politician, and local historian. A. J. Turner was warmly admired by his son and had a strong influence on the boy, to whom he always commended the virtues of initiative, self-reliance, and hard work. Fritz, as young Turner was called, was given the best education the state had to offer, yet he stated in later years that his real education had come from his father's newspaper office, where he had worked as a typesetter. There he gained a firsthand knowledge of life in Portage and especially of frontier politics.

Turner received his B.A. degree from the University of Wisconsin in 1884, and for a brief time he was employed as a reporter on Chicago and Milwaukee newspapers. Dissatisfied with this work, Turner decided to return to the university and prepare for a career as an historian. He completed the requirements for his M.A. degree in 1888 and immediately enrolled at Johns Hopkins University for his doctoral work. In 1890, he was awarded the Ph.D. degree for his dissertation, "The Character and Influence of the Indian Trade in Wisconsin."

It was during these years of work on his advanced degrees that Turner came into contact with the influences that contributed so heavily to the development of his views of history. At the University of Wisconsin he was fortunate in having the opportunity to study with some remarkable professors, such as the renowned historian William F. Allen. Professor Allen was teaching the new and radical view that society was an evolving organism—an idea which had an unusually strong impact on Turner and became the foundation of his later historical concepts regarding the American frontier.

While Turner was pursuing his studies at Johns Hopkins, his concepts were further molded by the teachings of Woodrow Wilson, a political scientist, by Richard Ely, an economist, and by his principal instructor, Herbert Adams. Professor Adams, a confirmed believer in the "germ theory" of history, contended that the origins of democratic institutions in America could be traced all the way back to "germs" in medieval Europe. Turner found himself nourishing a negative attitude toward this concept. He did not deny the germ theory, but he believed that equal emphasis had to be given to environmental forces which not only altered the original germs, but oftentimes produced mutations. Many years later, Turner remarked of Adams' teaching, "The frontier [thesis] was pretty much a *reaction* from that due to my indignation."[2]

It was during his early years as an instructor at the University of Wisconsin that Turner gave expression to his famous frontier hypothesis. In the summer of 1893, he was invited to present a paper at a special meeting of the American Historical Association held at the World's Columbian Exposition in Chicago. In "The Significance of the Frontier in American History," Turner presented a fresh approach to the understanding of American history. At first the essay attracted very little attention, but time soon brought recognition, and eventually it became a landmark in American historical writing.

In his essay, Turner held that the imported institutions of the United States and the inherited traits of its people had been altered by three hundred years of frontier experience, an experience that was coming to an end in the 1890's. As a result of this experience, he suggested, Americans were more mobile, more materialistic, and more inventive than their European forbears. Democracy, individ-

Frederick Jackson Turner in 1906.

[2]Frederick Jackson Turner, *Frontier and Section: Selected Essays of Frederick Jackson Turner*, edited by Ray Allen Billington (Englewood Cliffs, N.J.: Prentice-Hall, 1961), p. 3. © 1961. By permission of Prentice-Hall, Inc., Englewood Cliffs, New Jersey.

ualism, and nationalism were all strengthened by the frontier. But the most accurate way to explain the frontier thesis is to allow Turner to speak for himself. The following quotations are selected from his famous 1893 essay.

### [Definition of the Frontier]

Up to our own day American history has been in a large degree the history of the colonization of the Great West. The existence of an area of free land, its continuous recession, and the advance of American settlement westward, explain American development. . . . The peculiarity of American institutions is, the fact that they have been compelled to adapt themselves to the changes of an expanding people—to the changes involved in crossing a continent, in winning a wilderness. . . . American development has exhibited not merely advance along a single line, but a return to primitive conditions on a continually advancing frontier line, and a new development for that area. American social development has been continually beginning over again on the frontier. . . . In this advance, the frontier is the outer edge of the wave—the meeting point between savagery and civilization. The most significant thing about the American frontier is, that it lies at the hither edge of free land. In the census reports it is treated as the margin of that settlement which has a density of two or more to the square mile. The term is an elastic one, and for our purpose does not need sharp definition. . . . This paper will make no attempt to treat the subject exhaustively; its aim is simply to call attention to the frontier as a fertile field for investigation, and to suggest some of the problems which arise in connection with it. . . .

### [The Power of the American Environment]

In the settlement of America we have to observe how European life entered the continent, and how America modified and developed that life and reacted on Europe. Our early history is the study of European germs developing in an American environment. . . . The wilderness masters the colonist. It finds him a European in dress, industries, tools, modes of travel, and thought. It

A prosperous frontier town in Wisconsin, drawn in 1857.

takes him from the railroad car and puts him in the birch
canoe. It strips off the garments of civilization and arrays
him in the hunting shirt and the moccasin. It puts him in
the log cabin. . . . Before long he has gone to planting
Indian corn and plowing with a sharp stick. . . . In short, at
the frontier the environment is at first too strong for the
man. He must accept the conditions which it furnishes, or
perish, and so . . . little by little he transforms the
wilderness, but the outcome is not the old Europe. . . . The
fact is, that here is a new product that is American . . .
Moving westward, the frontier became more and more
American. . . . Thus the advance of the frontier has meant
a steady movement away from the influence of Europe. . . .
And to study this advance, the men who grew up under
these conditions, and the political, economic, and social
results of it, is to study the really American part of our
history. . . .

### [The Successive Frontier Waves]

The Atlantic frontier was compounded of fisherman,
fur-trader, miner, cattle-raiser, and farmer. Excepting the
fisherman, each type of industry was on the march toward
the West. . . . Each passed in successive waves across the

continent. Stand at Cumberland Gap and watch the procession of civilization, marching single file—the buffalo following the trail to the salt springs, the Indian, the fur-trader and hunter, the cattle-raiser, the pioneer farmer—and the frontier passed by. Stand at South Pass in the Rockies a century later and see the same procession with wider intervals between. The unequal rate of advance compels us to distinguish the frontier into the trader's frontier, the rancher's frontier, or the miner's frontier, and the farmer's frontier. When the mines and the cow pens were still near the fall line [the eastern foothills of the Appalachians] the traders' pack trains were trickling across the Alleghenies. . . . When the trappers scaled the Rockies, the farmer was still near the mouth of the Missouri.

[Effects of the Frontier on American Government]

First, we note that the frontier promoted the formation of a composite nationality for the American people. . . . In another way the advance of the frontier decreased our dependence on England. . . . The legislation which most developed the powers of the national government, and played the largest part in its activity, was conditioned on the frontier. . . . The growth of nationalism and the evolution of American political institutions were dependent on the advance of the frontier. . . . The pioneer needed goods of the coast, and so the grand series of internal improvement and railroad legislation began, with potent nationalizing effects. . . . Loose construction [liberal interpretation of the Constitution] increased as the nation marched westward. . . . The purchase of Louisiana was perhaps the constitutional turning point in the history of the Republic, inasmuch as it afforded both a new area for national legislation and the occasion of the downfall of the policy of strict construction. But the purchase of Louisiana was called out by frontier needs and demands. As frontier states accrued to the Union the national power grew. . . . In 1789 the States were the creators of the Federal Government; in 1861 the Federal Government was the creator of a large majority of the States. . . . The most important effect of the frontier has been in the promotion of democracy. . . . The frontier is productive of individualism. Complex society is [diluted] by the wilderness into a kind of primitive organization based on the family. . . .

[Effects of the Frontier on American Character]

From the conditions of frontier life came intellectual traits of profound importance. . . . That coarseness and strength combined with acuteness and inquisitiveness; that practical, inventive turn of mind, quick to find expedients; that masterful grasp of material things, lacking in the artistic but powerful to effect great ends; that restless, nervous energy; that dominant individualism, working for good and for evil, and withal that bouyancy and exuberance which comes with freedom—those are traits of the frontier, or traits called out elsewhere because of the existence of the frontier. . . . The people of the United States have taken their tone from the incessant expansion. . . . The stubborn American environment is there with its imperious summons to accept its conditions; the inherited ways of doing things are also there; and yet, in spite of environment, and in spite of custom, each frontier did indeed furnish a new field of opportunity, a gate of escape from the bondage of the past; and freshness, and confidence, and scorn of older society, impatience of its restraints and its ideas, and indifference to its lessons, have accompanied the frontier.

[Conclusion]

And now, four centuries from the discovery of America, at the end of a hundred years of life under the Constitution, the frontier has gone, and with its going has closed the first period of American history.[3]

Although he was only thirty-two years old and had just begun his teaching career, Frederick Jackson Turner presented a thesis which revolutionized social studies and became one of the most widely known essays in American history. During the three decades following the delivery of his address, the entire framework of American historical writing and teaching was altered. For a whole generation

[3]Ibid., pp. 37–62.

American historians studied the development of the United States in relationship to the frontier process.

The new urban-industrial society of the 1890's had already reached the stage of nostalgia for a vanished frontier, and its myths were treasured as a national heritage. The dime novel with a western theme had created an exciting stereotype of the West. Consequently, Turner's essay captured the imagination of the reading public as well as the attention of professional historians.

To the theme of his early address, "The Significance of the Frontier in American History," Turner referred again and again in his later writings and speeches. On each of these occasions, Turner either clarified or expanded his original thesis. In 1896, for example, he added a new dimension to the thesis by describing the frontier as a "safety valve":

> Americans had a safety valve for social danger, a bank account on which they might continually draw to meet losses. This was the vast unoccupied domain that stretched from the borders of the settled area to the Pacific Ocean. . . . No grave social problem could exist while the wilderness at the edge of civilizations opened wide its portals to all who were oppressed. . . .

Another of Turner's major arguments regarding the frontier was that it developed a distinctive style of American democracy. He expressed this argument very clearly in an address given at the University of Washington in 1914:

> American democracy was born of no theorist's dream; it was not carried in the *Susan Constant* to Virginia, nor in the *Mayflower* to Plymouth. It came out of the American forest, and it gained new strength each time it touched a new frontier. Not the Constitution, but free land and an abundance of natural resources open to a fit people, made the democratic type of society in America for three centuries. . . .[4]

---

[4] Ibid., pp. 100–101.

Even after his retirement, Turner continued to elaborate on the subject of his thesis. In a letter to a friend during the late 1920's, he wrote:

As you know, the "West" with which I dealt, was a *process* rather than a fixed geographical region: it emphasized the way in which the East colonized the West, and how the "West," as it stood at any given period affected the development and ideas of the older areas to the East. . . .[5]

As the years passed, Turner became aware that he was being increasingly identified as the "western" or "frontier" historian. He disliked being labeled because he felt this oversimplified and distorted his true concepts. Never did Turner claim that his frontier theory was the only key to the interpretation of American history. On the contrary, he repeatedly emphasized the notion of multiple causation in history. To Turner, there was no single key or simple explanation of human behavior—not in terms of economics, politics, sociology, or even the frontier. All were interwoven as motivating forces and each force had to be thoroughly investigated and its interrelationship with all other forces exactly understood. While writing to a former student, Carl Becker, in 1925, Turner pointed out how his treatment of the frontier had been misinterpreted:

Although my work has laid stress upon two aspects of American history—the frontier and the sections—I do not think of myself as primarily a western historian. . . . I have stressed these two factors, because it seemed to me that they had been neglected, but fundamentally I have been interested in the interrelations of economics, politics, sociology, culture in general, with the geographic factors, in explaining the United States of today by means of its history thus broadly taken.[6]

Earlier, in 1922, while introducing a lecture on section-

<hr />

[5] Quoted in Wilbur Jacobs, "Frederick Jackson Turner," *The American West* 1, no. 1 (1964): 32.

[6] Quoted in ibid., p. 34.

alism to his students, Turner revealed his impatience with the divisions in the social sciences:

> Whether to call this lecture a historical, geographical, political, economic or sociological discussion, I do not know, and I don't much care, for I am one of those who believes in breaking line fences, even at the risk of arrest for trespass, or disclosure of being an amateur, or something worse, breaking into the professional's game.[7]

To suggest that Turner explained American history solely in terms of the frontier is to distort the truth and discredit the man's true breadth of understanding. In the early 1920's, Turner prepared a companion essay to the one he delivered in 1893. In this second essay, entitled "The Significance of Sections in American History," he gave his finest analysis of the interrelationship of forces:

> No single factor is determinative. Men are not absolutely dictated to by climate, geography, soils, or economic interests. The influence of the stock from which they sprang, the inherited ideals, the spiritual factors, often triumph over the material interests. There is also the influence of personality.[8]

Turner used this essay to set forth his second great and challenging concept. As people moved westward, he wrote, they settled in a series of regions or subnations, each differing in soil, climate, and natural resources. These differences resulted in a nation of *sections,* each with its own economic interests, social customs, and political problems.

Reputation and opportunity continued to increase for Turner. During the late 1890's, he received a steady flow of offers to teach at such leading institutions as Princeton, Amherst, the University of Chicago, Johns Hopkins, Stanford, and the University of California. The pressure of these offers forced the Wisconsin regents to lessen his teaching load. In 1906, his only book published during

---

[7] Turner, *Frederick Jackson Turner's Legacy,* p. 47.

[8] Frederick Jackson Turner, "Sections and Nation," *The Yale Review* 12 (October 1922): 15. Copyright © 1922 by Yale University Press.

his lifetime, *The Rise of the New West: 1814–1829,* made its debut. In 1909, Turner became president of the American Historical Association, and the following year he accepted a teaching position at Harvard University.

As a teacher, Turner was very successful. He radiated an extraordinary personal influence over his students, always showing a keen interest in their work. Students flocked to his seminars, which they affectionately referred to as the "Wild West Show." Turner maintained his sense of humor, however, and did not misinterpret these occasional ribbings. His approach to teaching the West was neither dramatic nor romantic, but rather intellectual and scholarly.

Turner's interest in his students was not confined to the work they did in his classroom. He always found time to give them advice and criticism. To one of his students, who had just entered the teaching profession, Turner wrote the following words of encouragement:

> I have taught general history and medieval history, and English history, and recent modern history, and elocution, and have run a correspondence course in Oriental history! So I know some of your trials. But such things do broaden the view, if you live through them, and better men than either of us have been all the better for having occupied a settee instead of a chair. Cheer up, and take Dr. Walter Camp's Daily Dozen Exercises (price 10 cents).[9]

Some notes for a lecture Turner gave at Harvard in 1923 on "the West as a process rather than an area."

Turner taught at Harvard from 1910 until his retirement in 1924. In 1927 he became a research associate at the Huntington Library in California, where he remained until his death on March 14, 1932.

In the final analysis, Turner was concerned with every aspect of civilization. He was as much interested in literature and the arts, and in immigration and industrialization, as he was in the West. Because of his unusually wide range of interest and research, he understood the history of

---

[9]Quoted in Wilbur R. Jacobs, "Frederick Jackson Turner," in *Turner, Bolton, and Webb: Three Historians of the American Frontier* (Seattle: University of Washington Press, 1965), p. 30.

America better than most historians of his generation. It is highly significant that shortly before his death, he outlined a new essay to match his previous essays on the frontier and the section. The title of the work was "The Significance of the City in American Civilization."

## The Turner Critics

The Turner thesis remained almost unchallenged until the 1920's. But during that decade a whole procession of scholars began to publish savage attacks upon the frontier thesis which soon took the form of an anti-Turnerian revolt. Throughout the next twenty years, the bulk of scholarly opinion ran heavily against the Turner thesis.

The principal attacks on Turner and his ideas were mounted after his death in 1932. By that time the Great Depression had produced an intellectual climate that was not receptive to his views. In a world where internationalism rather than nationalism seemed to be the key to mankind's survival, where cooperation rather than individualism offered relief from economic depression, where industrial-urban problems were of such magnitude that they completely overshadowed the rural past—in such a world the frontier thesis lost its glamor and its hold on historians. So the assault began. Turner was charged with using inadequate definitions, inexact language, implausible analyses, and insufficient evidence. Critics argued that neither the move westward nor the changed environment had significantly affected the American character, and that the alleged "frontier traits" were actually European importations.

Although the critics held great respect for Dr. Turner, they felt justified in drawing certain critical conclusions about his thesis. Some of them based their attacks on "contradictions" within the thesis. One of Turner's own disciples remarked:

> He traced the spread of human slavery from old to new regions, there to become more fixed in a stratified western society, and still talked of a growing democracy. He pointed out the hostility of western men to governmental

interference and then told of the tendency among frontiersmen on the plains and in the semiarid regions to call on the central government to do things for them which did violence to all laissez faire attitudes. He emphasized the barn-raising, the husking bee, the logrolling, and the neighborhood roundup as normal cooperative efforts among those he depicted as extreme individualists. Everywhere there is contradiction. . . .[10]

After considering a number of frontier phenomena such as the spread of slavery, the hacienda system, lawlessness, vigilante law, trial without jury, and racial intolerance—many of the critics questioned Turner's suggestion that the frontier was productive of democracy. Others condemned Turner for his omission or neglect of certain forces in American western history such as the influence of the Spanish in the Southwest. Finally there were the critics who contended that Turner's thesis contributed a disservice to the nation by turning the country's attention inward just when it needed to begin thinking on a world scale.

At this point, the views of the Turner critics should be heard. The following selected quotations are representative of the major criticisms. As in the case of Turner, each critic will speak for himself.

Louis M. Hacker:

> Turner and his followers were the fabricators of a tradition which is not only fictitious but also to a very large extent positively harmful. . . What is of greater concern is the perverted reading Turner gave to American history in his insistence upon the uniqueness of American experience and his emphasis upon sectional development as a sort of flywheel to balance all political, social and economic disparities. The unhappy results, for forty years, were the following: a turning inward of American historical activity at exactly the time when all trained eyes should have been on events going on beyond the country's physical borders;

---

[10] Avery Craven, "Frederick Jackson Turner," in *Marcus W. Jernegan Essays in American Historiography,* edited by William T. Hutchinson (New York: Russell & Russell, 1958), p. 68.

an accumulation of supposed evidences of the development
of American institutions entirely in nativistic terms without
an understanding of how closely American institutional
growth paralleled the European; an almost complete
disregard of the basic class antagonisms in American
history; and a profound ignorance of the steps by which
monopolistic capitalism and imperialism were being
developed in the country. . . . Had Turner not so boldly cut
himself loose from the currents of European thought, . . .
had he given more attention to the activities of some of his
contemporaries instead of to the Wisconsin fur trade, . . .
then our own past, in the light of America's current needs,
might not be the sealed book it is today. . . . Only by a
study of the origins and growth of American capitalism and
imperialism can we obtain insight into the nature and
complexity of the problems confronting us today. And I am
prepared to submit that perhaps the chief reason for the
absence of this proper understanding was the futile hunt for
a unique "American spirit" which Frederick Jackson Turner
began forty years ago and in which he involved most of
America's historical scholars from that time until now.[11]

## George Wilson Pierson:

Turner stated and restated many times a conviction that . . .
Old World germs were not the really significant factors in
our national evolution . . . they were merely the roots, the
remote background, the undistinguished platform from
which a new departure could be taken. . . . A few queries
may legitimately be raised at this point. . . . It would
appear that the woman suffrage idea originated in Europe
and found but slim support in the Ohio Valley. The direct
dependence of our belated Civil Service legislation on the
earlier English movement will be apparent to anyone who
cares to investigate that subject. As for manhood suffrage,
whatever may have been the contributions of the wilderness
frontier, is it not hard to believe that the American
democrat sprang, as it were, full-armed, ballot in hand, out

[11] Louis M. Hacker, "Sections or Classes," *The Nation,* 26 July 1933,
pp. 108–110.

of the Western woods? Surely one cannot today dismiss the long evolution of Parliament, the history of Colonial legislatures, the methods of the New England town meeting, the self-government of Congregational churches, and the voting habits of trading-company stockholders without a thought. This leads to another disconcerting observation. Turner nowhere seriously credits Anglo-American Protestantism with democratic tendencies. One is left to infer that such equalitarian and humanitarian interests as American Christianity has displayed must have derived from the experience of conquering the West. . . . Turner himself did make a number of flat-footed and dogmatic statements, did put forward some highly questionable interpretations, did on occasion guess and not verify, did exaggerate—and stick for more than twenty years to the exaggerations. . . . Did Turner, perhaps on the other hand, put his effort into theory and philosophy, into developing and revising his first grand vision and interpretation? Once again, curiously, our examination indicates that he did not. For not only did he republish his first essay without substantial alteration, but his later essays show little if any advance beyond the position taken in his first. Not only is there small proof of fresh research; there is as little proof of fresh thinking. Elaboration, progress in application, repetition, certainly, but distressingly little in the way of genuine reconsideration or modification. If anything, the later essays are more general, sweeping, and blurred. . . . One of the most striking weaknesses of the essays as a whole is internal inconsistency . . . the frontier theory in its full development does not hang together. The nationalism of the frontier does violence to its sectional tendencies, innovations are derived from repetition, the improvement of civilization is achieved via the abandonment of civilization, and materialism gives birth to idealism. . . . In what it proposes, the frontier hypothesis needs painstaking revision. By what it fails to mention, the theory today disqualifies itself as an adequate guide to American development.[12]

[12] George Wilson Pierson, "The Frontier and American Institutions," *New England Quarterly* 15 (June 1942): 34–35.

## Benjamin F. Wright, Jr.:

In their choice of political institutions the men of this section [the Middle West] were imitative not creative. They were not interested in making experiments. Their constitutional, like their domestic, architecture was patterned after that of the communities from which they had moved westward. . . . It will be remembered that in his original essay on the influence of the frontier Turner wrote in the crusading mood of one who battles for a dear and a long neglected cause. It was with vigor and enthusiasm that "he hitched his star to a covered wagon."

. . . The conception of the "transforming influence" of the frontier, as it appears in Turner's essays, is largely a myth. Indeed, I believe that a much better argument can be made out that the hardships of pioneer living transformed a large proportion of the restless and discontented who migrated to the free and promised land into men ambitious to be prosperous citizens in the image of the bankers and merchants and landowners back home. . . . Furthermore it [the frontier thesis] is in good part a Middle West–sectional interpretation. . . . One has but to compare the differences between the institutions of the English and those of the French, Dutch and Spanish colonies in America to see that the foundations, and more, of our democracy were brought in the *Susan Constant* and *Mayflower*. That democracy did not come out of the American forest unless it was first carried there. On some frontiers democracy was not strengthened, rather the reverse. Free land gave the opportunity to establish slavery in Louisiana, oligarchy in the Mormon state, the hacienda system in Mexican California, while it was furnishing the opportunity for a "fit" people in the Middle West to establish the particular degree and kind of democracy that they favored.[13]

Frederick Jackson Turner interpreted the frontier as a process of Americanization in which the force of environ-

---

[13] Benjamin F. Wright, Jr., "Political Institutions and the Frontier," in *Sources of Culture in the Middle West,* edited by Dixon Ryan Fox (New York: Appleton-Century-Crofts, 1934), pp. 192–193.

ment forged a variety of character traits in the American personality. Most of his critics interpreted the frontier as a geographic area which slowly became Europeanized as civilization gradually overcame the hostile environment.

Several pertinent questions emerge from the controversy. Did the West originate new ideas or did it imitate old ones? Did the West assist in the development of democracy or hinder its growth? Finally, did the whole frontier experience leave any imprint at all on the American character? Subsequent chapters detail the frontier experience from the 1840's to the 1890's. In them, the reader will perhaps find his own answers to these questions.

## SUGGESTED READINGS

Babcock, C. Merton, ed. *The American Frontier: A Social and Literary Record.* Holt, Rinehart & Winston.

Billington, Ray Allen. *America's Frontier Heritage.* Holt, Rinehart & Winston.

Curti, Merle E. *The Making of an American Community: A Case Study of Democracy in a Frontier County.* Stanford University Press.

Hofstadter, Richard, and Lipset, Seymour. *Turner and the Sociology of the Frontier.* Basic Books.

Noble, David W. *Historians Against History: The Frontier Thesis and the National Covenant in American Historical Writing Since 1830.* University of Minnesota Press.

Potter, David M. *People of Plenty: Economic Abundance and the American Character.* University of Chicago Press, Phoenix Books.

Turner, Frederick Jackson. *Frontier and Section: Selected Essays of Frederick Jackson Turner.* Prentice-Hall, Spectrum Books.

This painting by George Catlin, probably made in the 1830's, shows Plains Indians at council. Among most American Indians, important decisions affecting the whole band or community were reached democratically, as in ancient Athens.

## CHAPTER TWO

# THE WARRIORS

In his native village, on the war path, and when raiding upon our frontier settlements and lines of travel, the Indian forfeits his claim to the appellation of the *noble* red man. We see him as he is, and, so far as all knowledge goes, as he ever has been, a *savage* in every sense of the word; not worse, perhaps, than his white brother would be, similarly born and bred, but one whose cruel and ferocious nature far exceeds that of any wild beast of the desert.[1]

The man who wrote these words in 1872 had, four years earlier, led a cavalry charge against an encampment of peaceful Cheyenne Indians and had massacred them— men, women, and children. George Armstrong Custer was by no means unsympathetic to Indian life. But he was an extremely ambitious man, and leading victorious cavalry charges against "savages" was a good way to advance one's military career and puff up one's public image. It is surely one of the bitterest ironies in American history that Custer's words about the cruelty, ferocity, and bestial nature of his Indian foe apply with equal accuracy to Custer himself and to the predominant white culture which made a hero of him.

In 1868, Tosawi, or Silver Knife, a chief of the Commanches, surrendered his people to General Philip Sheridan. In broken English, Tosawi introduced himself as a

[1] George Armstrong Custer, *My Life on the Plains,* edited by Milo Milton Quaife (Lincoln: University of Nebraska Press, 1971), p. 22. © 1971. Reprinted by permission of the University of Nebraska Press.

Chief Joseph surrendering his people in the Bear Paw Mountains, Montana, in 1877.

"good Indian." Sheridan replied that the only good Indian he ever saw was dead. And so, late in the history of Indian-white relations, a popular and truly savage aphorism was born: *The only good Indian is a dead Indian.* But almost from the beginning, private and governmental policies toward the Indian peoples had been murderous and dishonorable.

The Nez Percé Indians of Oregon had welcomed and succored the ailing Lewis and Clark expedition in 1805. Some sixty-five years later, they were driven out of their ancestral home and chased nearly a thousand miles by half the U.S. Army because they dared to prefer freedom in Canada to prisoner status on a malarial reservation in the United States. They were finally cornered, and their leader, Chief Joseph, surrendered rather than let his starving women and children freeze to death in a snowstorm. A young army officer, observing the surrender, wrote that in his opinion Chief Joseph could not accuse the United

States government of a single act of justice. This comment may perhaps serve as a sort of epitaph for the entire history of Indian-white relations in the United States. But Joseph's speech to government officials in Washington, D.C., is even more to the point:

> I have heard talk and talk, but nothing is done. Good words do not last long unless they amount to something. Words do not pay for my dead people. They do not pay for my country, now overrun by white men. . . . Good words will not give my people good health and stop them from dying. Good words will not get my people a home where they can live in peace and take care of themselves. I am tired of talk that comes to nothing. It makes my heart sick when I remember all the good words and broken promises. . . . You might as well expect the rivers to run backward as that any man who was born a free man should be contented when penned up and denied liberty to go where he pleases. . . . I have asked some of the great white chiefs where they get their authority to say to the Indian that he shall stay in one place, while he sees white men going where they please. They cannot tell me.
>
> Let me be a free man—free to travel, free to stop, free to work, free to trade where I choose, free to choose my own teachers, free to follow the religion of my fathers, free to think and talk and act for myself—and I will obey every law, or submit to the penalty.[2]

Chief Joseph.

Heinmot Tooyaleket, called Chief Joseph, was never allowed to return to his home or to his people. He died, a broken-hearted exile, in 1904. Heinmot Tooyaleket was a wise, humane man, and there was much greatness in him. But there were many such Indian men. The white civilization which lied to, robbed, and murdered these men—and sought to destroy the people and cultures they spoke for—was technologically and numerically a superior one. Ethically and spiritually, however, this civilization seems to have been by no means superior.

[2]Quoted in Dee Brown, *Bury My Heart at Wounded Knee: An Indian History of the American West* (New York: Bantam Books, 1972), pp. 113–114.

## Indian Cultures

The American Indian contribution to Western civilization is frequently underestimated. It is sometimes pointed out that stores of Indian corn helped the Plymouth colony survive its first disastrous winter in 1620, or that the introduction of tobacco as a money crop enabled the Jamestown plantation to prosper economically. But less frequently mentioned is the influence of Indian culture as an immensely varied whole—as a cultural entity extending in space from the tip of South America to beyond the Arctic Circle, and extending in time from perhaps 25,000 years ago to the present moment.

Part of the Indian cultural influence has been of a concrete or tangible nature. Most of the tangible contributions have already been made, and have become part of everyday Western life:

The earliest known (1542) European illustration of maize or Indian corn.

From the moment of Columbus's landfall in the Bahamas, the Indian made possible the European's first precarious footholds in every part of the Americas. He supplied the newcomer with Indian foods that were new to him, taught him to plant, fish, and hunt with Indian methods, guided him through the wilderness over Indian trails and in Indian-style watercraft, and introduced him to Indian implements, utensils, tools, clothing, and ways of life that made existence easier and more secure. By friendly trade he supplied the white man with furs and other goods that helped revolutionize styles and materials in the Old World; and his art forms, crafts, and cultural objects heavily influenced certain aspects of European artistic and intellectual life. Indian gold and other treasures built up the courts, armies, and navies of European rulers and nations, and financed intrigues, rivalries, and wars among imperial powers for generations.

Among the world's total food supply today, almost half the crops grown were first domesticated by American Indians and became known to white men only after 1492. Two of those crops, corn and potatoes, are now—with rice and wheat—the most important staples in the world. Not far behind them in present-day importance are two other

PAUL WEATHERWAX, INDIANA UNIVERSITY

Indian-developed crops—manioc, which has become a staple in parts of Africa, and the American sweet potato. In addition, Indians introduced to the white man more than eighty other domesticated plants, including peanuts, squashes, peppers, tomatoes, pumpkins, pineapples, avocados, cacao (for chocolate), chicle (for chewing gum), many kinds of beans, and other vegetables and fruits that are common to most people today. All cotton grown in the United States, as well as the long-fiber cotton raised in Egypt and in other parts of Africa, is also derived from species cultivated by the American Indians; tobacco—first seen in use by Columbus in the form of cigars in Cuba—came from the Indians; and at least fifty-nine drugs, including coca (for cocaine and novocaine), curare (a muscle relaxant), cinchona bark (the source of quinine), cascara sagrada (a laxative), datura (a pain-reliever), and ephedra (a nasal remedy), were bequeathed to modern medicine by the Indians.

In addition, people today make use of numerous Indian devices, including canoes, snowshoes, moccasins, hammocks, kayaks, smoking pipes, ponchos, rubber syringes, dog sleds, toboggans, and parkas. Indian designs have affected many manufactured goods, from beach backrests to jewelry, and both the rubber ball and the game of lacrosse were adopted from Indians. Thousands of names for cities, states, lakes, mountains, rivers, and other geographical sites and features in the Western Hemisphere are Indian, and European languages contain many words, like the French *apache*, that derive from American native tongues. Indian contributions to the English language include wigwam, succotash, tobacco, papoose, chipmunk, squash, skunk, toboggan, opossum, tomahawk, moose, mackinaw, hickory, pecan, raccoon, cougar, woodchuck, hominy, and hundreds of other words. . . .[3]

But there are other, less tangible aspects of Indian culture which, though formerly scoffed at, may yet prove

[3] Alvin M. Josephy, Jr., *The Indian Heritage of America* (New York: Bantam Books, 1969), pp. 30–31. Copyright © 1968 by Alvin M. Josephy, Jr. Reprinted by permission of Bantam Books, Inc.

relevant and indeed crucially important in the coming decades. Among the Indian peoples of North America alone, there were many different cultural groups, with widely varying social organizations and cultural practices. For example, the town-dwelling northeastern woodlands Indians formed sophisticated political alliances whose ideals and practices impressed and influenced colonial thinkers; many of these woodlands tribes were matriarchal in structure, women being the ultimate repositories of social and religious authority. On the other hand, some Indians in the Subarctic and the American Southwest were extremely primitive Stone Age gatherers, with no agriculture or any other complex forms of social organization. But despite this great cultural diversity, some generalization is nonetheless possible.

Many Indian societies had—and continue to have—forms of social organization that anthropologists call "synergistic." In a synergistic society, an individual achieves his personal goals—self-respect, social approval, fulfillment of one's potential, and so on—by acting in such a way as to benefit the entire community. In such societies, it is not possible for an individual to amass wealth, power, or social esteem at the expense of other members of the community: the more his actions benefit the community, the more his status improves, and vice versa. To take a very simple example, an expert hunter would get no social recognition for being the best shot or best tracker; these skills would have no positive value in and of themselves. Being a great hunter meant catching game and *sharing* it with other members of one's family group or with the community as a whole: the ability to give or share one's catch was the whole point of being a great hunter. As a great hunter—as a man whose skills enabled him to add to the communal food supply—the individual was praised and made to feel a valuable and respected member of the community. That is, social "reward" in the form of approval, and social "punishment" in the form of disapproval, were distributed in a pattern that differs considerably from that of most modern Western societies. The resulting tone of life was also different: many Indian communities reinforced or

A Minnetaree warrior in ceremonial costume. Minnetarees were related to eastern woodland Indians, but lived along the upper Missouri in North Dakota. They were wiped out by a smallpox epidemic in 1837.

made valuable behavior that was cooperative rather than competitive, sharing rather than acquisitive, open rather than aggressive. In her lovely book on the Pawnee Indians, Gene Weltfish has provided an interesting example of what the Pawnees considered an act of high social courage. A Pawnee man heard that another was making slanderous remarks about him. He thereupon dressed up in his best, and took his only horse and wagon to the slanderer—and gave them to him. "How," asks Dr. Weltfish,

> can one possibly call this an act of courage? Let us look at this action through Pawnee eyes. For one thing, by his action, the victim had cleared the society of a disruptive social element that could have grown into a more general net-work of hostilities and polluted the whole social climate so that they might no longer defend themselves effectively from outside attack nor coordinate their efforts for their mutual survival. It took real courage, from the Pawnee point of view, for a man to curb his anger and to make a material sacrifice as well. How different from our reaction which would lead a man to plant his fist forcibly into the face of the slanderer or perhaps counter with a more devious plan to get back at his opponent. The obvious result must necessarily be a continuation and augmentation of the social irritant.[4]

Although sometimes not particularly good conservationists, many Indian peoples were excellent ecologists. Indians were sometimes careless with campfires, or wasted natural resources, but their general understanding—their "big picture"—of natural processes and relationships was far more realistic and accurate than our own. They understood quite well man's ultimate dependence upon "the web of life"—the incredibly intricate interconnections that link all living and nonliving systems into one self-sustaining whole. The white man's notion about the human species as being set apart from and in control of the natural world struck Indians as both arrogant and fatally mistaken, as

[4]Gene Weltfish, *The Lost Universe* (New York: Ballantine Books, 1971), p. 17. Copyright © 1965 by Basic Books, Inc., Publishers.

indeed it is. Black Elk, an Oglala Sioux, provides a beautiful example of Indian thinking on this point. In the following excerpt, Black Elk prepares to tell his life-story and explains to his interviewer the significance of a pipe they will smoke together:

> So I know that it is a good thing I am going to do; and because no good thing can be done by any man alone, I will first make an offering and send a voice to the Spirit of the World, that it may help me to be true. See, I fill this sacred pipe with the bark of the red willow; but before we smoke it, you must see how it is made and what it means. These four ribbons hanging here on the stem are the four quarters of the universe. The black one is for the west where the thunder beings live to send us rain; the white one for the north, whence comes the great white cleansing wind; the red one for the east, whence springs the light and where the morning star lives to give men wisdom; the yellow for the south, whence come the summer and the power to grow.
>
> But these four spirits are only one Spirit after all, and this eagle feather here is for that One, which is like a father, and also it is for the thoughts of men that should rise high as eagles do. Is not the sky a father and the earth a mother, and are not all living things with feet or wings or roots their children? And this hide upon the mouthpiece here, which should be bison hide, is for the earth, from whence we came and at whose breast we suck as babies all our lives, along with all the animals and birds and trees and grasses. And because it means all this, and more than any man can understand, the pipe is holy.[5]

Although much of Indian life was hedged about by intricate rituals and procedures governing kinship relations and general social functioning, many Indian societies seemed able to encourage individual differences and indi-

[5] *Black Elk Speaks, Being the Life Story of a Holy Man of the Oglala Sioux,* as told through John G. Neihardt (Flaming Rainbow) (Lincoln: University of Nebraska Press, 1961), pp. 2–3. © 1961. Reprinted by permission of the University of Nebraska Press.

vidual self-fulfillment far more effectively than do so-called "nonconformist" modern nations. Among many Indian groups, child-rearing practices were considerably more appealing and sophisticated than our own: to physically discipline a child—or to frighten or otherwise traumatize him—was considered a serious and sometimes unforgivable error. Children were loved, guided, and cherished far more deeply and wisely than is the norm in Western families. At the same time, children were given genuine responsibility early in life, and adolescents were never denied meaningful roles in the community or family affairs. On the other hand, growing old was not something to be feared or denied; the old, as well as the young, were neither superfluous nor unwanted.

Many Indian groups practiced medicinal and religious techniques whose efficacy in psychological or psychosomatic terms is only now being understood and accepted by Western scientists. Many Indians were—and remain— open to what may be called the poetry or mystery of life. They did not exclude the wide range of sacred, visionary, or extrasensory experiences that a narrow and infertile rationalism has been able neither to explain on its own terms nor to laugh or bully away. The Indian openness or receptivity to the unexplained may yet prove to be the more scientific attitude, and has in any case already proved to be the less intolerant and impoverished one.

> After the . . ceremony, I came to live here where I am now between Wounded Knee Creek and Grass Creek. Others came too, and we made these little gray houses of logs that you see, and they are square. It is a bad way to live, for there can be no power in a square.
>
> You have noticed that everything an Indian does is in a circle, and that is because the Power of the World always works in circles, and everything tries to be round. In the old days when we were a strong and happy people, all our power came to us from the sacred hoop of the nation, and so long as the hoop was unbroken, the people flourished. The flowering tree was the living center of the hoop, and the circle of the four quarters nourished it. The east gave

peace and light, the south gave warmth, the west gave rain, and the north with its cold and mighty wind gave strength and endurance. This knowledge came to us from the outer world with our religion. Everything the Power of the World does is done in a circle. The sky is round, and I have heard that the earth is round like a ball, and so are all the stars. The wind, in its greatest power, whirls. Birds make their nests in circles, for theirs is the same religion as ours. The sun comes forth and goes down again in a circle. The moon does the same, and both are round. Even the seasons form a great circle in their changing, and always come back again to where they were. The life of a man is a circle from childhood to childhood, and so it is in everything where power moves. Our tepees were round like the nests of birds, and these were always set in a circle, the nation's hoop, a nest of many nests, where the Great Spirit meant for us to hatch our children.

But the Wasichus [white men] have put us in these square boxes. Our power is gone and we are dying, for the power is not in us any more. You can look at our boys and see how it is with us. When we were living by the power of the circle in the way we should, boys were men at twelve or thirteen years of age. But now it takes them very much longer to mature.

Well, it is as it is. We are prisoners of war while we are waiting here. But there is another world.[6]

The words quoted above were spoken by Black Elk in the early 1930's, when he was living in a shack on the Pine Ridge Reservation in South Dakota. Black Elk was an important man among his people; he was respected as a visionary and a healer, and was, incidentally, a cousin of Crazy Horse. The image or metaphor Black Elk has provided here is one of enormous force, integration, and richness. It is to be wondered what terms our civilization might choose to identify itself in the way that Black Elk has "summed up" his.

In an overcrowded world that threatens to strangle on its own waste products, and will shortly have to unlearn

6 Ibid., pp. 198–200.

its credo that growth is a social good *per se;* in a world in which increasingly large numbers of people of all ages feel cut off from useful work, from human companionship, and from the other wellsprings of a sane, meaningful, and happy life; in a world that occupies a flyspeck of space in a universe so enormous that the existence of other highly intelligent cultures is a virtual certainty—in such a world some of the American Indian beliefs and practices may prove useful, if not essential, to survival.

## Indians of the Great Plains

At the time of Columbus's first voyage, there were perhaps no more than one million Indians in North America. Some scholars have, however, put the number as high as three million, and suggest that disease introduced by explorers or fishermen wiped out whole populations before actual colonization began. By 1800—some 180 years after the first Atlantic seaboard colonies were planted—the native Indian population was outnumbered by at least four to one. By 1850, most Indian nations had been exterminated or defeated and penned up on land that nobody else wanted.

An Indian healer preparing medicine. Indian ointments and herbal medicines were greatly in demand among early white settlers. The later patent medicines and miracle elixers attempted to capitalize on the well-established reputation of the Indian medicines.

The last holdouts were the nomadic tribes of the Great Plains—the Pawnees, the Cheyennes, the Sioux, the Arapahoes, the Kiowas, and the Comanches. The land they called their own was the last frontier, and these Indians were among the last to lose their freedom.

Among the Plains Indians, there were considerable linguistic and cultural differences. Some of these tribal groups were traditional enemies, and most could not understand each other's languages; because of this, Plains Indians developed a sign language that served as a sort of Esperanto for trading, parleys, and other purposes. We cannot adequately examine all of these Indian cultural groups, and will for this reason select the Teton-Dakota, one of the most powerful of the Siouan-speaking groups, as representative of the kind of Indians encountered by the settlers of the last frontier, the northern Great Plains. We should emphasize once again, however, that the Teton-Dakota, or the Plains Indians in general, were not "typical" Indians. As Robert H. Lowie has written,

> Most of us, when we think of Indians, envision such items as tipis, war bonnets with trailing feathers, Sitting Bull, ponies, and buffaloes. In other words, we have all come to think of the Plains Indians as the genuine Indian, the ideal Indian—the very quintessence of Indian-ness. In many ways, however, the Plains Indians were a highly distinctive group and lived in a rather specialized way or at least in a manner quite different from other kinds of Indians. They were no more typical of the American Indian than the Navajo, the Hopi, or the Iroquois. Yet through the accidents of history, perhaps also by their own role, often heroic, in the epic of the West or indeed as the result of the insistent stereotype of the movies, they have come to usurp in the public mind all other Indians and to represent *the* Indian way of life.[7]

[7] Robert H. Lowie, *Indians of the Plains* (Garden City, N.Y.: Natural History Press, 1963), p. 7. Copyright 1954 by the American Museum of Natural History. Reprinted by permission of Doubleday & Company, Inc.

Walter Prescott Webb calls our attention to another of the reasons why the Indians of the Great Plains have come to symbolize the typical American Indian:

> The Plains Indians constituted for a much longer time than we realize the most effectual barrier ever set up by a native American population against European invaders in a temperate zone. For two and a half centuries they maintained themselves with great fortitude against the Spanish, English, French, Mexican, Texan, and American invaders, withstanding missionaries, whisky, disease, gunpowder, and lead.[8]

## The Sioux

The Siouan language family included many tribes of the north-central United States. The most powerful of the Sioux family were the Dakota— the Santee-Dakota east of the Missouri River, and the Teton-Dakota west of the Missouri. The French fur trappers first noted the Sioux as being woodland Indians living in the region of the upper Minnesota River in the 1600's. There they had acquired the horse and the gun—without coming into extensive contact with whites—and had then pushed onto the plains, driving before them Indians who had horses or guns but not both. By 1800, the Teton-Dakota had completed their westward migration, and had adopted the nomadic and colorful warrior-hunter style which then came to be considered characteristically "Indian." It may be noted in contrast that by 1800 the Hopi-Zuñi-Pueblo cultures of the Southwest were over a thousand years old. In migrating west of the Missouri River, the Teton-Dakota split into many tribes: Brulés, Oglalas, Miniconjous, Sans Arcs, Two Kettles, Hunkpapas, and Blackfeet. These tribes claimed as their hunting lands the plains of western South Dakota in the early 1800's. The area hunted by the Teton-Dakota was however only a part of the Great Plains, which

[8] Walter Prescott Webb, *The Great Plains* (Waltham, Mass.: Blaisdell, 1959), p. 48. Copyright © 1959 by Walter Prescott Webb. Reprinted by permission of Xerox College Publishing. All rights reserved.

cover a vast area from the Missouri River on the east to the Rocky Mountains on the west. From the Rio Grande in the south, these nearly level, treeless, and semiarid grasslands extend north into Canada.

The relatively new culture of the Indians of the Great Plains, and particularly the culture of the Sioux, was ironically enough among the last to be destroyed. Professor Walter Prescott Webb lists the following features of the culture of the Plains Indians:

1. They were nomadic, they were not farmers.
2. Often called "the buffalo Indians," they depended upon the great herds of these animals to supply all their necessities.
3. Their weapons were adapted to the hunting of big game, the buffalo.
4. Theirs was a "horse culture." This animal revolutionized their way of life long before the coming of white civilization.[9]

The Indians of the high plains had no permanent homes, though they retained favorite hunting and camping areas. They moved about constantly in search of food—their food being primarily the buffalo. This continual movement in following the buffalo affected nearly every aspect of their existence.

The term *tipi* is Dakota in origin, and this conical tent was well adapted to a people always on the move. The foundation of a Teton-Dakota tipi was three poles with some twenty additional poles used as supports. The Teton-Dakota used more poles in their tipis than most Plains Indians because of the availability of timber in the Black Hills and Bighorn Mountains. Ten to twelve buffalo hides sewn together served as the cover of a tipi. The foundation poles were laid on the ground and tied together near one end and raised. The supporting poles were then tied to the foundation poles. The buffalo-hide cover was raised by the last pole and pulled around the tipi until it met in front. The overlapping cover was held together by

[9]Ibid., p. 52.

wooden pegs. The cover was pulled taut by moving the supporting poles tightly against it. The two gaps on either side of the smoke hole could be adjusted by movement of the two outside poles to which they were attached. A tipi was fifteen to eighteen feet high and approximately fifteen feet in diameter.

The tipi covering was decorated with porcupine quill trimming (beads often replaced quills after the coming of white traders) and painted with various symbols. A skin curtain shielded the narrow opening in the cover of the tipi; this entrance usually faced east and the place of honor was opposite the entrance.

All the work of erecting the tipi, or of taking it down, was performed by the women. A tipi could be taken down, packed, and loaded with its furnishings on a travois in fifteen minutes. Two Indian women could raise a tipi and set up a household in about an hour's time. The tipi's conical shape made it easy to heat during the long, cold winters. On hot summer days, the sides of the tipi could be rolled up to provide more ventilation.

With the availability of food in the summer, camps tended to be larger than in the winter, when food sources were limited and the increased need for firewood dictated somewhat smaller villages. Particularly severe winters brought starvation and the necessity for individual hunters to set out in search of food. Winter was the time for making tools and bows and arrows, December was referred to by some as the Moon of Frost in the Tipi; January was the Tree Popping Moon because the extreme cold would cause trees to split with a loud noise; February caused snow blindness and was referred to as Sore Eyes Moon. March—the Moon When the Grain Comes Up—and April—the Moon of the Birth of Calves—saw the Dakota still in their sheltered winter camps. The coming of spring meant increased activity, dances, ceremonial affairs, communal hunts.

Summer was the time of vision-seeking and the sun dance. A young man sought power and personal identity from some supernatural being or spirit. If the vision were great enough, the young man might, like Black Elk, be-

A detail of a Plains Indian camp, painted in the 1870's.

A painting, made in the 1930's by Olaf Seltzer, entitled "Medicine Man."

come a *wichasha wakon*—a sort of poet-prophet-priest, usually with the gift of healing the sick. The vision quest usually lasted four days, in which time the Indian fasted and thirsted. In some instances, he sought the pity of a spirit by self-mutilation. In his vision, the Indian was sometimes befriended by a supernatural being, usually some animal or bird. Thereafter, he might wear a token of this vision or paint it on his shield cover. The young Indian might also be instructed in the vision as to the sacred objects which should be assembled for his "medicine bundle."

The sun dance was common to nearly all the Plains Indians. Participants would fix their gaze upon the top of the sun-dance pole—upon which a buffalo skull or other symbolic object had been placed—while rising up and down on their toes, or shuffling backward and forward. They sought to bring about a vision which might give them power, or remove some worry or problem. A Dakota would sometimes participate in a sun dance in fulfillment of a vow. In this ceremony, the Dakota was known to use self-torture. The torture consisted of running skewers through

A buffalo hunt in Wyoming, possibly showing one of the last of the great herds.

the muscles of the chest or back, attaching the skewers to the sun-dance pole with thongs, and pulling on the thongs until the skewers were torn through the flesh.

Fall was the busiest time of year for the Plains Indians. Hunting was most important, for a large food supply had to be laid up for the winter. Women cut up the meat and dried it or made pemmican of it by mixing it with dried, crushed berries. After melted fat and marrow were added, the pemmican was stored in skin bags. With the snows of winter, the Indian bands again moved to favorite sheltered camp sites.

## The Buffalo

That Plains Indians were dependent upon the buffalo for their way of life was a fact fully appreciated by frontiersmen familiar with the Great Plains and, of course, by the Indians themselves. Frank H. Mayer, one of the old "runners," as professional buffalo hunters were called, observed that

> the buffalo served his mission, fulfilled his destiny in the history of the Indian, by furnishing him everything he needed—food, clothing, a home, traditions, even a theology. But the buffalo didn't fit in so well with the white man's encroaching civilization. . . . The buffalo was hunted and killed with the connivance, yes, the cooperation, of the Government itself. . . .

Indians moving their things on a travois.

Don't understand that any official action was taken in Washington and directives sent out to kill all the buff on the plains. Nothing like that happened. What did happen was that army officers in charge of plains operations encouraged the slaughter of buffalo in every possible way. Part of this encouragement was of a practical nature that we runners appreciated. It consisted of ammunition, free ammunition. . . . All you had to do to get it was apply at any frontier army post. . . .

One afternoon I was visiting this man [a high-ranking officer in the plains service] in his quarters. . . . We smoked and talked. He said to me: "Mayer, there's no two ways about it: either the buffalo or the Indian must go. Only when the Indian becomes absolutely dependent on us for his every need, will we be able to handle him. He's too independent with the buffalo. But if we kill the buffalo we conquer the Indian. It seems a more humane thing to kill the buffalo than the Indian, so the buffalo must go," he concluded.[10]

Watercolor sketch by George Catlin of a painted buffalo robe.

When buffalo were near, the Indians lived well. There was more than enough to eat. There was leisure time to paint tipis and to embroider clothing, moccasins, and parfleches (skin bags) with the glass beads secured from white men eager to trade for buffalo robes. There was time for gambling, horse racing, and storytelling. But when the buffalo were not around, the Indians often went hungry. The Plains Indians were, quite literally, "buffalo Indians."

The Plains Indians utilized nearly every part of the animal. Tipi coverings, blankets, shield covers, clothing, moccasins, and containers were all made from buffalo skins, either rawhide or leather. The hides were first staked out on the ground with the hairy side down, and the women would scrape away fat, muscle, and tissue with a bone tool. The clean hide was bleached in the sun for several days and again scraped to an even thickness. Sometimes the hair was removed from the rawhide. If leather was desired for

THE THOMAS GILCREASE INSTITUTE OF AMERICAN HISTORY AND ART

[10] Frank H. Mayer and Charles B. Roth, *The Last of the Buffalo Hunters* (Chicago: The Swallow Press, 1972), pp. 27–30. Copyright © 1972. Reprinted by permission of The Swallow Press.

clothing or soft pouches, the rawhide had to be tanned. A mixture of buffalo fat and brain was rubbed thoroughly into the surface of the rawhide, which was then dried in the sun, stretched, and rubbed with a stone to make the leather pliable.

Buffalo bones were made into tools such as arrow shaft straighteners—and sometimes arrowheads—and awls which the women used to punch sinew through hides in sewing them together. Sinew, from the tendons of the buffalo, was made into bowstrings and used where strong bindings were necessary. Buffalo horns were worn in head-dresses and as ornaments; horn spoons and dishes were also fashioned. Lariats were woven from the hair of the buffalo. Glue was secured from boiled horns and hoofs. Dried buffalo dung was burned as fuel. Even the rough side of the buffalo's tongue was put to use—as a hair brush.

An Indian woman ornamenting a robe or blanket with beads.

During the early decades of the 1800's the buffalo may have numbered as many as sixty million on the Great Plains. The buffalo were slaughtered in such great numbers that by 1897 there were *twenty* of the animals left in the United States—a tiny herd in Yellowstone National Park. Runners like Mayer killed the buffalo for their hides or for their tongues, which were shipped back by the trainload to restaurants in the East. The carcasses were left to rot on the plains.

The buffalo has been described as "unquestionably the stupidest game animal in the world." Its eyesight was extremely poor, its hearing was little better, and even its scent was faulty. Buffalo runners were not referred to as hunters because the animal was so easy to kill. A runner could lie off from a herd at a distance of several hundred yards and drop great numbers of the animals before the herd took alarm.

Four major forms of collective hunting were practiced by the Plains Indians: surrounding the buffalo; driving them over a cliff; impounding the animals; or encircling them with fire. The horse greatly aided the surround method; the mounted Indians would surround the herd, get the animals to milling around, then shoot them down with bows and arrows. Running buffalo over a cliff's edge was a favorite method of securing large amounts of meat. If the cliff was not high enough to kill the animals, a corral was built at the bottom and the animals that had been stampeded over the cliff and into the corral were then killed. Much the same technique was used in the method of impounding the buffalo. Men and women would be strung out in two converging lines; these two lines would funnel the buffalo into a natural or man-made enclosure. The buffalo might be lured into the enclosure by Indians who covered themselves with buffalo robes and imitated the bleat of a buffalo calf while moving in the direction of the enclosure. Before they had acquired the horse, the Indians would often start the buffalo toward the enclosure by firing the grass behind them.

The weapons employed in the buffalo hunt had to be capable of bringing down an animal which weighed some eighteen hundred pounds. Bows and arrows, clubs, spears, and shields were the weapons used both in hunting and in warfare. Wood of the ash tree was considered by the Sioux to be best for bow-making. The wood was shaped and dried for about two weeks. Final shaping began at the grip, and the ends of the bow were tapered later. The bow was cut to about the height of the owner's waist and the thickness depended upon his grip. The sinew-backed bow was favored by most western Indians. These bows had three to five layers of sinew glued to their backs, and were harder hitting than one-piece bows. Bowstrings were made of sinew which had been shredded, soaked, and rolled together into one string which was three times the length of the bow. The bowstring was then folded into thirds, braided together forming a three-ply bowstring, stretched, and then dried.

In the time it would take a white man to fire and reload a muzzle-loading cap and ball rifle, an Indian could discharge up to twenty arrows and ride three hundred yards. Indian males learned early—usually by the age of eleven or twelve—how to use the bow, and in general how to make and repair their weapons. Among some Plains Indians, however, certain tasks, like arrow-making, were performed by a very few specialists within the tribe or band.

Only men could touch such sacred items as weapons, for a woman's touch would contaminate them and destroy their efficiency.

After a buffalo hunt each man knew which animals he had killed, because each hunter painted his arrows in his own fashion. Arrow shafts were made of various woods—gooseberry, cherry, and juneberry were preferred by the Sioux. The shaft was measured from the elbow to the tip of the little finger; it was smoothed and straightened by running it through a flat bone in which a hole had been cut. Three feathers, usually of the turkey buzzard or wild turkey, were cut and attached to the shaft by sinew and glue. After the coming of the white trader, metal points began to replace those made of chipped stone.

Circular shields were made of buffalo hide. The Dakota covered theirs with buckskin and painted them with designs which had often been revealed to the owner in a vision. Feathers often decorated the shields. As a newly made shield dried in the sun, the lacings holding the cover to the wooden hoop were tightened over a mold, giving the shield a convex shape which helped deflect an arrow.

## The Horse

Historians differ somewhat about the extent to which the horse constituted a major influence upon the culture of the Plains Indians. In an article for *The American West*, a magazine published by the Western History Association, Francis Haines states:

An Appaloosa horse, of the type bred by the Nez Percés.

> To the Plains tribes horses did not bring a new way of living, but a great enrichment of the old way. They still lived off the buffalo, but now they could kill the animals more easily and in greater numbers. They could follow the herds more closely, and could transport larger lodges, more food, and many more personal belongings. Their adjustments to the new servants were small and easily made.[11]

[11]Francis Haines, "Horses for Western Indians," *The American West* 3, no. 2 (1966): 14.

Reflecting a somewhat less contemporary view, Walter Prescott Webb wrote:

> Then came the horse and overnight, so to speak, the whole life and economy of the Plains Indians was changed. Steam and electricity have not wrought a greater revolution in the ways of civilized life than the horse did in the savage life of the Plains.[12]

Clark Wissler, Dean of the Scientific Staff at the American Museum of Natural History, wrote that

> the importance of the horse lay, not in fighting, but in mobility. Baggage, tents, the aged and children could be transported rapidly. The changes in Indian life brought about by this new mode of travel were even greater than those produced by the automobile in our time.[13]

To settlers moving westward out onto the Great Plains, it seemed that the Indians must have been mounted from time immemorial. Actually, many of the Plains Indians had acquired the horse less than two centuries before. The first horses had been brought to North America with Coronado's expedition of 1540. Not until the establishment of large ranches in northern New Mexico by the Spanish colonists did horses appear in large numbers. The Spanish were well aware of the threat which might be posed by Indians on horseback and thus made it an offense punishable by death for the agricultural Pueblo Indians, who worked the Spanish farms and ranches, to possess horses.

From the upper Rio Grande river valley in the vicinity of Santa Fe, the horse culture spread throughout the grasslands of the Great Plains. With the revolt of the Pueblo Indians against the Spanish in 1680, many animals were traded to the Plains Indians; during the next century the use of horses spread rapidly north to Canada. By the time of the American Revolution almost all North American Indians had horses.

[12] Webb, *Great Plains*, p. 53.

[13] Clark Wissler, *Indians of the United States* (Garden City, N.Y.: Doubleday, 1940), p. 262. Copyright © 1940 by Doubleday & Company, Inc. Reprinted by permission.

The horse became a standard of value among the Indians of the plains. An individual's wealth depended upon the horses he owned. It was traditional that a young man would offer horses in acquiring a bride. In addition, his prestige rose according to the number of horses he presented as gifts to the less fortunate. Of utmost importance, a man's standing as a warrior and his reputation for bravery depended upon his ability in the art of horse stealing.

Warfare among the Plains Indians had different objectives than those of Western peoples. The Indian normally went to war in order to gain revenge or personal glory, or to acquire horses, but rarely to extend dominion over others. The Crow Indians, nomadic neighbors to the west of the Dakota, recognized four categories of personal exploits: (1) leading a successful war party—one in which no warriors were lost; (2) counting coup upon an enemy (to count coup was to strike a blow with the hand or with a special stick upon an armed enemy); (3) taking a bow from an enemy in hand-to-hand combat; (4) stealing picketed horses. A distinguished warrior had to have one of each exploit to his credit. One of the most admired acts of personal bravery was the theft of a horse picketed outside the tipi of an enemy warrior. The recovery of stolen horses constituted the major cause for revenge. Indians could break a wild horse in one day; however, they much preferred to steal them from rival tribes after they had been trained.

The Indian was an expert horseman. Indian horses were trained to run next to a fleeing buffalo while the rider, with both hands free, sent arrows into the heart of the animal. While hanging from the back of his horse by one leg, the Indian would throw his bow arm over the horse's neck, and from underneath he would shoot at the enemy with very little of his own body exposed. An Indian warrior could rescue a dismounted friend by reaching down and picking him up by one hand and dragging him to safety.

If, as Frederick Jackson Turner pointed out, the frontier provided a military training school for the frontiersmen, the most competent of instructors were the Indians of the Great Plains. The two great gifts of the white man—the

LIBRARY OF CONGRESS

An old Indian, and his ghostlike memories of the hunt.

horse and the gun—made the Indian the most formidable of enemies.

> The horse glorified the Plains Indian and brought him a golden age of glory, ease, and conquest which he had never known before. Through long ages the horse has been the symbol of superiority, of victory and triumph. The "man on horseback" rides through the military history of the world; and wherever the horseman appears in statuary or painting he is the central or foremost figure.[14]

By the 1830's, the Black Hills and the hunting grounds to the east had become overcrowded as more Sioux moved west across the Missouri. The numbers of buffalo were declining when, in 1834, white traders from the newly constructed Fort William, at the junction of the Platte and Laramie rivers, appeared in the Sioux villages. One hundred lodges of the Oglalas were persuaded to move south and west of the Black Hills and into the region of the North Platte River near the fur trading post which was later to be called Fort Laramie. More Sioux were attracted to this

---

[14]Webb, *Great Plains,* p. 493.

region when they learned of the opportunity to trade with the white men and of the great numbers of buffalo to be hunted.

The Sioux who moved westward came into conflict with the Crow Indians, who had been hunting the plains east of the Bighorn Mountains. The Crows and the Snake Indians to the west, always friendly to the white trappers and traders, were soon displaced by the aggressive Sioux. Cheyenne and Arapaho Indians who had hunted the Upper Platte were counted as allies by the Sioux against their common enemy, the Pawnees. This alliance of Sioux and Cheyenne-Arapaho was maintained in the Indian wars against the whites.

## The Intruders

Their early associations with the white men often benefited the Sioux, who traded horses and buffalo hides for metal tools, coffee, flour, and weapons. But the fur trade was declining by the early 1840's and the fierce rivalry between competing fur companies for the Indian trade led to uncontrolled use of liquor as a lure to the Indians. The sale of liquor often resulted in demoralization of the Indians. The killing of one Sioux by another had been a rarity; but under the influence of liquor drunken brawls, murder, and quarreling between factions within a band became commonplace.

As the fur trade in the northern Rockies died out, the trappers were soon replaced by newcomers. The first of the Oregon-bound home seekers, numbering only eighty, passed through Sioux hunting grounds in 1841. Two years later, a wagon train made up of one thousand men, women, and children passed by Fort Laramie on their way to Oregon. Mormon pioneers, persecuted and driven from Illinois, rested at Fort Laramie on their way to Salt Lake Valley. Twenty-five thousand gold seekers bound for California added their numbers to the Oregon and Utah-bound settlers. The tide of emigration reached a peak in 1850, when fifty-five thousand emigrants traveled over South Pass in the Rocky Mountains.

Mormon settlers entering the Great Salt Lake Valley in 1852.

The Oregon Trail through the hunting grounds of the Sioux had become a highway; a treaty with the Indians was needed, one which would guarantee safety to the white emigrants on the Oregon Trail. Accordingly, in 1851, a treaty was signed in which the Indians agreed not to molest wagon trains and to permit the stationing of soldiers along the trail. The government agreed to pay the Indians $50,000 in goods every year and to respect their hunting rights. But good terms between Indians and whites lasted only three years. The Grattan Massacre of 1854 touched off a war between the Plains Indians and the United States Army which was to last for the next thirty-five years.

The Grattan Massacre, to which a young warrior named Red Cloud was said to have been a witness, resulted from the theft of a cow by a band of Sioux. The Sioux chief reported to the commander at Fort Laramie that the guilty man had been punished, but the commander sent Lieutenant John L. Grattan and thirty men to the Sioux camp to arrest the offender. When the Indians refused to surrender the guilty man, a dispute ensued and the Sioux annihilated Grattan and his entire command.

The arrival of General William S. Harney with a large force of troops quickly crushed growing Sioux opposition to white incursions. General Harney proposed the organization of an Indian police force and the establishment of a tribal government under direction of the United States, but the government refused to consider the plan—one which was years ahead of the Indian policies of that time.

The outbreak of the Civil War in 1861 brought about the removal of federal troops from the frontiers. The following year a major uprising of Santee-Dakota occurred near their reservation in southwestern Minnesota. Many eastern Dakota fled west to the country of the Teton and brought stories of the massacres and the hanging of the Indian offenders. Territorial governors demanded that troops be sent from the East, and at the same time they began organizing the frontier settlers into volunteer units. These large numbers of troops helped to bring on the bloody Plains Indian war of 1864. Red Cloud was correct when he said, "The white soldiers always want to make war." Life at a frontier post on the Great Plains was monotonous, and the inexperienced and bored soldiers often seized upon any excuse to start a fight with the Indians, most of whom had been friendly toward the whites.

Following the Civil War, railroads began to push west. Cattle ranching was spreading over the grasslands of the Great Plains. Mining communities were springing up in the Rockies. Mining centers such as Helena and Bozeman, in southwestern Montana, had to be supplied from the east. The most direct route followed was an old trail that ran north from Fort Laramie on the main overland trail, to Bozeman, skirting to the east of the Bighorns. The Bozeman Trail was a route familiar to old trappers and traders. It was also a route which cut through the heart of the "Powder River country," the hunting grounds which had been guaranteed to the Sioux in the Treaty of 1851.

The Indians became alarmed as the government sent out surveyors and road builders. A treaty commission was sent by the government to obtain permission of the Indians to build the road. The commissioners, however, failed to obtain the signatures of the Indians. A meeting was called in 1866 to be held at Fort Laramie. As negotiations proceeded, Red Cloud learned that seven hundred soldiers were being led into the Powder River country under the command of Colonel H. B. Carrington. To Red Cloud it appeared that the government was going to build a road through the Indians' hunting grounds and build forts along the road whether the Indians agreed or not. In anger, Red Cloud addressed the treaty-makers:

> I will talk to you no more. I will go now, and I will fight you. As long as I live I will fight you. As long as I live I will fight you for the last hunting grounds of my people.[15]

Red Cloud walked out of the meeting and began what was to be referred to as "Red Cloud's War." Red Cloud and his braves were experts in guerrilla warfare; they outmaneu-

---

[15] Quoted in Jack Guinn, "The Red Man's Last Struggle," *Empire* Magazine, *The Denver Post,* 1966.

vered U. S. troops, inflicting heavy casualties upon them, and finally forced the United States government in 1868 to come to terms on conditions laid down by Red Cloud.

In July of 1866, Colonel Carrington moved his men to the Powder River to begin construction of Fort Phil Kearney. Red Cloud sent word that if the soldiers packed up and left, no harm would come to them. Carrington ordered the area of the fort to be staked out. Then Red Cloud's warriors stampeded part of the soldiers' horse herd. Two soldiers in a rescue party were killed. Within a month, five emigrant trains had been attacked, and fifteen whites killed. Carrington was forced to ask for reinforcements. When, in August, two companies of soldiers were sent north to the Bighorn River to establish Fort C. F. Smith, the Indians stepped up their attacks. Wood trains, sent seven miles into the hills for needed timber, had to be heavily guarded; and any stray white man who wandered far from the fort was in danger of being killed or captured.

Capture by the Indians was the greatest fear of the soldiers. Colonel Richard I. Dodge, an experienced Indian fighter, wrote:

> The Indian is thoroughly skilled in all methods of torture, and well knows that that by fire is the most exquisite if it can only be prolonged. He therefore frequently resorts to it when time and opportunity serve. The victim is "staked out" and pleasantly talked to. (The man is laid on his back on the ground; his arms and legs, stretched to the uttermost, are fastened by ropes to pins driven into the ground. The victim is not only helpless, but almost motionless.) It is all the best kind of joke. Then a small fire is built near one of his feet. When that is so cooked as to have little sensation, another fire is built near the other foot; then the legs and arms and body, until the whole person has been crisped. Finally, a small fire is built on the naked breast, and kept up until life is extinct.[16]

[16] Richard Dodge, *Our Wild Indians: Thirty-Three Years' Personal Experience Among the Red Men of the Great West* (New York: Archer House, 1956), pp. 525–526.

In November, more reinforcements were sent Carrington. Among them was Captain William J. Fetterman, an infantry officer who held a low opinion of Indians and who, like most men recently assigned to the West, was eager for action. In early December, a wood train was attacked, and Captain Fetterman led the rescue party from the fort. The Indians resorted to their usual tactic of fleeing when opposed by superior numbers. Fetterman ordered his men to pursue the Indians. When they were out of sight of the fort, the Sioux turned and attacked Fetterman's command. When Fetterman disappeared from sight, Colonel Carrington took what men could be spared from the fort and rode to his rescue. After the fight, Fetterman was heard to make this statement: "Give me eighty men and I'll ride through the whole Sioux nation."

On Friday morning, December 21, word was received at the fort that the work detail of ninety men sent to gather wood was being attacked. Fetterman volunteered to lead the rescue party. His orders were to relieve the wood train, and under no circumstances to pursue the Indians. Ironically, Fetterman rode out of the fort with eighty men. Ten young Sioux warriors rode out in front of Fetterman and his men and lured them into a chase.

A sign erected by the state of Wyoming records the fate of Fetterman's command:

Along this ridge on Dec. 21, Brevet Lt. Col. Fetterman, 2 officers, 76 enlisted men and 2 civilians were decoyed into ambush and overwhelmed by a superior force of Sioux, Cheyenne and Arapahoe Indians. . . . Fetterman, disobeying orders not to pursue the Indians, issued forth on his ill-fated foray. Although termed a massacre, the fight was actually a pitched battle. The final stand was made behind the large boulders. . . . There were no survivors.[17]

Colonel Carrington, before riding out to relieve Fetterman, gave orders to the undermanned fort that in case of attack the women and children were to be taken into the

[17] Wyoming Historical Marker, U.S. Highway 87, near Banner, Wyoming.

LIBRARY OF CONGRESS

An encampment of Brulé Sioux, near Pine Ridge, in 1891.

powder magazine which was to be blown up if the fort
was overwhelmed. Carrington found that all but six of the
men in Fetterman's command had been killed by arrows,
lances, clubs, or old muzzle-loading muskets. Only six men
had been killed by bullets from guns which were equivalent to those carried by the troops. One body carried 105
arrows.

The Fetterman disaster emphasized the need to arm and
equip troops stationed in the West with weapons better
adapted to frontier warfare. In August of 1867, a large
force of Sioux and Cheyennes under Red Cloud attacked
thirty-two men guarding the wood train sent from Fort
Phil Kearney. These few men, armed with new Springfield
breech-loading rifles and Colt revolvers, overturned their
wagons and prepared a defense-works of wagon boxes. The
first charge by eight hundred Indians—designed primarily
to draw the defenders' fire—was broken up; the second
attack and a third attack of over twelve hundred Indians
was stopped before they ever reached the wagon boxes.
The whites had been able to fire and reload at unprecedented speed, thus confounding the Indians' usual technique—causing whites to fire, and then charging with a
second group before the whites could reload. Indian losses

that afternoon numbered between two hundred and three hundred. Only seven soldiers had been killed.

Although the last battle in Red Cloud's war had been a defeat for the Indians, they continued their attacks all along the Bozeman Trail. Traffic was brought to a standstill, road building stopped, and the forts which had been built to protect the road stood useless. The Treaty of 1868 gave Red Cloud what he demanded: the Indians were to retain their hunting grounds in the Powder River country; no whites were to trespass without the Indians' permission, and all the forts built by the sacrifice of many lives were to be abandoned. Before he signed the treaty, Red Cloud was taken on a grand tour of Washington, and it was proposed to the Sioux chief that he settle on a reservation on the Missouri River. Red Cloud made a speech in which he told how the Indians felt:

> When we first had this land we were strong; now we are melting like snow on a hillside, while you are grown like spring grass. Now, I have come a long distance to my Great Father's house. See if I have left any blood in his land when I go. When the white man comes to my country he leaves a trail of blood behind him. . . .
>
> I have two mountains in that country. The Black Hills and the Big Horn Mountain. I want the Father to make no roads through them. I have told these things three times and now I have come here to tell them the fourth. I do not want my reservation on the Missouri. This is the fourth time I have said so. . . .[18]

Red Cloud was settled on a new reservation—Pine Ridge—created for his people on the Platte River near Fort Laramie; but he continued to serve his people, even after the United States government deposed him as a chief for his opposition to the Black Hills Treaty. Red Cloud lived to be an old man. He witnessed the breaking of the Treaty of 1868 by railroad builders surveying a route for the Northern Pacific Railroad on the south side of the Yellowstone River, in the Powder River country. Red Cloud

---

[18] Quoted in Guinn, "Last Struggle," p. 11.

Red Cloud in very old age. After 1868, Red Cloud was true to the treaty and never fought the white man again. But he had this advice for those of his people who wanted to live like whites: "When your house is built, your store-room filled, then look around for a neighbor whom you can take advantage of and seize all he has."

witnessed the gold rush to his Black Hills, which had been inspired by Colonel George Armstrong Custer's 1874 reconnaissance mission into the region, a violation of the Treaty of 1868. Black Elk has provided an interesting and harsh perspective on the gold rush into the Black Hills:

When I was older, I learned what the fighting was about that winter and the next summer. Up on the Madison Fork the Wasichus had found much of the yellow metal that they worship and that makes them crazy, and they wanted to have a road up through our country to the place where the yellow metal was; but my people did not want the road. It would scare the bison and make them go away, and also it would let the other Wasichus come in like a river. They told us that they wanted only to use a little land, as much as a wagon would take between the wheels; but our people knew better. And when you look about you now, you can see what it was they wanted.

Once we were happy in our own country and we were seldom hungry, for then the two-leggeds and the four-leggeds lived together like relatives, and there was plenty for them and for us. But the Wasichus came, and they have made little islands for us and other little islands for the four-leggeds, and always these islands are becoming smaller, for around them surges the gnawing flood of the Wasichu; and it is dirty with lies and greed.

A long time ago my father told me what his father told him, that there was once a Lakota [Dakota-Sioux] holy man, called Drinks Water, who dreamed what was to be; and this was long before the coming of the Wasichus. He dreamed that the four-leggeds were going back into the earth and that a strange race had woven a spider's web all around the Lakotas. And he said: "When this happens, you shall live in square gray houses, in a barren land, and beside those square gray houses you shall starve." They say he went back to Mother Earth soon after he saw this vision, and it was sorrow that killed him. You can look about you now and see that he meant these dirt-roofed houses we are living in, and that all the rest was true. . . .[19]

[19] *Black Elk Speaks,* pp. 9–10.

In 1875, the government ordered the Sioux to leave their Powder River hunting grounds and warned all who did not withdraw to the reservations along the Platte that they would be "deemed hostile and treated accordingly by the military force." This military force was placed under the command of General Crook, who had just won victories over the Apache Indians in Arizona. Sitting Bull's Sioux and Cheyenne warriors stopped General Crook in a battle along the Rosebud River in June of 1876. In July of that year, the hundredth anniversary of the United States, Custer and 264 men of the 7th Cavalry were killed in a twenty-minute battle near the banks of the Little Big Horn River in southern Montana.

The defeat of Custer only intensified the demands for placing all the Sioux on reservations. In August of 1876, the government took the Black Hills and sent a treaty commission to negotiate with Red Cloud, Spotted Tail, and other chiefs who were at peace with the white man. The commission reported, in part:

> While the Indians received us as friends and listened with kind attention to our proposition, we were painfully impressed with their lack of confidence in the pledges of the government.
>
> At times they told their story of wrongs with such impressive earnestness that our cheeks crimsoned with shame.[20]

Between 1876 and 1881, eight thousand hostile Sioux, including Sitting Bull and Crazy Horse, gave themselves up and went to live on reservations in South Dakota. Crazy Horse—never really defeated in battle—was murdered after having been placed under arrest. Robert M. Utley describes the reservation life of the Sioux:

> . . . During the following decade, the white man cut the very heart out of the only life they knew. Resentful and suspicious, the old life fresh in their memories, they resisted, not altogether successfully, the substitute offered.
>
> At once, they surrendered a large group of customs on

On November 27, 1868, Colonel George Armstrong Custer led the Seventh Cavalry in a surprise attack against Chief Black Kettle (above) and his band of Cheyennes, who had set up their winter camp south of the Canadian River in Indian Territory. The cavalrymen killed more than one hundred Cheyennes and took fifty women and children prisoners. This massacre, called the Battle of the Washita, helps to account for the ferocity of the Little Big Horn confrontation.

[20] Quoted in Guinn, "Last Struggle," p. 14.

which the old life had focused. Warfare was an activity no longer possible. Planning and conducting raids, performing attendant rituals, celebrating success, and mourning failure had once consumed much of the time, interest, and ambition of the Tetons. Now, except when men gather to reminisce, it consumed none. The principal means of attaining prestige, wealth, and high rank vanished the moment they arrived at the agency. . . .

The tribal economy promptly collapsed. The annual buffalo hunt was no more, not only because officials in Washington regarded it as barbaric but also for the very practical reason that buffalo were growing increasingly scarce. That the vanishing herds symbolized their own vanishing way of life cannot have escaped the Sioux.[21]

In the late 1880's, many Plains Indians, sick, starving, and anguished on their reservations, yet knowing that they were no longer able to rise up effectively against their oppressors, turned to religion for solace. Quite literally, they began to dance.

An obscure messiah among the Nevada Paiutes—Wovoka by name—prophesied that if the Indians partook in a complex dance ritual called the Ghost Dance, the white man would disappear from the earth and the buffalo would return. For the most part, Wovoka's message was that Christ—about whom he had learned from missionaries—had been rejected by whites and would this time return as an Indian. He would return if Indians danced the Ghost Dance and followed Christ's precepts: nonviolence and brotherly love. Wovoka's Ghost Dance message spread rapidly among the incarcerated Plains Indians, and white officialdom became alarmed. In 1890, orders went out for the arrest of Sitting Bull, who had in fact been rather skeptical about the whole movement; Sitting Bull, also a holy man, had been afraid that the Ghost Dance would bring new sorrows to his people, and had recognized it for what it was—Indianized missionary

---

[21] Robert M. Utley, *The Last Days of the Sioux Nation* (New Haven, Conn.: Yale University Press, 1963), p. 22. Copyright © 1963 by Yale University. Reprinted by permission of the Yale University Press.

Christianity. Nevertheless, Sitting Bull was considered to be a "fomenter," and Indian police were sent for him. During the arrest, Sitting Bull was killed.

The death of Sitting Bull frightened many Indians, and a band of Sioux under Big Foot fled their own reservation, hoping to find sanctuary with Red Cloud—one of the last great Sioux chiefs—at Pine Ridge. At Wounded Knee Creek, near Pine Ridge, Big Foot was halted and surrounded; he ordered the white flag of surrender to be flown. The army ordered the Indians to disarm. Rifles, knives, axes, and even tent stakes were heaped up in compliance with these orders. The soldiers then insisted upon searching the camp more thoroughly, going through the Indians' personal belongings. A scuffle ensued, and a shot was fired. The army opened fire on Big Foot's encampment with, among other things, two cannons. Men, women, and children were gunned down in the first fire, and then were systematically ridden down and murdered. Big Foot's band included about a hundred warriors and some two hundred and fifty women and children. There were about five hundred soldiers. It has been estimated that as many as three hundred men, women, and children were killed at Wounded Knee.

A portion of Big Foot's Sioux encampment following the massacre at Wounded Knee.

Black Elk was living in Pine Ridge at the time, and he and some of his friends heard the shooting and rode over to Wounded Knee to help. He and a friend managed to save a few infants from the soldiers. Speaking some forty year later, Black Elk had this to say about Wounded Knee:

And so it was all over.

I did not know then how much was ended. When I look back now from this high hill of my old age, I can still see the butchered women and children lying heaped and scattered all along the crooked gulch as plain as when I saw them with eyes still young. And I can see that something else died there in the bloody mud, and was buried in the blizzard. A people's dream died there. It was a beautiful dream.

And I, to whom so great a vision was given in my youth,—you see me now a pitiful old man who has done nothing, for the nation's hoop is broken and scattered. There is no center any longer, and the sacred tree is dead.[22]

In 1890, the year of the Wounded Knee Massacre, the U.S. Bureau of the Census declared the American frontier to be officially closed.

## Indians Today

American Indians today are still fighting a battle for survival. They are fighting to retain what lands they have left, and to preserve their identity as people. Alvin Josephy, Jr., has examined this ongoing struggle in the following terms.:

> Since 1492, Indians have been uninterruptedly on the defensive, fighting for their lives, their homes, their means of sustenance, their societies, and their religions. During that time, on both continents, many of them were assimilated into the white men's civilizations. . . .
>
> Nevertheless, the Indian has survived, still posing to the white conqueror a challenge that not all non-Indians, particularly in the United States, wish happily to tolerate, even, indeed, if they understand it: acceptance of the right to be Indian. That right suggests, at heart, the right to be different, which in the United States runs counter to a traditional drive of the dominant society. Ideally, the American Dream in the United States offers equal opportunities to all persons; but in practice the opportunities imply a goal of sameness, and the Indians, clinging to what seems right and best for them, have instinctively resisted imposed measures by non-Indians designed to make them give up what they want to keep and adopt what they have no desire to acquire. That has been—and continues to be—the core of the so-called "Indian problem" in the United States, which many Indians characteristically refer to as "the white man's problem." Essentially, the Indian recognizes the problem better than the white man. The best-meant aim of the non-Indian is to get the Indian thoroughly assimilated into white society. . . . To the Indian, the concept that being different means being inferior remains—as it has for almost five hundred

[22] *Black Elk Speaks,* p. 276.

years—one of the principal obstacles to his survival. But, ironically, he now views it increasingly—with one eye on the rest of the world—as a concept which the white man must soon shed if he, the white man, expects to survive.

There are other facets to the Indians' resistance to assimilation. To many of them, the argument that they should assimilate (implying detribalization, loss of cultural heritage, and dispersion) is not alone an appeal for them to give up their identity as Indians, but an excuse for the taking of the rest of their lands from them and the ending of their treaty rights and guarantees. The white man may insist that he has other motives that can only be achieved by assimilation: he wants to raise the Indians' standards of living; he wants to give them education, technological know-how, managerial ability, and purchasing power with which to share the white man's affluence. To such arguments, Indians remain deaf: assimilation still means dispossession. Moreover, while most Indians want also to raise their standards of living, they do not see that assimilation is required to do so. More real to them is the need for a new point of view by white men which accepts the right of Indians to manage their own affairs in communities (i.e., reservations) of their own. It is not a new concept. Indians have pleaded in its behalf for years. But they have had little or no response from the non-Indian population, in or out of government, which has failed to recognize the inhibitions, deadening of initiative, and lack of motivation that exist inevitably when an individual or an institution is not vested with responsibility for success or failure.

In contrast to what most Indians would consider a realistic appraisal of the roots of their stagnation, non-Indians generally have made no change for almost a century in their basic point of view concerning the nature of "the Indian problem," but still endorse a national policy founded on the maxims that reservations are intolerable enclaves of different peoples within the nation's boundaries, and that Indians who choose to remain unassimilated on the reservations are incapable of managing their own affairs.[23]

[23] Josephy, *The Indian Heritage,* pp. 346–348.

Perhaps John F. Kennedy, who spoke often about *new* frontiers, also recognized the "Indian problem" as being really the white man's problem when, in the following passage, he emphasized the task of learning that many Americans have before them:

American Indians defy any single description. They were and are far too individualistic. They shared no common language and few common customs. But collectively their history is our history. . . .

When we forget great contributors to our American history—when we neglect the heroic past of the American Indian—we thereby weaken our own heritage. We need to remember the contributions our forefathers found here and from which they borrowed liberally.

When the Indians controlled the balance of power, the settlers from Europe were forced to consider their views and to deal with them by treaties. . . .

But when the American Indians lost their power, they were placed on reservations, frequently lands which were strange to them, and the rest of the nation turned its attention to other matters.

Our treatment of Indians during that period still affects the national conscience. We have been hampered—by the history of our relationship with the Indians—in our efforts to develop a fair national policy governing present and future treatment of Indians. . . .

Before we can set out on the road to success, we have to know where we are going, and before we can know that we must determine where we have been in the past. It seems a basic requirement to study the history of our Indian people.

America has much to learn about the heritage of our American Indians. Only through this study can we as a nation do what must be done if our treatment of the American Indian is not to be marked down for all time as a national disgrace.[24]

[24]John F. Kennedy, "Introduction," *The American Heritage Book of Indians* (New York: American Heritage Publishing Company, 1961), p. 1. Copyright © 1961 by the American Heritage Publishing Company, Reprinted by permission.

Oglala Sioux doing the Ghost Dance at Pine Ridge, 1890.

LIBRARY OF CONGRESS

## SUGGESTED READINGS

Andrist, Ralph K. *The Long Death: The Last Days of the Plains Indians.* Macmillan Co., Collier Books.

*Black Elk Speaks, Being the Life Story of a Holy Man of the Oglala Sioux.* As told through John G. Neihardt (Flaming Rainbow). University of Nebraska Press, Bison Books.

Brown, Dee. *Bury My Heart at Wounded Knee: An Indian History of the American West.* Bantam Books.

Custer, George Armstrong. *My Life on the Plains.* University of Nebraska Press, Bison Books.

De Loria, Vine, Jr. *Custer Died for Your Sins.* Avon Books.

Josephy, Alvin M., Jr. *The Indian Heritage of America.* Bantam Books.

Josephy, Alvin M., Jr. *The Patriot Chiefs: A Chronicle of American Indian Resistance.* Viking Press, Compass Books.

Lowie, Robert H. *Indians of the Plains.* Natural History Press.

Sandoz, Mari. *Crazy Horse: The Strange Man of the Oglalas.* University of Nebraska Press, Bison Books.

Utley, Robert M. *The Last Days of the Sioux Nation.* Yale University Press.

Weltfish, Gene. *The Lost Universe.* Ballantine Books.

One fur trapper is remarking to the other, "I took ye for an Injin." Although
Frederic Remington made this drawing in 1890, long after the trapping frontier
had closed, he captured the look and the spirit of the early mountain men.

## CHAPTER THREE

# THE MOUNTAIN MEN

Frederick Jackson Turner wrote that the frontier stripped the garments of civilization from the frontiersman and arrayed him in the hunting shirt and the moccasin:

> . . . At the frontier the environment is at first too strong for the man. He must accept the conditions which it furnishes, or perish, and so he fits himself into the Indian clearings and follows the Indian trails.[1]

The Indian trader, the fur trapper, or, as he preferred to be called in the West, the mountain man, was the vanguard of the advancing frontier. He was the pathfinder. Turner grew up in a part of the country first explored by the French *voyageurs*, who traded with the Indians for furs, and he wrote his master's thesis on "The Influence of the Fur Trader in the Development of Wisconsin." "The Indian trade pioneered the way for civilization," wrote Turner.

> The buffalo trail became the Indian trail, and this became the traders "trace"; the trails widened into roads, and the roads into turnpikes, and these in turn were transformed into railroads.[2]

[1] Frederick Jackson Turner, *Frontier and Section: Selected Essays of Frederick Jackson Turner,* edited by Ray Allen Billington (Englewood Cliffs, N.J.: Prentice-Hall, 1961), p. 29. © 1961. By permission of Prentice-Hall, Inc., Englewood Cliffs, New Jersey.

[2] Ibid, p. 37.

## The Fur Trade

Meriwether Lewis.

The fur trade was concentrated in the upper Mississippi Valley at the time Meriwether Lewis and William Clark explored the upper Missouri River, the northern Rockies, and the headwaters of the Columbia River from May of 1804 to September of 1806. The journals of Lewis and Clark recorded the possibilities of a profitable fur trade in the West. Only three days after the expedition had departed from its winter camp at the Mandan Indian villages, Lewis wrote:

> At 1 P.M. we overtook three French hunters who had set out a few days before us with a view of trapping beaver; they had taken 12 since they left Fort Mandan. These people avail themselves of the protection which our numbers will enable us to give them against the Assinniboins who sometimes hunt on the Missouri; and intend ascending with us as far as the mouth of the Yellowstone river and continue their hunt up that river. This is the first essay of a beaver hunt on this river. The beaver these people have already taken is by far the best I have ever seen.[3]

William Clark.

Before Lewis and Clark returned to St. Louis, two men, Joseph Dickson and Forest Hancock, set out from Illinois to follow the trail blazed by the Lewis and Clark expedition. These two trappers were camped near the mouth of the Yellowstone River when Lewis and Clark met them on August 12, 1806. They told Clark that they had been hunting and trapping along the Missouri. Although they had had very little luck as yet in taking beaver they were still determined to proceed. Lewis gave them a description of the upper Missouri River and directed them to places where beaver abounded. Three days later, Captain Clark recorded the beginning of the first expedition of mountain men into the wilderness of the Rockies:

Colter one of our men expressed a desire to join [Dickson

[3] Bernard De Voto, ed., *The Journals of Lewis and Clark* (Boston: Houghton Mifflin, 1953), p. 94.

and Hancock] who offered to become shearers with [him] and furnish traps &c. The offer [was] a very advantagious one, to him, his services could be dispenced with . . . and as we were disposed to be of service to any one of our party who had performed their duty as well as Colter had done, we agreed to allow him the privilage provided no one of the party would ask or expect a Similar permission to which they all agreed that they wished Colter every suckcess. . . . We gave Jo Colter Some Small articles which we did not want and some powder and lead. The party also gave him several articles which will be usefull to him on his expedition.[4]

At President Jefferson's request, Lewis and Clark carefully observed the plant and animal life they encountered. On this page of his journal, Clark described the heath cocks of the plains, "which go in large gangues or singularly and hide remarkably close when pursued."

John Colter and his companions trapped along the Yellowstone and spent the winter of 1806–1807 in what is now southern Montana.

In 1808 the first fur trading company of Americans to operate in the Rockies was formed by an experienced trapper of French and Spanish origins, Manuel Lisa. The Missouri Fur Company built Fort Lisa near present-day Omaha in 1812, and this fur trading post remained the most important on the Missouri River until Lisa's death in 1820. Before organizing his company, Lisa employed John Colter and another member of the Lewis and Clark expedition to act as guides and to build a fort at the mouth of the Bighorn River. From Fort Manuel, as this first post in the Rocky Mountain region was known, John Colter traveled through wilderness areas bearing the present-day names of Yellowstone Park, Jackson's Hole, and Pierre's Hole on the upper Snake River. His stories of earth which boiled under one's feet, water which spouted out of the ground, valleys steaming with sulphur fumes, and mountains made of glass resulted in the name "Colter's Hell" being applied to the area. "Out thar in Yellowstone thar's a river that flows so fast it gets hot on the bottom" was the way another mountain man, Jim Bridger, described a portion of the beaver country.

Ray Allen Billington, in his book *The Far Western Frontier,* said of the mountain men:

[4] Ibid., p. 456.

In the 1840's, soldiers commanded by Colonel Kit Carson, the most famous of the mountain men, patrolled the Santa Fe Trail to guard travelers against Indian attacks. In this painting by Charles M. Russell, the clothing and equipment used by Carson's men have been carefully detailed.

Their hour of glory was brief; the trade flourished only between the mid-1820's and the early 1840's. But during those years the fur trappers played a heroic role in opening the land to more permanent settlers. Theirs was the task of spying out fertile valleys that needed only man's touch to yield bountiful harvests, of spreading word of the West's riches throughout the Mississippi Valley, of pioneering routes through mountain barriers, and of breaking down the self-sufficiency of the Indians by accustoming them to the firearms and firewater of civilization. When their day was done all the Far West was readied for the coming of the pioneer farmers.[5]

Billington identified three jumping-off points where the trappers began their invasions of the beaver country. From Taos, in what is now New Mexico, trappers worked the streams from the Pecos on the east to the Gila on the west and virtually exterminated the beaver from this portion of the Rocky Mountains. From Fort Vancouver on the Columbia River, the men of the Hudson's Bay Company of Canada trapped the streams of the Pacific Northwest. St. Louis was the jumping-off point for most American

[5]Ray Allen Billington, *The Far Western Frontier: 1830–1860* (New York: Harper & Row, 1956), p. 41.

trappers and traders, and credit for opening up the northern Rockies should belong to a group of trappers brought together by General William H. Ashley and his partner Andrew Henry. Ashley, lieutenant governor of the new state of Missouri, brought to the partnership business experience and imagination. Henry had been a member of the American Fur Company party which had followed much the same route as Lewis and Clark in proceeding to the mouth of the Columbia to establish Fort Astoria. This group had camped in the Green River Valley of what is today southwestern Wyoming on their return trip east, and in this valley they had discovered some of the finest beaver country in the West.

## The Mountain Men

On February 13, 1822, the following advertisement appeared in the St. Louis *Missouri Gazette & Public Advertiser:*

To

Enterprising Young Men

The subscriber wishes to engage one hundred men, to
ascend the river Missouri to its source, there to be
employed for one, two or three years.—For particulars
enquire of Major Andrew Henry, near the Lead Mines, in
the County of Washington, (who will ascend with, and
command the party) or to the subscriber at St. Louis.

Wm. H. Ashley[6]

By 1822 the fur trade had already made St. Louis the largest and busiest town on the frontier, and Mexico's successful rebellion against Spain in 1821 promised to make it even more important. Unlike the Spanish colonial government, the new Mexican government welcomed settlers from the United States, and St. Louis was the logical starting point for the journey from the American East to

[6]Quoted in Dale L. Morgan, *Jedediah Smith and the Opening of the West* (Lincoln: University of Nebraska Press, 1953), pp. 19–20. Copyright © 1953 by Dale L. Morgan. Reprinted by permission of the Bobbs-Merrill Company, Inc.

the Southwest. At the time Ashley's advertisement appeared, William Becknell was preparing the first wagon caravan to Santa Fe, an undertaking which would make him "Father of the Santa Fe Trail."

Ashley had little difficulty recruiting men for his enterprise. St. Louis's population of five thousand included boatmen, trappers, traders, soldiers, visiting Indians, farmers, miners, and peddlers. The recruits, for the most part, were young and inexperienced in trapping. Among those who survived the first years were the greatest names in the history of fur trapping in the West.

Jim Bridger, a twenty-year-old barkeeper in St. Louis— "Old Gabe" as he was to be called—established Fort Bridger on the Oregon Trail and helped guide the Mormons into the valley of the Great Salt Lake in the late 1840's.

Thomas Fitzpatrick, a native of Ireland, joined Ashley's band at the age of twenty-four. Fitzpatrick's left hand was shattered when his rifle barrel burst accidently, and the Indians called him "Broken Hand" thereafter. But the Indians also referred to Fitzpatrick as "the man who never lied to us, the best agent we ever had." Fitzpatrick became Indian agent for the tribes on the upper Platte and Arkansas rivers in 1846, and from Bent's Fort he dealt with the Cheyennes, Arapahoes, and Kiowas justly and fairly. When the first settlers and miners entered the central Rockies these tribes were friendly, thanks to the work of Fitzpatrick.

Louis Vasquez signed on with Ashley when he was twenty-one. A native of St. Louis, he was half French and half Spanish. Vasquez spent the remainder of his life in the Rocky Mountains. In 1837 he built Fort Vasquez on the South Platte. Later, he went into partnership with Jim Bridger to build Fort Bridger. When the gold rush of 1859 brought swarms of miners into his old hunting grounds, Vasquez made investments in the new town of Denver.

James Beckwourth, whom the nineteenth-century historian Francis Parkman described as "a ruffian of the first stamp, bloody and treacherous," became a co-chief of the Crow Indians and led them against their enemies, the

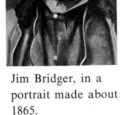

Jim Bridger, in a portrait made about 1865.

Blackfeet. Beckwourth, a mulatto, had earned the reputation of a tough hombre, a daredevil, and a liar when he narrated his experiences as a mountain man for the book *The Life and Adventures of James P. Beckwourth.* Another historian, Bernard DeVoto, said of the book, "It is one of the gaudiest in our literature and may well be the goriest."

The Sublette brothers gave their name to many locations in the West and added legends to the lore of the mountain man. William Sublette, with his partners Dave Jackson (for whom Jackson Hole, Wyoming, was named) and Jedediah Smith, bought out Ashley when he retired wealthy from the trapping business. It was William Sublette who brought the first wagons over what would become the Oregon Trail. His brothers, Milton and Andrew, also became prominent in the fur trade.

Jim Beckwourth, photographed about 1860.

Perhaps the greatest of all the mountain men, in terms of lasting contributions to the history of the West, was Jedediah Smith. Smith was a relatively old man at twenty-four when he joined Ashley and Henry. He was also as much a greenhorn as any member when he joined, but within a year he was appointed the leader of a brigade of sixteen men sent overland from the Missouri River to the valley of the Green River. In his book *Jedediah Smith and the Opening of the West,* Dale Morgan introduces the reader to this deeply religious, natural leader of men:

> In the exploration of the American West, Jedediah Strong Smith is overshadowed only by Meriwether Lewis and William Clark. During his eight years in the West Jedediah Smith made the effective discovery of South Pass; he was the first man to reach California overland from the American frontier, the first to cross the Sierra Nevada, the first to travel the length and width of the Great Basin, the first to reach Oregon by a journey up the California coast. He saw more of the West than any man of his time, and was familiar with it from the Missouri River to the Pacific, from Mexico to Canada. He survived the three worst disasters of the American fur trade, the Arikara defeat of 1823, the Mojave massacre of 1827, and the Umpqua massacre of 1828, in which no less than forty men fell

around him, only to die a lonely death on the Santa Fe Trail under the lances of the Comanches.[7]

The object of the mountain man's wanderings was beaver fur, which was much in demand for the tall beaver hats or "stovepipes" that were fashionable in Europe and the eastern United States from about 1800 through the early 1840's. Beaver pelts brought an average of four dollars per pound at the trading posts; one pelt weighed about a pound and a half, thus the standard "six dollars a plew, prime." A "plew" was a whole pelt and "prime" referred to the condition of the pelt. The best time to trap beaver was when the coat was thick or prime for winter; but since winter trapping was nearly impossible, most pelts were taken in the late fall or early spring.

Generally, a brigade of trappers broke up into smaller parties which worked independently of each other for several days. These smaller parties broke into pairs for the actual trapping; the trappers then rejoined the larger party or the brigade to move on to other streams which had not been trapped out. The trappers usually moved upstream when setting their traps because signs of beaver such as tree shavings would float downstream, as would signs of other trappers or Indians. Usually the higher the trappers moved into the mountains the safer it became for them.

A pair of trappers with their catch.

The most authentic accounts of the life of a fur trapper in the Rocky Mountains are those of Osborne Russell. Russell was one of the very rare trappers who possessed an education and who documented his travels. He accompanied Nathaniel J. Wyeth's trading caravan to the Rocky Mountains in 1834. The purpose of the expedition was to trade with the men of the Rocky Mountain Fur Company, but the cut-throat competition between that company and the American Fur Company left no market for Wyeth's trade goods. In order to dispose of his merchandise, Wyeth constructed Fort Hall on the Snake River in eastern Idaho. It was from Fort Hall that Russell embarked on his career as a mountain man, a career which lasted until 1843. Dur-

[7] Ibid., p. 7.

ing that time the young trapper maintained a journal of his experiences and observations which included the following account of the beaver:

> The Beaver . . . is an amphibeous animal but the instinct with which it is possessed surpasses the reason of a no small portion of the human race. Its average size is about 2½ feet long from the point of the nose to the insertion of the tail, which is from 10 to 15 inches long and from 5 to 9 broad, flat in the shape of a spade, rounded at the corners, covered with a thick rough skin resembling scales. The tail serves the double purpose of steering and assisting it thro. the water by a quick up and down motion. The hind feet are webbed and the toe next the outside on each has a double nail which serves the purpose of a toothpick to extract the splinters of wood from their teeth as they are the only animals that cut large trees for subsistence. . . . Its color is of light brown generally but I have seen them of a jet black frequently and in one instance I saw one of a light cream color having the feet and tail white. The hair is of two sorts, the one longer and coarser, the other fine, short and silky. Their teeth are like those of the rat but are longer and stronger in proportion to the size of the animals.[8]

Traps were set in the late afternoon. The beaver is a nocturnal animal, and by working near dusk the trapper could avoid warning the animals of his presence. This also helped to prevent other trappers from discovering the location of the traps, which, along with the pelts, were too valuable to risk being stolen.

Before setting his traps, the mountain man smeared castoreum, or "medicine" as he called it, on the bank or near the trap to act as bait. The trapper extracted this substance from the beaver and carried it in a small wooden box. The particularly pungent odor of castoreum added to the many other odors accumulated by the typical mountain man. Russell described how castoreum worked as bait.

[8]Osborne Russell, *Journal of a Trapper,* edited by Aubrey L. Haines (Portland: Oregon Historical Society, 1955), pp. 149–150. Reprinted by permission of the Oregon Historical Society, Portland.

[The beaver has] 4 glands opening forward of the arms, two
containing oil with which they oil their coats, the others
containing the castorum, a collection of gummy substance
of a yellow color which is extracted from the food of the
animal and conveyed thro. small vessels into the glands. It
is this deposit which causes the destruction of the Beaver by
the hunters. When a Beaver Male or female leaves the
lodge to swim about their pond they go to the bottom and
fetch up some mud between their forepaws and breast carry
it on to the bank and emit upon it a small quantity of
castorum. Another Beaver passing the place does the same
and should a hundred Beaver pass within the scent of the
place they would each throw up mud covering up the old
castorum and emit new upon that which they had thrown
up. The Trapper . . . sets his trap in the water near the
bank about 6 inches below the Surface, throws a handful of
mud on the bank about one foot from it and puts a small
portion of the castorum thereon. After night the Beaver
comes out of his lodge, smells the fatal bait 2 or 300 yds.
distant and steers his course directly for it; he hastens to
ascend the bank but the trap grasps his foot and soon
drowns him. . . .[9]

After wading into the water to set his traps, the trapper
splashed water over his tracks on the bank to eliminate
all man-scent. When trapping was poor, many mountain
men repeated some ritualistic phrase whose magical effect,
they believed, would ensure a good catch. The Indians
believed that all animals possessed supernatural powers
and that the beaver was among the wisest of animals.
Trappers who had lived for a while among the Indians often
picked up some of their beliefs and superstitions.

Beaver pelts were scraped free of flesh and stretched on
round willow frames to dry in the sun for a day or two.
When the pelt was dry it was folded with the fur on the
inside and marked with the company's symbol or the trapper's name. At the trading post, the pelts were pressed into
packs or bales of one hundred pounds for transportation
back to St. Louis.

[9] Ibid., p. 150.

The trapper's clothing was usually made of buckskin, well fringed at the seams and often highly decorated with beads and porcupine quills. The leather fringes could be used in repairing clothing, moccasins, and equipment. The trapper's buckskin trousers sometimes became so black and greasy that it was difficult to tell, by looking, what they were made of. Because buckskin stretched out of shape in the water, the trapper usually cut the trouser legs short and substituted buffalo-skin leggings before the trapping season began. Stockings were pieces of blanket wrapped around the feet. The mountain man's shirt was of flannel or cotton if he was fortunate; if not, antelope skin served the purpose. Moccasins of elk or buffalo skin were usually decorated with colored beads. Buffalo robes served as blankets and as heavy coats in cold weather. During the winter, the trapper wore a fur cap with a brim and flaps which turned down to protect his ears; in warm weather he wore an old felt hat with a slouched brim and an eagle feather stuck in the band for good luck. When his clothing became too covered with vermin, the trapper laid it across an ant hill and waited for the vermin to be exterminated by the ants.

Equipment included a riding saddle and bridle, a couple of apishamores (square pieces of buffalo robe used as saddle blankets), a sack containing six traps, a powder horn slung under one arm on a strap, and a leather belt from which hung a bullet pouch, a tobacco pouch, and a butcher knife—usually the "Green River" knife made popular by the fur traders. The trapper also carried a small wooden box containing the necessary castoreum and a "fixens" or "possibles" bag filled with everything he might possibly need such as an awl, flints, and a bullet mold. A hatchet attached to the pommel of his saddle and a rifle completed the outfit. A horse and one or more mules were needed to transport the trapper, his equipment, and his pelts.

The trapper purchased necessary supplies and occasional luxury items like beads, trinkets, and sugar from the trading posts, the medium of exchange being "hairy bank notes"—beaver pelts. *Engagés,* the recruits hired by the fur companies at salaries of $200 to $400 a year, received their

A deer trap.

A stretcher for muskrat pelts.

equipment from the *bourgeois* or chief trader of the fur company. Many of the *engagés* were raw recruits from Canada who signed five-year contracts to trap or act as camp tenders. Few of these men completed their engagements. Those who survived blizzards, grizzly bears, Indians, thirst, starvation, and bad treatment at the hands of such employers as the American Fur Company either returned to civilization or became "free trappers." Two categories of free trappers were recognized. Those who purchased their outfits on credit from a fur company and who agreed to sell all their pelts to that company alone were known as "skin trappers." The elite of all trappers were those who trapped for themselves wherever they wished and sold their pelts to the company offering the highest price.

Many terms employed by the mountain men were French in origin. *Bourgeois* was soon corrupted by Americans to "booshway." A *cache* was a hiding place. When a trapper lost his horses to the Indians, he was forced to cache his "fixens" and pelts in a hollow tree, a cave, or more commonly in a hole in the ground which was then filled and well concealed. A cache, as well as a scalp, could be "lifted" or "raised." A trapper might refer to himself as "this child," and to refer to another trapper as "old" showed a form of respect. "Fofaraw" was a term used for trinkets, beads, little metal bells, or any decoration of clothing or personal adornment. Indian wives were preferred by the mountain men because white women were too "fofaraw" for the mountain wilderness; they couldn't take care of a camp or make clothing or prepare buffalo meat. Also an Indian wife was obedient and would accept such punishment as a "lodgepoling" (severe beating) with good grace.

The trapper's speech reflected the type of life he led. On one occasion a group of trappers found a friend's horse and one of them remarked: "Well, it ain't nothin' else, it's the old boy's hoss as sure as shootin' and them Rapahos has rubbed him out at last and raised his animals. Ho, boy! let's lift their hair." In Frederick Ruxton's *Life in the Far West,* Old Bill Williams was quoted on the subject of butchering buffalo meat: "Do 'ee hyar, now, you darned greenhorn, do 'ee spile fat cow like that whar you was raised? The doin's won't shine in this crowd, boy, do 'ee hyar, darn you? What! butcher meat across the grain! why whar'll the blood be goin' to, you precious Spaniard? Down the grain, I say, and let your flaps be long or out the juice'll run slick, do 'ee hyar now?"[10] And Osborne Russell recorded the following bit of mountain wisdom:

> There is a proverb among Mountaineers "That It is better to count ribs than tracks." That is to say it is better to fasten a horse at night untill you can count his ribs with poverty than turn him loose to fatten and count his tracks after an Indian has stolen him.[11]

## The Rendezvous

William Ashley's company, which later became the Rocky Mountain Fur Company, introduced a major change in the western fur trade by abandoning the fixed trading post in favor of the rendezvous system. Jedediah Smith suggested to his partner Ashley that the trading company send a caravan of supplies and equipment to the trappers, thus saving them the journey to a distant trading post to dispose of their pelts and purchase their necessities. An annual summer rendezvous held at a prearranged location would also save the company the expense of maintaining a permanent trading post.

The first rendezvous was held at Henry's Fork on the Green River in 1825. Ashley's trading party, consisting of twenty-five men, fifty pack horses, and a wagon and team, left Fort Atkinson on the Missouri River in November, 1824. The party followed the Platte River to the mountains of northern Colorado, crossed the continental divide at Bridger Pass, and arrived on the Green River in April. Ashley's men, including Tom Fitzpatrick, Jim Clyman,

---

[10] Quoted in George Frederick Ruxton, *Life in the Far West,* edited by LeRoy R. Hafen (Norman: University of Oklahoma Press, 1951), p. 22. Copyright 1951 by the University of Oklahoma Press.

[11] Russell, *Journal of a Trapper,* p. 71.

Zacharias Ham, Robert Campbell, and Jim Beckwourth, crossed the Great Plains and the Rockies at the most difficult time of the year. Snowstorms, bitter cold winds, and the scarcity of meat led Beckwourth to write:

> After passing six days without tasting food, the men were weak and disheartened. I listened to all their murmurings and heart-rending complaints. They often spoke of home and friends, declaring they would never see them more. Some spoke of wives and children whom they dearly loved, and who must shortly become widows and orphans. They had toiled, they said, through every difficulty; had risked their lives among wild beasts and hostile Indians in the wilderness, all which they were willing to undergo; but who could bear up against actual starvation?

Ashley's men learned much from the first rendezvous. The trading caravan for future rendezvous would travel in the spring. It would bring enough trade goods to supply all of Ashley's men as well as trappers employed by other companies who might be attracted to the rendezvous. In future rendezvous, the traders would be better supplied with items in demand by trappers and Indians. The first caravan did not even include a quantity of rum; it carried only sugar, coffee, tobacco, lead, powder, knives, bar iron, and Indian trinkets. Still, this first rendezvous was a financial success, as the *Missouri Advocate* reported on October 5, 1825:

> Our fellow-citizen, Gen. Ashley, has just returned from his adventurous enterprize to the Rocky Mountains, bringing with him one of the richest cargoes of fur that ever arrived at St. Louis. He spent the past winter in the bosom of the mountains, and made excursions in the spring down several of the rivers which go to the Pacific ocean. The furs obtained by him were brought on horses to the waters of the Big Horn, where they were embarked about the middle of Aug. and after a voyage of three thousand miles arrived at St. Louis on the 4th inst.[12]

---

[12] Quoted in Morgan, *Jedediah Smith,* p. 174.

Ashley had returned with eighty to one hundred packs of beaver pelts valued at between $40,000 and $50,000.

Every year for the next fifteen years, a rendezvous was held somewhere in the vicinity of the Green River in southwestern Wyoming. The last rendezvous took place in 1840 at Horse Creek, near the site of an unsuccessful fur trading post which had been dubbed "Fort Nonsense" by the mountain men.

The scene at a rendezvous was one of gambling, horse racing, wrestling, drinking, storytelling, and general carousing. Men who had been in the mountains away from civilization for months looked forward to the annual rendezvous when they could renew acquaintances, relax, and have a good time. In two weeks or less of riotous living, they usually managed to spend everything they had received for their pelts. They purchased their supplies on credit and returned to the mountains even more in debt to the fur company than before, but with pleasant memories to last another year of the fun they had had at the rendezvous.

The trapper paid "mountain prices" for everything he purchased at the rendezvous. The trading companies made profits as high as 2,000 percent on the articles they sold, as this comparison of mountain prices and St. Louis prices shows:

|                    | Mountain Price | St. Louis Price    |
|--------------------|----------------|--------------------|
| Alcohol (diluted)  | $5 pint        | 15¢ gallon         |
| Coffee             | $2 pound       | 15¢ pound          |
| Sugar              | $2 pound       | 9¢ to 13¢ pound    |
| Coarse cloth       | $10 yard       | 14¢ yard (calico)  |
| Flour              | $2 pound       | 2¢ to 3¢ pound     |
| Lead               | $2 pound       | 6¢ pound           |
| Gunpowder          | $2 pound       | 7¢ pound           |

Osborne Russell described those in attendance at a rendezvous:

Here we found the hunting Parties all assembled waiting for the arrival of Supplies from the States. Here presented what might be termed a mixed multitude. The whites were chiefly Americans and Canadian French with some Dutch, Scotch, Irish, English, halfbreed, and full blood Indians, of nearly every tribe in the Rocky Mountains.[13]

Indians usually outnumbered whites at the rendezvous. Lodges and sometimes whole villages of Crows, Snakes, Nez Percés, Bannocks, Flatheads, and perhaps a few Teton-Sioux, Utes, and Cheyennes camped along the tributary streams of the Green, the Snake, and the Wind rivers. The Indians were anxious to trade beaver pelts, buffalo robes, and horses (usually stolen from other Indians or from trappers themselves) for beads, hatchets, kettles, and all too often for liquor. The liquor used in trading was well diluted and the traders made certain that Indians received less than full measure. Often, the bottom of the tin measuring cup was coated with a thick layer of hardened cooking fat. The trader might also thrust a thumb (or even all four fingers) into the cup as he filled it to cheat the Indians still further. Ruxton observed that the traders set to work immediately to induce the Indians to trade on favorable terms:

> In opening a trade a quantity of liquor is first given "on the prairie" [free], as the Indians express it in words, or by signs in rubbing the palm of one hand quickly across the other, holding both flat. Having once tasted the pernicious liquid, there is no fear but they will quickly come to terms; and not unfrequently the spirit is drugged, to render the unfortunate Indians still more helpless. Sometimes, maddened and infuriated by drink, they commit the most horrid atrocities on each other, murdering and mutilating in a barbarous manner, and often attempting the lives of the traders themselves.[14]

Gambling took most of the trappers' profits for the year. Seated in Indian fashion around a fire with a blanket spread out before them, the mountain men gambled away

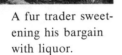

A fur trader sweetening his bargain with liquor.

COURTESY OF THE AMERICAN MUSEUM OF NATURAL HISTORY

---

[13] Russell, *Journal of a Trapper,* p. 58.
[14] Ruxton, *Life in the Far West,* p. 99.

their pelts, mules, rifles, hunting packs, shirts, and breeches. The gamblers even challenged each other to play for the highest stakes: the trapper's squaw, if he had one, his horses, or, as once happened, his scalp. When all his possessions had been lost, the trapper exclaimed: "There goes hoss and beaver!" "Hoss and beaver" usually became the possessions of the fur company's traders.

One of the quickest ways to lose "hoss and beaver" was the Indian game of "hand."

> A small piece of carved bone . . . was held by the gambler, who joining his closed fists together one above the other, could thus pass it into either, he then separated them and threw his arms wide apart, singing and jerking his body up and down, and again bringing his hands together, and changing or pretending to change the bone, the gamblers choosing only when the hands were held wide apart. If the guess is right, the guesser pulls away his pile with that of the bone holder.[15]

The most enjoyable aspect of the rendezvous, to most of the trappers, was the conversation, the swapping of stories around the fire at night. Few of the stories told by mountain men have been preserved in American folklore as have the legends of rivermen, lumberjacks, and cowmen. The average trapper was illiterate, and he appreciated the rare instances when someone like Jed Smith would read aloud from the Bible. Jim Bridger loved to listen to someone read the classics and remarked that Shakespeare, in writing of the murder of two young princes, must "have had a bad heart and been as devilish mean as a Sioux, to have written such scoundrelism as that." In *Across the Wide Missouri,* Bernard De Voto gives this description of the yarn-spinning of the mountain men:

> It was shop talk, trapping, hunting, trailing, fighting Indians, escaping from Indians, the lore of animals and plants, and always the lay of the land and old fields revisited and new fields to be found, water and starvation and trickery and

[15] Bernard De Voto, *Across the Wide Missouri* (Boston: Houghton Mifflin, 1947), p. 98.

feasts. How Long Hatcher had lifted those Apache scalps. How one who was with us last year was eviscerated by a grizzly or gutshot by a Blackfoot. How Old Gabe outsmarted a Blackfoot war party, or Tom Fitzpatrick lay in his crevice while the Gros Ventres looked for him, or a Delaware . . . had taunted the Arikaras who were killing him piecemeal. How one's partner had wandered into a canyon quite unknown even to these masters of geography, how another had stolen the daughter of a Sioux medicine man or a Taos rancher, how a third had forted up behind his slaughtered horse and held off fifty Comanches. How we came into Taos or the Pueblo of Los Angeles and the . . . brandy we drank and the horses we stole.[16]

Their pelts traded, their money spent, outfitted with new strings of traps, and with fresh supplies of tobacco, powder, and lead, the trappers left the rendezvous. Traveling in groups, or in pairs, or singly, they headed back to the mountains to search out new beaver grounds, to hole up for the winter in some isolated valley, and to return in the summer—if they were lucky—to the next rendezvous.

### Primitive Existence

To a greater extent than any other group of pioneers, the mountain men reverted to the most primitive existence. For much of his life the fur trapper lived in an environment completely cut off from all contacts with civilization; in order to survive, he was forced to adapt himself to the environment of nature and not of man. Enemies were everywhere, and the trapper had to be constantly on the alert. He was completely on his own. His food and water supply depended upon his ability to secure them, and any injury which he or his animals might sustain had to be treated by the mountain man himself. He had to provide his own clothing, repair his own equipment, build his own shelters, and gather his own firewood in a country often barren of timber.

In order to survive in the wilderness, it is often said, the

---

[16] Ibid., p. 45.

fur trapper was forced to adopt the way of life of the Indian. It is true that the trapper did adopt many of the Indian's techniques for survival and some of the Indian's beliefs and customs. Many trappers took Indian wives. But the life of the average mountain man was far more primitive than that of any Indian. Despite dislocations and deprivations caused by the white man, the Indian was part of a community. He had a medicine man to attend him when he was sick; he had neighbors whose work contributed to his comfort; he had a family and friends with whom to share his hopes and fears and imaginings; he had tribal elders to advise him, praise him, or rebuke him when he did not live up to his responsibilities. He had an ancient tradition that defined his spiritual relationship to his environment in addition to giving him the tactical knowledge to survive there. He was, in short, a civilized man, a member of an organized society—although that society lived closer to nature than the white man's. The mountain man, on the other hand, had left civilization behind. There was no one to help him, no one to judge him. Much of what he had learned as proper or decent behavior in the East proved unsuitable in the West, so he dropped it. He seldom attempted to replace the white man's notions of civilized behavior with the Indian's notions of civilized behavior. As a result, the mountain man's personal habits and his treatment of other people and animals were often shocking to white men and Indians alike.

In leading a war party of Crow Indians against a party of Blackfoot Indians, a trapper was seen cutting off the hands of the wounded enemy and gouging out their eyes. In more than one instance trappers who were starving were known to have resorted to cannibalism. The story is told of "Cannibal Phil" who was lost in a winter blizzard but reappeared in camp with the leg of his Indian companion packed on his mule; throwing the leg to the ground, Phil was reputed to have said: "There, I won't have to gnaw on you any more."

A mountain man was as expert in taking a scalp as any Indian warrior. Taking a firm hold of the scalp with one hand, he would make two semicircular incisions on either side, loosen the skin with his knife, and place his feet against the dead man's shoulders until the scalp pulled loose.

At the rendezvous of 1829, held at Pierre's Hole on the Snake River, a trapper purchased a small kettle of alcohol and passed it around the campfire. After the kettle had made several rounds, one of the mountain men seized it and poured the contents over another trapper. Then he picked up a lighted stick and touched it to the other's clothing.

A battle took place at Pierre's Hole in 1832 when a large number of trappers who had just left the rendezvous ran into an entire village of Gros Ventre Indians, who were on their way to the country of their allies, the Blackfoot Indians. During the battle both sides "forted up" and neither group could dislodge the other. The mountain men decided that the best way to take care of the Gros Ventres was to set fire to the surrounding dry grass and brush. But Indian allies of the mountain men argued against burning the enemy to death, not because of any feeling of humanity toward their enemy but because too much valuable loot would also be burned up in the process. In this one instance practicality won out over savagery.

The mountain men gorged themselves on meat when the hunting was good. When they had plenty, they ate the best pieces first for fear "of being killed by some brat of an Indian before we have enjoyed them. . . ." The best pieces of the buffalo were the hump ribs which were given a peppery flavor by being roasted over a fire of buffalo chips. Warm buffalo blood reminded the mountain men of fresh milk. The liver, flavored by the contents of the full bladder, was eaten raw. Bones were cracked, and the marrow extracted. Meat was pulled off the ribs and gulped down while grease dripped off the trapper's chin and ran down his clothing. From time to time he might wipe his hands on his clothing or his long hair, but he would continue eating until he had devoured about eight or nine pounds of buffalo meat.

Frederick Ruxton wrote of watching two Canadian trappers eating buffalo intestines, or *"boudins"*:

They commenced at either end of such a coil of grease, the
mass lying between them on a dirty apishamore like the
coil of a huge snake. As yard after yard glided glibly down
their throats, and the serpent on the saddle-cloth was
dwindling from an anaconda to a moderate-sized
rattlesnake, it became a great point with each of the feasters
to hurry his operation, so as to gain a march upon his
neighbor and improve the opportunity by swallowing more
than his proportion; each at the same time exhorting the
other, whatever he did, to feed fair and every now and
then, overcome by the unblushing attempts of his partner to
bolt a vigorous mouthful, would suddenly jerk back his
head, drawing out at the same moment, by the retreating
motion, several yards of *boudin* from his neighbor's stomach
and, snapping up the ravished portions, greedily swallowed
them.[17]

When food was scarce "meat was meat," as the trapper
said, and he would eat anything—boiled beaver tail, his
own moccasins, a puppy dog, or the ears off his own mule.
During "starvin' times" a trapper might bleed his horse
and drink the blood. One trapper held his hands over an
ant hill until they were covered with ants, then "greedily
licked them off." And, like the Indians of the Great Basin,
trappers sometimes gathered large black crickets, threw
them into a kettle of boiling water, and, when they stopped
kicking, ate them.

Even when meat was available, lack of firewood or a
storm might make preparation of it difficult. Such an occasion was described by Osborne Russell:

We sat down round the fire with each holding a piece of
beef over it on a stick with one hand while the other was
employed in keeping up the blaze by feeding it with wet
sage and weeds until the meat was warmed thro. when it
was devoured with an observation that "Bull Meat was dry
eating when cooked too much." After supper (if I may be
allowed to disgrace the term by applying it to such a
Wolfish feast) we spread the Bull skin down in the mud in

---

[17]Ruxton, *Life in the Far West*, p. 41.

Trappers around a campfire. Notice the shelter dug into the hill and the heavy double-jawed steel traps.

the dryest place we could find and laid down upon it. Our fire was immediately put out by the rain. . . . We lay tolerably comfortable whilst the skin retained its animal warmth and remained above the surface but the mud being soft the weight of our bodies sunk it by degrees below the water level which ran under us on the skin but we concluded it was best to lie still and keep the water warm that was about us. . . .[18]

The trapper became used to hardships. When he suffered from attacks of arthritis, he accepted them as a natural result of wading around in icy streams to set his traps. The attack of a huge grizzly bear upon Jedediah Smith would have killed a lesser man, but the incident offers an example of the mountain man's acceptance of misfortune and his toleration of pain. Such was the attitude described by Smith's companion, Jim Clyman:

Grissly did not hesitate a moment but sprang on the Capt taking him by the head first pitc[h]ing sprawling on the earth he gave him a grab by the middle . . . breaking several of his ribs and cutting his head badly none of us

[18] Russell, *Journal of a Trapper,* p. 75.

having any sugical Knowledge what was to be done one Said come take hold and he wuld say why not you so it went around I asked the Capt what was best he said one or 2 [go] for water and if you have a needle and thread git it out and sew up my wounds around my head which was bleeding freely I got a pair of scissors and cut off his hair and then began my first Job of d[r]essing wounds upon examination I [found] the Bear had taken nearly all his head in his capcious mouth close to his left eye on one side and close to his right ear on the other and laid the skull bare to near the crown of the head leaving a white streak whare his teeth passed one of his ears was torn from his head out to the outer rim after stitching all the other wounds in the best way I was capable and according to the captains directions the ear being the last I told him I could do nothing for his Eare. O you must try to stitch up some way or other said he then I put in my needle stitching it through and through and over and over laying the lacerated parts togather as nicc as I could with my hands. . . .[19]

Although Jed Smith recovered from his wounds, other mountain men were less fortunate. It mattered little whether a man died from a grizzly's claws, an Indian's arrows, or a blizzard; his death was accepted with little comment and less mourning by his companions. Each man knew that death was to be expected as part of the kind of life he led. "Poor fellow! Out of luck" was the usual reaction to a friend's death.

The mountain man's speech took on some characteristics of Indian speech. A trapper's "wagh" was the equivalent of the Indians' "ugh" and indicated agreement or approval. The trapper's voice was also usually high pitched, like that of the Indian, and his manner of emphasizing each spoken syllable reflected the Indian pattern of speech.

Indian names for geographic places were colorful and descriptive. So, too, were place names applied by trappers: Hell Roaring Creek, Stinkingwater River, Sweetwater Valley, Sunlight Basin, Medicine Lodge, Two-Ocean Pass,

[19] Quoted in Morgan, *Jedediah Smith*, p. 84.

Beaverhead Rock, and the Bighorn Mountains. Water dirtied by the fine sand blown into it by the wind, so muddy that it was scarcely drinkable, gave the Powder River its name.

By the late 1830's, there were few beaver left in the western mountains. Every valley and river had been explored and trapped by the mountain men. They had become familiar with every geographic feature, every Indian trail, and every mountain pass. When the silk topper replaced the beaver hat as the fashionable headwear, the era of the mountain man was at an end. Few of the trappers returned to "the States." They preferred instead to hunt buffalo, guide emigrant trains, or scout for the American army in the Mexican War. Perhaps returning to civilization was not really possible for the kind of man described by Osborne Russell:

A trading post in Canada, photographed near the end of the nineteenth century.

Here [on the Platte] we had plenty of wood water meat and dry grass to sleep on, and taking everything into consideration we thought ourselves comfortably situated—comfortably I say for mountaineers, not for those who never repose on anything but a bed of down or sit or recline on anything harder than Silken cushions for such would spurn at the idea of a Hunter's talking about comfort and happiness. But experience is the best Teacher hunger good Sauce and I really think to be acquainted with misery contributes to the enjoyment of happiness and to know ones self greatly facilitates the Knowledge of Mankind. One thing I often console myself with and that is the earth will lie as hard upon the Monarch as it will on a Hunter and I have no assurance that it will lie upon me at all. My bones may in a few years or perhaps days be bleaching on the plains in these regions like many of my occupation without a friend to turn even a turf upon them after a hungry wolf has finished his feast.[20]

Frederick Jackson Turner considered Hiram Chittenden's study *The American Fur Trade of the Far West,* published in 1902, the best general account of this phase of

BROWN BROTHERS

---

[20] Russell, *Journal of a Trapper,* p. 76.

WALTERS ART GALLERY

A trapper and his wife, painted by A. J. Miller in 1853.

the frontier. Turner utilized Chittenden's work on the fur
trade in his own writings and included it in his list of
references for his students. Turner stated that at the frontier
the environment is too strong for the man. He must accept
the conditions which it furnishes, or perish. Chittenden
observed that the very nature of the fur trade determined
the character of the frontier trader and trapper:

> It was the roving trader and the solitary trapper who first
> sought out these inhospitable wilds, traced the streams to
> their sources, scaled the mountain passes, and explored a
> boundless expanse of territory where the foot of the white
> man had never trodden before. The Far West became a
> field of romantic adventure, and developed a class of men
> who loved the wandering career of the native inhabitant
> rather than the toilsome lot of the industrious colonist. The
> type of life thus developed, though essentially evanescent,
> and not representing any profound national movement, was
> a distinct and necessary phase in the growth of this new
> country.[21]

[21]Hiram Chittenden, *The American Fur Trade of the Far West* (San
Francisco: Academic Reprints, 1954), 1: xxiv.

The environment influenced the trader and trapper, but what influence did these early frontiersmen have upon the course of national development? Chittenden emphasized the following influences: The traders and trappers were the real "pathfinders" of the West; they were the first explorers and they established the routes of travel; their knowledge of the West aided Brigham Young in selecting the Great Salt Lake Valley as the home of the Mormon people; they guided the military forces of the United States into New Mexico and to Santa Fe, which had been virtually won to the Americans as a result of years of trade; they guided the emigrant trains to Oregon and the forty-niners to California; and they acted as guides for government exploring parties.

As he adopted the ways of the Indian, so too did the mountain man influence the Indian's destiny. This influence was, according to Chittenden, "profound and far-reaching":

A mountain man in search of fresh beaver country, his supplies loaded on his pack horse. Drawn by Frederic Remington.

If the traders brought with them corrupting vices and desolating disease, they also brought to the Indian his first lessons in the life that he was yet to lead. They mingled with his people, learned his language, and customs, understood his character, and, when not impelled by business rivalry, treated him as a man and as a brother. . . . It was only in these early years that the white man and the Indian truly understood each other.[22]

[22] Ibid., p. xxvi.

## SUGGESTED READINGS

Billington, Ray Allen. *The Far Western Frontier: 1830–1860.* Harper & Row, Torchbooks.

Carson, Kit. *Kit Carson's Autobiography.* University of Nebraska Press, Bison Books.

De Voto, Bernard. *Across the Wide Missouri.* Houghton Mifflin, Sentry Editions.

De Voto, Bernard, ed. *The Journals of Lewis and Clark.* Houghton Mifflin, Sentry Editions.

Gregg, Josiah. *Commerce of the Prairies.* Edited by Milo Milton Quaife. University of Nebraska Press, Bison Books.

Morgan, Dale L. *Jedediah Smith and the Opening of the West.* University of Nebraska Press, Bison Books.

Russell, Osborne. *Journal of a Trapper.* University of Nebraska Press, Bison Books.

Tibbles, T. H. *Buckskin and Blanket Days: Memoirs of a Friend of the Indians.* University of Nebraska Press, Bison Books.

Vestal, Stanley. *Jim Bridger: Mountain Man.* University of Nebraska Press, Bison Books.

Vestal, Stanley. *The Missouri.* University of Nebraska Press, Bison Books.

## CHAPTER FOUR

# THE PROSPECTORS

In 1838, in a speech to the United States Senate, Daniel Webster asked:

> What do we want with this vast worthless area, this region of savages and wild beasts, of deserts, shifting sands and whirlwinds of dust, of cactus and prairie dogs? To what use could we ever hope to put these great deserts or those endless mountain ranges, impregnable and covered to their very base with eternal snow? What use have we for such a country?
>
> ... I shall never vote one cent from the public treasury to place the Pacific Coast one inch nearer Boston than it is now.[1]

Webster's attitude toward the far West, although widespread, was not universal. In the early 1840's, worried by increasing French and British interest in the Pacific Coast, President James K. Polk attempted to buy California from Mexico. Failing in that, he instructed his consul at Monterey, a wealthy merchant named Thomas Oliver Larkin, to work toward the peaceful annexation of the region. Before Larkin could get this plan underway, however, California was proclaimed a "sovereign republic" by a

[1]Quoted in Robert L. Perkin, *The First Hundred Years* (Garden City, N.Y.: Doubleday, 1959), p. 12. Copyright © 1959 by the Denver Publishing Company. Reprinted by permission of Doubleday & Company, Inc.

In the photograph on the opposite page, a prospector is panning for gold.

LOS ANGELES COUNTY MUSEUM OF NATURAL HISTORY

99

BROWN BROTHERS

John C. Frémont ran for the presidency as the first candidate of the new Republican party in 1856, losing to James Buchanan.

group of Americans—led by the soldier-explorer John C. Frémont—who had succeeded in taking over the town of Sonoma on June 14, 1846, in an armed uprising known as the Bear Flag Revolt. In time, the Americans (or "Anglos," as the native Californians called them) would probably have extended their control throughout the territory, and California would have become an independent, Texas-style republic. As it was, however, the Mexican War intervened, and California was occupied by American troops in less than a month.

Despite the success of the Bear Flag Revolt and the relative ease with which the American army occupied the region, there were not many Anglos in California in 1846—probably no more than 1,500. A few were fur trappers who had settled in the valleys where they had once sought beaver, a few were ranchers who had obtained large tracts of land from the Mexican government, but most were businessmen and craftsmen in the larger settlements such as Monterey and San Francisco. Pioneer farmers generally preferred the Oregon territory, where the countryside and climate were more like the eastern parts of the nation. Instead, California's rich farms, ranches, and orchard lands were occupied by "Hispanos," or Californians of Mexican and Spanish descent—about 10,000 of them scattered from San Diego up through the San Joaquin Valley to Sacramento and beyond. It was the Hispanos' isolation from one another, together with the absence of a strong territorial government, that made the American takeover so easy.

In 1846, both Anglos and Hispanos were outnumbered by the third element of California's population, the Indians. About 5,000 "Hispanized" Indians worked as craftsmen and laborers in coastal villages near the old missions, which had been reduced to the status of ordinary parish churches when the Mexicans took over from the Spanish in 1821, or as servants and vaqueros on the large ranches. The great majority of the Indians, however, lived in the foothills and valleys of the interior. Their number has been estimated at 200,000 to 300,000. Although their territories had been reduced somewhat by the settlers' ranches, for the most part their traditional way of life remained undisturbed. They had neither horses nor guns and were divided into very small tribes or "tribelets"—a tribe might consist of no more than a single village. Each group had its own fairly well-defined hunting territory, its own leaders and customs, and usually its own language. The California Indians did not practice agriculture but lived by hunting, fishing, and gathering wild fruits, berries, and nuts. Acorns served as substitute for corn and grain; the acorns were ground into a meal which was washed to remove the tannic acid and then cooked into a porridge or baked into flat cakes. The white settlers considered this way of life very primitive and often referred to the California Indians as "diggers" because the Indians dug up edible roots and insects with sharp sticks. Digging was never the Indians' primary means of subsistence, although they were forced to resort to it more frequently after the settlers came and took their best lands. On the whole, the California Indians were a remarkably peaceful people, with very little history of warfare among themselves and no organized or efficient means of defending themselves against intruders.

On February 2, 1848, Mexico signed the Treaty of Guadalupe Hidalgo, ceding California and most of the rest of the present American Southwest to the United States. Two weeks earlier, an event had taken place near Sacramento on the estate of John Augustus Sutter which was to bring nearly a hundred thousand people into California within a year, nearly a quarter of a million within three years. It brought statehood to California in two years. Sutter was a Swiss immigrant who had obtained a land grant of about seventy-five square miles from the Mexican government and had enlarged this vast holding by buying up Fort Ross, the Russians' last possession in California. He described what happened on January 28, 1848:

John Sutter.

I was sitting one afternoon just after my siesta, engaged . . . in writing a letter to a relation of mine at Lucerne, when I was interrupted by Mr. Marshall, a gentleman with whom I had frequent business transactions—bursting into the room. From the unusual agitation in his manner I imagined that something serious had occurred, and, as we involuntarily do in this part of the world, I at once glanced to see if my rifle was in its proper place. You should know that the mere appearance of Mr. Marshall at that moment in the Fort, was quite enough to surprise me, as he had but two days before left the place to make some alterations in a mill for sawing pine planks, which he had just run up for me some miles higher up the Americanos [River]. When he had recovered himself a little, he told me that, however great my surprise might be at his unexpected reappearance, it would be much greater when I heard the intelligence he had come to bring me. "Intelligence," he added, "which if properly profited by, would put both of us in possession of unheard-of wealth—millions and millions of dollars, in fact." I frankly own, when I heard this that I thought something had touched Marshall's brain, when suddenly all my misgivings were put at an end by his flinging on the table a handful of scales of pure virgin gold.[2]

Marshall had discovered the gold when widening the tail-race of Sutter's mill. Telling no one of his discovery, he rode the forty miles to Sutter's fort with the news which he hoped would bring wealth to himself and his employer. Instead, it brought ruin to Sutter, who in 1848 was the most powerful man in California and a candidate for territorial governor. His estate was overrun by gold seekers, who settled on his land and stole his cattle. Although his land grant was confirmed by the United States Supreme Court, he could not afford the litigation necessary to evict the hundreds of squatters and recover his property. In 1864 the California state legislature voted him a pension of $250 a month. Sutter died in Washington, D.C., in 1880, still trying to persuade Congress to compensate him for his losses.

At first, however, only a few people learned about the discovery at Sutter's mill. Some of these first prospectors were members of a Mormon battalion which had been recruited by President Polk to fight in the Mexican War. After the battalion was disbanded, most of its members

---

[2]Quoted in Harry T. Peters, *California on Stone* (Garden City, N.Y.: Doubleday, 1935), p. 67.

BROWN BROTHERS

Sutter's sawmill on the American River.

made their way back to the Mormon settlements in Utah. But a few stayed behind and began prospecting up the south fork of the American River. According to tradition, news of success at these Mormon diggings was brought to San Francisco by a prominent merchant of that town, Sam Brannan. Brannan was said to have rushed through the plaza shouting, "Gold! Gold! Gold! from the American River." For proof he displayed a bottle of gold dust to the excited onlookers.

## The Forty-Niners

BUREAU OF PRINTING AND ENGRAVING

Within a month, San Francisco was all but depopulated as its inhabitants abandoned homes, shops, and even schools, in their rush to the Sierras. Sailors deserted their ships in San Francisco harbor; men from Oregon abandoned the farms they had traveled two thousand miles to claim. Mexicans from Sonora and Kanakas from the Hawaiian Islands joined the Californians and Oregonians in washing over five million dollars' worth of gold dust out of the Sacramento River and its tributaries in 1848. News of gold strikes on the Sacramento spread rapidly through the States. When the presence of gold in California was given official recognition by President Polk himself, even the most cautious of would-be prospectors were

President James K. Polk.

caught up in the fever. The president informed Congress in December of 1848 that the abundance of gold in the California territory would scarcely command belief. The gold rush of 1849 was underway.

By midsummer of 1849, over forty thousand "forty-niners" were on the overland trails headed for the diggings. By 1850, as many as eighty thousand gold seekers had reached California by way of the Oregon, California, Santa Fe, or other trails, some of which crossed northern Mexico. Another thirty-five thousand had reached California by ship, either by way of the Cape Horn route or by way of Panama, where they crossed the isthmus and awaited ships on the Pacific side.

Travelers who could afford the time and expense of the Cape Horn route preferred it for its relative comfort and safety. The Panama route was favored by those who wanted, for one reason or another, to beat the crowds to the gold fields. Gamblers, speculators, businessmen, and politicians usually favored the quickest possible route. One such forty-niner was Bayard Taylor, a twenty-four-year-old writer for the *New York Tribune*. Arriving on the Pacific side of the isthmus, Taylor found nearly three hundred men competing for the fifty-two available steamship passages to California. A few months before, three thousand men had awaited passage on a ship of any kind.

Many of the ships were not seaworthy. Conditions were crowded and dirty. Food was often ill-prepared and sometimes in short supply. Taylor wrote of his voyage:

Our vessel was crowded fore and aft: exercise was rendered quite impossible and sleep was each night a new experiment, for the success of which we were truly grateful. We were roused at daylight by the movements on deck, if not earlier, by the breaking of a hammock-rope and the thump and yell of the unlucky sleeper. . . . The breakfast hour was nine, and the table was obliged to be fully set twice. At the first tingle of the bell, all hands started as if a shot had exploded among them; conversation was broken off in the middle of a word; the deck was instantly cleared, and the passengers, tumbling pell-mell down the cabin-stairs, found every seat taken by others who had probably been sitting in them for half an hour. . . . There was a confused grabbing motion for a few seconds, and lo! the plates were cleared. A chicken parted in twain as if by magic, each half leaping into an opposite plate; a dish of sweet potatoes vanished before a single hand; beef-steak flew in all directions. . . .[3]

While the Panama route was quickest, taking six to eight weeks, the overland routes were most popular because overland travel required the least expenditure of money. Many a farm boy from the Mississippi Valley reached California on physical strength, determination, a wagon and oxen borrowed from his family, and a few dollars' worth of food and hand tools. Planning and organization characterized some journeys to the gold fields, however. "Stock companies" were organized in the East and even in Europe to raise enough money to purchase and outfit ships for the voyage. Once in the gold fields, the company members were supposed to share their profits.

Most forty-niners followed the trail established by the Oregon pioneers, usually to a point beyond Fort Hall in what is now Idaho. From the Snake River to the Sacramento, they encountered obstacles not included in such popular guidebooks of the day as Lansford Hastings' *Emigrants' Guide* and John C. Frémont's *Report of the Exploring Expedition to the Rocky Mountains in 1842*. A later guidebook gave the following advice:

We would recommend emigrants who have cattle to shoe them, and we would advise, not to take them further on the route than Fort Hall, or Great Salt Lake, but exchange them there for others, or horses. It is useless for men to start from either of these places with worn out cattle, as they never will get them to their journey's end. . . . The road from the States to Salt Lake or Fort Hall, is comparatively a railroad to the one from thence to California. We would recommend no man to overload his

Miners climbing a "corduroy road" of rough-hewn logs through the mountains to the gold fields.

[3]Quoted in Paul Angle, ed., *The American Reader* (Chicago: Rand McNally, 1958), p. 251.

wagon with tools, &c., for spades, shovels, picks, &c., can be purchased cheap in California. Throw away your old yokes, chains, boxes, &c., for you will do so before you cross the desert, no wagon should have more than 800 lbs. with three yoke of cattle.

. . . Pack animals are the best all the time, and single men had by all means better pack. Hard bread is the best to take from either of these places; also dried beef.

Clothes can be bought in Sacramento and Stockton, as cheap as in the States, and it is useless for men to overload themselves with such articles, to retard their movements. . . . Men carrying ploughs, anvils, gold washers, stoves, or any other article of weight, may as well throw them away, or dispose of them; as it is perfectly useless to wear out their cattle, and at last leave the cattle, and goods between this [Salt Lake City] and California.

After the emigrant settles on his winter diggins, he had better secure provisions enough to last him until April; together with pickles, vinegar, &c. as a preventive to the scurvy.

Emigrants had better not dispose of their animals when they are poor, but place them in good hands on ranches; as a poor horse or ox will not fetch over $10 or $15, while a fat ox or horse is worth $100.[4]

A pack train bringing supplies to a mining town.

Deviating from the established trails could be dangerous, and travelers who did so often lost equipment and livestock and sometimes their lives.

Came from Iowa to Calif. in '49 across the plains in ox teams, 7 Months Enroute—with 64 wagons. All went well till we reached Salt Lake. It being late in the season we concluded to winter at Utah Fort but learning that the Mormons were about to attack us we broke camp and with a Mexican guide took the south route for Los Angeles which was the pioneer train over that route being 5 days at times going 3 Miles. At Santa Clara Canyon the Indians

----

[4]Quoted in LeRoy R. and Ann W. Hafen, eds., *Journals of Forty-Niners* (Glendale, Calif.: Arthur H. Clark, 1954), pp. 324–325. Reprinted by permission of the Arthur H. Clark Company.

ran off 9 head Cattle and shot one full of arrows. We surprised one of the braves who had his bow bent to fire on us by shooting him on the spot, which threw the enemy into disorder and so we escaped further trouble. Soon after leaving this place we ran short of provisions and my brother and myself started in pursuit of rations. Instead of reaching the settlements in 3 days we were 13 days and for 3 days and nights had nothing to eat. . . .[5]

The author failed to explain what his party had done to provoke the Mormons into an attack upon their train. He did note, however, that upon arrival in California he engaged in mining and made "plenty of money." His account concluded: "In coming into Cal. I came as a poor boy and what fortune I have at the present was made by hard labor and industrious habits—being perfectly temperate all my life."[6]

Both his success as a miner and the temperance of his habits would have distinguished the forty-niner just quoted from most of his companions in the diggings. California society was decidedly masculine during the first years of the gold rush, and most of the men were under forty years of age. In the spring of 1849 there were very few respectable, "homelike" women in San Francisco, California's largest city. One seventeen-year-old miner rode thirty-five miles just to see a miner's wife who had recently arrived in the district. The young man was reminded of home when, after sewing on a button, the woman admonished him for gambling and drinking.

The mines of the Mother Lode district placed all men on the same level. Family background, manners, and style of dress and speech mattered little in the mining regions, at least during those early months. The richest man in camp might not be able to hire a servant because those who had been servants were working their own claims. Every man had the same start, and the least experienced miner of the camp might suddenly strike it rich.

This mock-serious portrait shows a miner with the tools of his trade, which include two pistols and a whiskey jug.

A cartoon entitled "The Independent Gold Hunter on His Way to California."

[5]Quoted in ibid., pp. 54–55.
[6]Quoted in ibid., p. 55.

Charles Howard Shinn was born in California during the gold rush. As a young man he became well acquainted with mining communities through teaching school in a number of them. In his book *Mining Camps, a Study in American Frontier Government,* he described the make-up of a typical camp:

> Take a sprinkling of sober-eyed, earnest, shrewd, energetic New-England business-men: mingle with them a number of rollicking sailors, a dark band of Australian convicts and cut-throats, a dash of Mexican and frontier desperadoes, a group of hardy back-woodsmen, some professional gamblers, whiskey-dealers, general swindlers, or "rural agriculturists" . . . and having thrown in a promiscuous crowd of broken-down merchants, disappointed lovers, black sheep, unfledged dry-goods clerks, professional miners from all parts of the world . . . stir up the mixture, season strongly with gold-fever, bad liquors, faro, monte, rouge-et-noir, quarrels, oaths, pistols, knives, dancing, and digging, and you have something approximating to California society in early days.[7]

Two prospectors examining a lucky find—a gold nugget.

But Shinn was far from disapproving of the miners or their camps. On the contrary, he praised the forty-niner as "an organizer of society":

> He often appears in literature as a dialect-speaking rowdy, savagely picturesque, rudely turbulent: in reality, he was a plain American citizen cut loose from authority, freed from the restraints and protections of law, and forced to make the defense and organization of society a part of his daily business.[8]

## Mining Techniques

The early gold discoveries in California, the Pikes Peak region, the Black Hills, and the other areas which experienced gold rushes, were all placer deposits. These deposits were located near the surface of the soil, in stream beds,

---

[7] Charles Howard Shinn, *Mining Camps, a Study in American Frontier Government* (New York: Harper & Row, 1965), p. 158.
[8] Ibid., pp. 134–135.

Miners working a placer deposit along the bank of a ravine.

and along the banks of gulches and ravines. Placer mining consisted, basically, of separating the gold from the gravel, clay, or dirt that surrounded it. Such gold, found in an almost pure state, was called "free gold" and ranged in size from nuggets to powderlike "flour gold."

Experienced miners, of whom there were very few among the forty-niners, knew that gold originated in lodes or veins, which were streaks of gold-containing ore extending down into the earth for long distances. To recover gold from a lode or vein it was necessary to tunnel deep into the earth, dig out the ore, and transport it back to the surface. Then the ore had to be crushed and smelted, or fired at high temperatures, to separate out the gold. This type of tunnel or hard-rock mining obviously required large expenditures of capital for labor and heavy equipment.

Placer mining, on the other hand, was cheap and relatively easy. The primary requirement was luck. The first miners into any district arrived with the simplest of equipment and employed the simplest of methods. The popular song of the day indicated the extent to which many forty-niners could afford to equip themselves:

Miners panning for gold.

Oh, California, that's the land for me;
I'm going to Sacramento
With my washbowl on my knee!

But what these prospectors lacked in tools and experience, they possessed in optimism:

I'll scrape the mountains clean, my boys,
I'll drain the rivers dry,
A pocketful of rocks bring home,
So brothers, don't you cry.

The "washbowl" or gold pan was the simplest tool used in placer mining and the easiest to operate. The pan was circular in shape, ten to eighteen inches in diameter, with sloping sides, and made of sheet iron. The prospector placed some gravel or dirt in the pan, throwing out the larger pebbles, and then filled it with water from a stream to break up the lumps of dirt or clay. Holding the pan firmly with both hands, he shook it gently from side to side. Any gold in the pan would be carried to the bottom because of its weight. Then, with a circular motion, the miner washed the lighter sand and dirt over the side until finally all that was left in the "V" formed by the sides and bottom of the pan was a black residue. If he was very lucky, he might find a nugget in this black sand, but ordinarily he would feel fortunate enough if he found "colors" in the pan. These were small particles of gold about the size of pinheads which could be picked out with forceps. The even finer flour gold could be separated from the residue by adding a bit of mercury, which has an affinity for gold; the mercury was then separated from the gold by evaporation in a closed container. The gold pan was the most primitive device for recovering gold, but in the hands of an experienced miner it was one of the best. The major disadvantage of the pan was the limited amount of soil and gravel that could be worked at one time.

With ingenuity and a few pieces of scrap wood and metal, the miner could create such devices as the rocker, the long tom, and the sluice box. The rocker, which was something like a child's cradle, had holes bored in it at one end near the bottom. At the other end was a "riddle," a tray punched full of holes. The operator shoveled dirt into the tray, poured water on top, and rocked the device back and forth. The heavy gold would settle between slats of wood or "riffles" at the bottom of the rocker as the water washed the lighter materials through. The long tom was a trough made of wood or sheet iron, elevated at the narrower end where the water entered, with a riddle at the wider downhill end to catch the gold washed from the dirt. The sluice box was also a trough about a foot wide and six to ten inches deep. But the sluice box was much longer, often over a hundred feet in length. Removable frames of riffles were placed the length of the sluice box. Operation of the long tom, and especially of the sluice box, necessitated the cooperation of a number of miners. Great amounts of water were needed to operate both devices, and ditches or "flumes" were constructed to carry the water, sometimes for miles. A sluice box would keep many men busy shoveling in the dirt to be washed.

In California, distinction was made between wet diggings, where all the gold was procured through washing, and dry diggings. In these dry diggings, which were usually located in ravines, the surface rocks and earth were removed to expose little crevices and holes. These "pockets" often contained free gold that could be dug out with a knife or sharp object. Every prospector dreamed of finding a rich pocket, and in the early days the dream sometimes came true:

> We had packed on the back of one of our mules a sufficient number of boards . . . to construct a machine, and the morning after our arrival placed two of our party at work for this purpose, while the rest of us were to dig; and taking our pans, crowbars, and picks, we commenced operations. Our first attempt was to search around the base of a lofty boulder, which weighed probably some twenty tons, in hopes of finding a crevice in the rock on which it rested, in which a deposit of gold might have been made; nor were we unsuccessful. Around the base of the rock was a filling up of gravel and clay, which we removed with

much labour, when our eyes were gladdened with the sight of gold strewn all over its surface, and intermixed with blackish sand. This we gathered up and washed in our pans, and ere night four of us had dug and washed twenty-six ounces of gold, being about four hundred and sixteen dollars.[9]

It has been said that men never worked so hard in all their lives to get rich without working. The forty-niner's belief in tales of riches to be picked off the ground soon gave way to the realization that mining was backbreaking work that offered no assurance of even making expenses. But the miners remained optimistic and listened eagerly to every new rumor of a big strike near Loafer Hill, Slap-jack Bar, Chicken-thief Flat, Git-up-and-Git, Rat-trap Slide, Sweet Revenge, Shirt-tail Canyon, You Bet, or Gouge Eye. The prospectors, like the mountain men, seemed to be always traveling—traveling in search of a new Eldorado.

An isolated ravine in the midst of a wilderness could be transformed overnight into a booming mining camp. The letters of "Dame Shirley" (Louise Amelia Knapp Smith Clappe) to her sister Molly, in "the States," provide some of the finest accounts of life in the mining camps. Dame Shirley described the founding of Rich Bar, the mining town in which her husband was a physician:

> On arriving at Rich Bar a [group of miners] camped there, but many went a few miles further down the river. The next morning two men turned over a large stone, beneath which they found quite a sizable piece of gold. They washed a small panful of the dirt, and obtained from it two hundred and fifty-six dollars. Encouraged by this success, they commenced staking off the legal amount of ground allowed to each person for mining purposes; and, the remainder of the party having descended the hill, before night the entire bar was "claimed." In a fortnight from that time, the two men who found the first bit of gold had each

---

[9] Quoted in Edwin R. Bingham, ed., *California Gold* (Boston: D.C. Heath, 1959), p. 20.

taken out six thousand dollars. Two others took out thirty-three pounds of gold in eight hours; which is the best day's work that has been done on this branch of the river; the largest amount ever taken from one panful of dirt was fifteen hundred dollars. In little more than a week after its discovery, five hundred men had settled upon the bar for the summer.—Such is the wonderful alacrity with which a mining town is built.[10]

## Mining Towns

Food, shelter, and clothing were as simple, and even crude, as the miners were willing to tolerate. There wasn't time for nonessentials, especially during the first few months when the prospects of making a paying strike were good. In the winter of 1848, outbreaks of "land scurvy" were widespread. Perhaps as many as half the miners in northern California experienced the disease, which resulted from a diet that consisted almost entirely of salt meat. Fresh vegetables were difficult to obtain and were too costly for most miners. Weakened by the disease and unaccustomed to living constantly exposed to the elements, many miners did not survive the winter.

Transportation to many of the mining camps was difficult. Primitive roads and long distances contributed to the high prices at the mines. Flour and sugar cost a dollar a pound and molasses cost four dollars a gallon. Tobacco was a luxury at two dollars a pound. In one recorded instance two miners, on their way to a sawmill, were unable to obtain a meal and were obliged to purchase the ingredients for their breakfast:

| | |
|---|---|
| One box of sardines | $16.00 |
| One pound of hard bread | 2.00 |
| One pound of butter | 6.00 |
| A half-pound of cheese | 3.00 |
| Two bottles of ale | 16.00 |
| | Total $43.00[11] |

[10] Quoted in ibid., p. 94
[11] Quoted in ibid., p. 24.

A party of four, planning for six months of prospecting, purchased the following items:

| | |
|---|---|
| 3 yoke of oxen at $75 per yoke [pair] | $225.00 |
| 1 wagon | 85.00 |
| 1 tent and poles—the latter iron | 15.00 |
| 1 Dutch oven, for baking bread | 1.25 |
| 1 wooden bucket | .25 |
| 4 steel picks, with handles | 9.50 |
| 4 steel shovels, Ames' make | 6.00 |
| 5 gold pans, largest size | 4.00 |
| Sheet iron for Long Tom | .75 |
| Pair of gold scales | 2.00 |
| 3 gallons of Brandy | 12.00 |
| 8 pounds of gunpowder | 3.20 |
| 25 pounds of lead | 2.50 |
| 10 pounds of shot | 1.00 |
| 2000 gun caps | 1.20 |
| 10 yards drilling, for sluice | 1.25[12] |

The merchants and the teamsters who transported the provisions often profited more from the miners' labor than the miners themselves.

An early tent camp.

The miners' first dwellings were tents which had been erected, taken down, and moved so many times that they were quite well worn. The tent camps gave way to more permanent dwellings. Brush and pole houses dug partially into a hillside and provided with a dirt roof were cool in the summer and warm in the winter. Log cabins eventually replaced these ruder habitations, especially after a long rainy season had turned the dirt roofs to mud that dripped continually on the miners who inhabited them. Until sawed lumber became available at prices the miner could afford, he had to be content with a hard-packed earthen or clay floor.

Some cabins were furnished with chairs and tables formed of split poles with the bark still on them. The cabin floor was often partially covered with a bearskin or raw

[12] Quoted in Perkin, *The First Hundred Years,* p. 14.

hides. The miner's bed was usually a wooden platform fastened to the log wall and covered with hay. There was always a shortage of wood in the immediate area of the mining camp. The available timber had been taken for cabins, firewood, sluice boxes, and, where lode mining was practiced, for shoring up mine tunnels.

The very new mining towns, particularly those of 1848, were usually quite law-abiding. The apparent abundance of gold inspired the inhabitants to long hours of feverish activity with their washing pans, long toms, and sluice boxes. There was little time for planning ahead, little time for formulating rules, little time for diversions—which might include washing clothes, observing the Sabbath, or reading a stray newspaper or book.

In these early camps, crime was almost unknown. It was easier for a man to wash gold than to steal it. Strangers were welcomed as equals. A man could go into another miner's cabin, help himself to a slice of bacon or cook a meal, roll up in a blanket, and go to sleep with the knowledge that he would be welcomed by the returning owner.

But as the mining towns grew and competition for the best claims increased, the original bonds of fellowship disappeared. All elements of society were attracted to the gold fields, lured there by reports that miners were making twenty to thirty dollars a day. Men who were making one dollar a day in the East found the temptation to go west irresistible. Swindlers, bandits, and gamblers were attracted by the free-spending habits of the miners, who were accustomed to paying a hundred dollars for a pair of boots and who thought little of gambling away nearly everything they earned.

"The typical camp of the golden prime of '49 was flush, lively, reckless, flourishing, and vigorous," wrote Charles Howard Shinn.

Saloons and gambling-houses abounded; buildings and whole streets grew up like mushrooms, almost in a night. Every man carried a buckskin bag of gold-dust, and it was received as currency at a dollar a pinch. Every one went armed, and felt fully able to protect himself. A stormy life ebbed and flowed through the town. In the camp, gathered as of one household, under no law but that of their own making, were men from North, South, East, and West, and from nearly every country of Europe, Asia, South America. They mined, traded, gambled, fought, discussed camp affairs; they paid fifty cents a drink for their whiskey, and fifty dollars a barrel for their flour, and thirty dollars apiece for butcher-knives with which to pick gold from the rock crevices.[13]

In a book called *Mountains and Molehills,* Frank Marryat described the saloons of the California mining towns in the early 1850's. The interior of the typical saloon in a prosperous town, he wrote, dazzled the eye with the brilliance of its chandeliers and mirrors.

> The roof, rich with giltwork, is supported by pillars of glass; and the walls are hung with French paintings of great merit. . . . Green tables are scattered over the room, at each of which sit two "monte" dealers surrounded by a betting crowd. The centres of the tables are covered with gold ounces and rich specimens from the diggings, and these heaps accumulate very rapidly in the course of the evening . . . the dealer is intently watched by a hundred eyes, whose owners, in revenge for having lost, would gladly detect a cheat, and fall upon him and tear him to pieces. . . .[14]

Gambling was the major form of entertainment in the mining towns, but the miners also enjoyed singing and dancing, fiddle-playing, cockfights, fights between bears and bulls, and the occasional visits of traveling shows.

Excessive drinking and gambling all too often indicated a general absence of social restraint. As the gold fields became more crowded and the placer deposits became harder to find, many miners resorted to coercion and even violence to enforce or enlarge their claims. As usual, the victims were members of minority groups, those least able to enlist public sympathy and support. The historian Ray

[13]Shinn, *Mining Camps,* p. 147.
[14]Quoted in Bingham, *California Gold,* p. 74.

Miners playing monte, a game in which the player picks any two of four cards laid out face up and bets that one of them will be matched before the other as cards are dealt from the pack. The dealer is probably a professional gambler.

Allen Billington commented on the undemocratic and often brutal behavior that resulted when the economic pressures on the miners were not counterbalanced by social pressures requiring some semblance of decency and fair play.

> Mexicans, Chinese, and Indians were shamefully abused by the "Yankee" majority, under the theory that "coloured men were not privileged to work in a country intended only for American citizens." In nearly all camps Mexicans were driven from their claims by mobs, Chinese were heavily taxed or forced to work mines abandoned by others, and Indians mercilessly slaughtered. That Americans could be converted into such heartless nativists was indicative of the corrosive effect of the environment.[15]

But the miner's frontier also provided its lessons in democracy, as Charles Howard Shinn pointed out:

> . . . There were times in almost every camp when the rowdy element came near ruling, and only the powerful and hereditary organizing instincts of the Americans present

[15] Ray Allen Billington, *The Far Western Frontier: 1830–1860* (New York: Harper & Row, 1956), p. 238.

ever brought order out of the chaos. . . . Side by side in the same gulch, working in claims of eight paces square, were, perhaps, fishermen from Cape Ann, loggers from Penobscot, farmers from the Genesee Valley, physicians from the prairies of Iowa, lawyers from Maryland and Louisiana, college-graduates from Yale, Harvard, and the University of Virginia. From so variously mingled elements, came that terribly exacting mining-camp society, which tested with pitiless and unerring tests each man's individual manhood, discovering his intrinsic worth or weakness with almost superhuman precision, until at last the ablest and best men became leaders.[16]

In the absence of established agencies of law enforcement, self-appointed "vigilance committees" were formed for the purpose of bringing order to districts threatened by lawless elements. These committees would often apprehend a suspected enemy of society, determine the punishment, and carry out the sentence. However, the committee members themselves were not always the most law-abiding residents of the community. In December, 1851, in a letter to her sister, Dame Shirley described the vigilance committee of San Francisco:

> . . . The Vigilance Committee had become absolutely necessary for the protection of society. It was composed of the best and wisest men in the city. They used their powers with a moderation unexampled in history, and they laid it down with a calm and quiet readiness which was absolutely sublime, when they found that legal justice had again resumed that course of stern, unflinching duty which should always be its characteristic. They took ample time for a thorough investigation of all the circumstances relating to the criminals who fell into their hands; and in *no* case have they hung a man, who had not been proved beyond the shadow of a doubt, to have committed at least *one* robbery in which life had been endangered, if not absolutely taken. . . .[17]

[16]Shinn, *Mining Camps,* pp. 148–149.
[17]Quoted in Bingham, *California Gold,* p. 102.

Eight months later, Dame Shirley wrote to her sister about the vigilance committee of Indian Bar, the mining camp in which she resided:

> . . . The state of society here has never been so bad as since the appointment of a Committee of Vigilance. The rowdies have formed themselves into a company called the "Moguls," and they parade the streets all night, howling, shouting, breaking into houses, taking wearied miners out of their beds and throwing them into the river, and in short, "murdering sleep," in the most remorseless manner. Nearly every night they build bonfires fearfully near some rag shanty, thus endangering the lives . . . of the whole community. They retire about five o'clock in the morning; previously to this blessed event posting notices to that effect, and that they will throw any one who may disturb them into the river. I am nearly worn out for want of rest, for truly they "make night hideous" with their fearful uproar.[18]

This town near South Pass, Wyoming, was once a booming gold mining center. When it was photographed in 1947, it was almost deserted.

In July, 1849, delegates from all over California met to write a state constitution, and the territory's request for statehood was approved by Congress the following year.

Although many of the mining camps quickly declined into ghost towns after the placers or lodes had been worked out, others attained permanence. Local governments were instituted, schools established, literary societies formed, newspapers published, and theaters or opera houses constructed. The cultural depth represented by these institutions was not always great. Frank Marryat remarked that the literary societies in many mining towns were established by "profane illiterates who were as unfamiliar with books as with morality," and gave as an example one "literary society" which provided entertainment for its members by spinning a hat to see who would pay for drinks.

The formation of mining districts and the drafting of mining codes were better indications of growing social and legal stability in the western mining regions.

[18]Quoted in Robert V. Hine and Edwin R. Bingham, *The Frontier Experience* (Belmont, Calif.: Wadsworth, 1963), p. 230.

### Mining Government

During the first year of the California gold rush, crimes were rare. The abundance of rich placer deposits and the relatively small number of miners in the Sierras made the establishment of rules and regulations unnecessary. Perhaps the first formal codes of behavior were those drawn up by groups of miners from Oregon who had organized small mining companies before setting out for the gold fields. The members of such companies usually agreed to abide by certain rules. One small mining company drew up the following code:

(1) That we shall bear an equal share in all expenses.
(2) That no man shall be allowed to leave the company without general consent till we reach the mines.
(3) That any one leaving with our consent shall have back his original investment.
(4) That we work together in the mines, and use our tools in common.
(5) That each man shall retain all the gold he finds, but must contribute an equal portion of our daily expenses.
(6) That we stand by each other.
(7) That each man shall in turn cook, and do his share of the drudgery.
(8) That any one guilty of stealing shall be expelled from tent and claim, with such other punishment as a majority of our company decide upon.
(9) That no sick comrade be abandoned.[19]

These small companies of miners considered no authority beyond that of the majority of their own members. Such was the first government in many mining camps.

In most camps, however, no attempt was made to formulate rules until a need for them became apparent:

> When we come back to dinner, Bill an' I, two strange
> fellers was at work in our claim. We sat down on the bank,
> an' told them there was plenty of good gravel, jest as good,
> a mile down the river, an' that was our diggin's. They didn't

---

[19] Quoted in Shinn, *Mining Camps,* p. 113.

stir, so one of us went an' asked Cap'n Bob Porter, the best
an' quietest man in camp, to come up; an' we all had a
drink outen the cap'n's flask, an' then we talked it over, he
bein' spokesman. Pretty soon they said it warn't no use
making a row, an' went off very friendly.[20]

Such informal agreements soon became impractical. The
miners began to hold meetings in order to draw up definite
rules and regulations pertaining to the size, ownership, and
working of the claims. These miners' meetings were the
first attempts at self-government in the frontier gold camps.
There was no authority to which a miner could appeal
beyond the majority of those in attendance at such a
miners' meeting.

Decisions involving civil complaints were made by
miners in attendance at a miners' "court." Such decisions
were reached by referring the issue to the judgment of the
majority and did not always reflect the merits of the case.
Bribing the miners in attendance by providing them with
whiskey was not uncommon, and personal rivalries and
friendships played a part in most decisions. Criminals were
also tried and punished by miners' courts. Lacking jails
and jailers, the courts were limited to three penalties for
serious crimes: whipping, banishment, and death. Lesser
offenses drew fines of varying amounts, although it was
customary to permit a miner to keep his basic tools up
to a value of about twenty dollars.

A miners' court in
session. The notice
on the wall says,
"Lawyers must not
be long-winded."

A miners' court could be assembled in minutes by dis-
patching a messenger through the diggings. If the mining
camp was large, a jury might be appointed to hear the
case and render a verdict, but more often the jury consisted
of the miners in attendance. A miners' court might reach
a verdict and carry out the punishment all within an hour's
time, as was once the case when a cold-blooded murder
was witnessed by twelve miners. The often-quoted remark,
"We needed no law until the lawyers came," reflected the
miner's desire for prompt justice unhampered by legal
technicalities and delays. In another instance, however, a

[20] Quoted in ibid., p. 174.

miners' court took four days to hear testimony and reach a verdict.

As the process of self-government became better established in the mining camps, written bodies of law were formulated to provide organized government. These written bodies of law, or constitutions, derived their authority from the consent of the miners. A constitution was drawn up after an assembly of miners within a general area formed a mining district. Forming an organized district involved (1) selecting a name for the district; (2) determining the boundaries of the district; (3) electing or appointing the officers who were to execute the laws of the district; and (4) drawing up laws to regulate the size and ownership of mining claims.

The boundaries of a mining district were of two general types. With the original discovery claim as its center, a district might have boundaries which formed a rectangular area. Or the boundaries of a district might be more irregular, following the summit of a ridge or perhaps a stream bed. Whichever the method chosen, the district assembly attempted to establish very definite boundaries. The size of the district usually depended on the extent and type of the gold deposits. Mining districts in Colorado, the Black Hills, Montana, and Idaho were often smaller than those in California because the gold was more often concentrated underground in lode deposits rather than scattered near the surface in placers.

The officers of a mining district, with some variations, included a president, a recorder, and a sheriff. In California, the president was often designated the *alcalde,* a Spanish word for the head man or mayor of a village. In addition to presiding at the miners' meetings, the president usually served as judge of the miners' courts and had the authority to settle minor disputes within the district.

The recorder, or secretary, kept records of claims filed or transferred within the district and prepared documents on the payment of a fee. Portions of the fees collected constituted the recorder's pay. His job also included taking minutes at the miners' meetings.

The sheriff was charged with preserving the peace, which

in some districts was a very hazardous occupation. The sheriff earned much of his pay by serving writs and summonses; he also received a percentage of the proceeds on sheriffs sales of properties on which there were judgments for bad debts.

The officers were elected at miners' meetings after publicly declaring themselves to be nominees. Many districts were lenient in voter requirements, establishing a minimum age of sixteen years and residence in the district for ten days. Some districts, especially those in the Rocky Mountain regions, allowed women to hold mining claims and these districts may have allowed women to vote.

In most mining districts, anyone over sixteen years of age could hold a mining claim. Making a legal claim was quite simple. First the discoverer marked off the boundaries of his claim by driving stakes into the ground. Then, on one of the stakes, he posted the name of the claim, the date and direction as well as the dimensions of the claim, and his own name. He had ten days to file his location with the district recorder and thirty days to prove that there was actually gold there. If it was a lode claim, the discoverer was required to expose the lode within the thirty days, which meant that he might have to hire other miners to help him with the tunneling. The discoverer was also allowed one additional claim before others were allowed to file on a lode. If a claim was not proved within the stipulated amount of time, the claim was declared vacant and another miner could file for ownership of it.

Many forty-niners participated in later gold rushes in other regions of the West. They took with them experience in mining techniques and the techniques of self-rule which they learned in the California mining camps. These experienced miners helped to make the constitutions of later mining districts. Some of these constitutions were so well formulated that their provisions were adopted without alteration by the territorial and state governments which followed.

A placer or "gulch" claim usually included the bed and both banks of a stream, gulch, or ravine for a distance of about fifty feet on either side of the first strike. A lode

A speaker addressing a miners' meeting.

or "mountain" claim was generally one hundred feet long and fifty feet wide, twenty-five feet on each side of the lode or vein.

Water was the life blood of mining. Water was necessary in washing placer gold and in the crushing and separating processes of lode mining. A claim to a section of a running stream was called a "water claim." Because room was needed to build and operate sluice boxes, rockers, and long toms, a portion of the adjoining land was also included in a water claim. If a miner wished to build a mill for compressing or stamping loose gold into bars, he made a mill site claim. The size of this type of claim was determined by the distance up and down the stream necessary to give sufficient head to a dam. In most cases, the dam had to raise the water fourteen feet, which was enough fall to turn a mill wheel.

Miners working a sluice box.

Claims to parcels of land containing loose gold that were not located in gulches or ravines were called "patch diggings" and were a hundred feet square. Many a greenhorn was sold a worthless claim of this type which had been "salted."

There were additional types of mining claims, and as mining became more complex, particularly hard-rock mining, the provisions of these claims also became more complex. In addition to mineral claims, there were also timber claims, ranch claims, and cabin claims. Although miners tended to regard lawyers with suspicion, it was obvious that a good many of the constitutions of later mining districts were drawn up by people with legal training.

After the first miners had taken the gold that was relatively easy to recover, the mining industry began to require expensive machinery for processing the ores. A large amount of capital was required to build mills, dig tunnels and shafts, and to hire men to work the mines. Eventually the prospector gave way to the industrialist. The forty-niners returned to their families in the East, or followed rumors of big strikes in Nevada, or Colorado, or the Dakota Territory, or moved to someplace in California where they could farm or practice other trades. And what had, for a short time, been the rip-roaring boom town of

Red Dog Camp, or Mad Mule Gulch, or Murderer's Bar soon became another ghost town.

"The saddest of all possible sights in the old mining region," observed one of the pioneers,

> is where there are not even half a dozen miners to keep each other company, but where, solitary and in desolation, the last miner clings to his former haunts. He cooks his lonesome meals in the wrecked and rotting hotel where a quarter of a century before, then young, gay, prosperous, and in his prime, he had tossed the reins of his livery-team to the . . . servant, and played billiards with the "boys," and passed the hat for a collection to build the first church.[21]

## The Gold Rush and the California Indian

There remains one more part of the gold-rush story to be told. It is not colorful or exciting, it deals with negative rather than positive accomplishments, and it reminds us that the nation was impoverished as well as enriched by the way in which California and much of the rest of the West was settled. For these reasons it is often omitted altogether.

A tunnel miner. Notice the candle attached by wires to his hat and collar.

The richest placer deposits were in the foothills and valleys of the interior—in precisely the places where the majority of California's Indians lived and hunted. The fate of these gentle people can be explained quite simply by saying that the forty-niners wanted their land and took it. But while the behavior of the thousands of miners who inundated these regions was primarily motivated by greed, it was also the expression of a definite attitude toward the Indians as people. Professor Sherburne F. Cook has described this attitude by contrasting it with that of the Hispanic Californians, who often recruited Indians from the interior to work in their missions and ranchos:

> . . . Despite the occasional appeal to violence, and a certain inherent ruthlessness, the Hispanic Californian attempted to gain two objectives: first, to convert the native race to Christianity, and, second, to exploit it as a great labor pool

[21]Ibid., pp. 146–147.

underlying the superstructure of white society. In theory at least, the Indian was, or should have become, a citizen, although perhaps of second class. In the long run, even this distinction would have vanished, for the Mexicans of Spanish origin felt no social or personal aversion to free intermarriage with the Indian. Even when confronting the unreduced, relatively wild tribes of the interior, both civilian and military groups, despite a sometimes liberal use of force, undertook to bring the native within the framework of a Europeanized society, rather than destroy him forthwith.

A profound change occurred when the Anglo-Americans submerged the Hispanic population, replaced its form of government, and drove its culture into the remnants of the missions and ranchos. The "Norteamericanos," as the Mexicans call them, had been engaged for two hundred years in murderous warfare with the indigenous peoples of North America. First came the struggle for a foothold, and then the long, slow, crushing advance over the breadth of a continent. The initial armed hostility rapidly crystallized a fundamental intolerance into an implacable hatred of the red race. This hatred was inflamed by the very competent resistance offered by the tribes of the Mississippi and Missouri basins, a resistance thoroughly punctuated by excessive atrocity on both sides.

When the pioneers who had crossed the plains reached the Pacific Coast, their unalterable policy toward the natives, any natives, had come to embody a point of view diametrically opposed to that of the Hispanic occupants of the area. While the latter had paid much attention to the religious welfare of the Indian, the Anglo-Americans were completely indifferent. While the Indian had supplied the basic labor for the Ibero-American economic system, in that of North America he was given no place, or at best was relegated to abject serfdom. While the Spaniard or Mexican found no moral or physical obstacle to marriage with the native, the American pioneer abjured such unions with finality, and regarded those who entered into them as beyond the pale of social recognition. Together with this repulsion, there developed the doctrine, accepted by many

M. H. DE YOUNG MEMORIAL MUSEUM, SAN FRANCISCO

Mission San Carlos del Rio Carmelo near Monterey, founded by Spanish priests in 1771. Mission Indians were often recruited by force and were made to work hard for their keep, but the missions existed for them, to teach them Christianity, European customs, and crafts useful to the Spanish and Mexican settlers.

people, that the Indian was inherently, congenitally wicked, a soul inevitably lost to damnation. Such a belief must have been that of D. N. Cooley, Indian Agent at the Tule River Farm, when he wrote in his annual report: "A cruel, cowardly vagabond, given to thieving, gambling, drunkenness, and all that is vicious, without one redeeming trait, is a true picture of the California Digger. . . ."[22]

In 1846, to take an average of the estimates of anthropologists and historians, there were 250,000 Indians in California. In 1873, after the turmoil of the gold rush had subsided sufficiently to permit a fairly accurate count, the

[22] Sherburne F. Cook, "The California Indian and Anglo-American Culture," in *Ethnic Conflict in California History*, edited by Charles Wollenberg (Los Angeles: Tinnon-Brown, 1970), pp. 26–27. Reprinted by permission of the author.

DENVER PUBLIC LIBRARY WESTERN COLLECTION

A typical mining town, photographed about 1865.

Commissioner of Indian Affairs reported a total of 17,000. The chief causes of this mass destruction of a people were, according to Professor Cook, disease and "rough treatment by the Americans."

The health factor had always been significant. Even prior to 1840, devastating epidemics of smallpox and malaria swept through the central valley and the coast ranges. Several thousand persons are reported to have died. Moreover, even at the missions, where living conditions were generally quite good, an extremely high mortality was caused by infections such as typhoid, measles, and tuberculosis, together with a virulent form of syphilis. These maladies, naturally, could not be confined to the mission environment, but quickly spread to the non-missionized tribes where they became endemic. The intensity of their attack upon the natives was amplified manyfold when the massive immigration of 1849 broadcast a host of new pathogens, with an accompaniment of universal bad sanitation, water pollution, and complete lack of social control. The ravages of disease, nevertheless, could probably have been tolerated without permanent and fatal consequences had the Indian not been subjected to a bitter interracial conflict with the Anglo-American, during the course of which he barely escaped extinction.

The actual destruction of life was most clearly manifested in military action. Small expeditions had been sent out for half a century by the Spanish and Mexican administrations to chastise and subdue recalcitrant natives in the interior. With the occupation of California by the United States Army in 1845–1848, however, such operations were greatly expanded, even though they still followed conventional lines. Bodies of troops at company strength were scattered through all parts of the territory, where they established "forts," the primary purpose of which was to hold in check and "pacify" the Indians. The latter, according to all previous experience on the continent, would soon initiate violent physical opposition. As one might expect, the least sign of armed hostility was countered by a crushing military campaign, in the course of which it was standard practice to burn the native villages and destroy all stored food.

During the 1850's, the army came to participate less and less in these affairs. The regular units were then replaced by local bodies of militia, acting under orders from the state, and eventually by groups of private citizens who went forth to fight the Indians clothed with little more authority than their own charitable inclinations. It would be of little value to recount in detail the series of atrocities perpetrated by these people, although there might be mentioned the notorious Clear Lake massacre in 1850 and the Humboldt Bay massacre in 1860. The former was committed by an army contingent under Captain (later General) Nathaniel Lyon, the latter by a company of local civilians. In both instances, several dozen helpless women and children were cut down without mercy.

The actual number of deaths directly referable to these operations is difficult to assess, but the available evidence leads to the conclusion that from 1848 to 1865 the casualties amounted to several (perhaps three to five) thousand Indians. At the same time there went on an insidious erosion due to personal homicide, the result of that ordinary, everyday quarrelling, fighting, and shooting, with or without benefit of liquor, which characterized the culture of the 1850's in California. The Indians were predestined victims, particularly since no white man was ever punished for killing one. The number of recorded cases reaches a few hundred, possibly not a huge total, but still suggestive of a precarious and brutal existence. In this context, it is illuminating to quote an item published in the *Alta California* (San Francisco) for August 8, 1854: "Two Indians were found murdered in our streets the past week, by persons unknown, and dumped into the common receptacle made and provided for such cases."

The effect of physical contact was not always sudden and violent death. More debilitating because more subtle was the steady movement of white settlers, farmers, cattlemen, and lumbermen, as well as miners, onto the lands held by the local Indian villages. First came displacement and dispossession with unceremonious explusion; then followed exclusion from the former home domains by means of barbed wire, dogs, and guns. The uprooting of ancient social units, with its unavoidable destitution, was a severe blow in numerous instances, but even more critical was the elimination of the primitive means of subsistence, together with the complete lack of any substitute.

The native sources of food were copious, but they required a precise adaptive mechanism on the part of the natives in order to be usable. The ecological balance over large areas was entirely destroyed by the newly entering civilization. Big game was driven out or killed; the salmon runs were reduced by placer mining in the streams; the acorn reserves of the valleys and foothills were dissipated by farming operations. But the most serious damage was inflicted by the simple occupation of the land, which in turn meant the denial of its use to the former occupants. Over the long run, this progressive mass eviction generated a horde of displaced persons, who roved about the countryside or moved into the settlements, trying to exist by scavenging and beggary, living in hopeless squalor and poverty, driven all too often to robbery for survival itself.

The most repulsive physical affront offered to the natives was the widespread practice of kidnapping. Before the American occupation of California, the Spanish-speaking ranchers had periodically abducted adults from the still-heathen villages in order to augment their labor supply. But the English-speaking settlers developed the technique of kidnapping small children, who were then sold as servants to respectable families for prices ranging from thirty to two hundred dollars. By 1860, this trade had reached the dimensions of an industry. In an editorial on July 19, 1862, the Sacramento *Union* charged that the purveyors to this traffic were actually killing the parents to secure the children for sale, and that such a child might be seen in the house of every fourth white man. . . .[23]

Indian women were frequently stolen from their families, raped, and then abandoned or killed, and Indians of both sexes were in constant danger of being arrested on vagrancy charges and then auctioned as laborers or servants to the highest bidder. The Indian had no civil rights whatever. As Professor Cook observed, "He could not vote, he could not hold office, he could not attend a white school, he had no police protection, he was not permitted to testify in court, he could not accuse a white man of any legal infraction nor could he claim any damages for injury."[24]

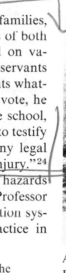

A woman of the Panamint Shoshone tribe, which lived in central California near the Nevada border.

Most of the Indians who survived all of these hazards eventually found themselves on reservations. Professor Cook has described the theory behind the reservation system and the way in which it was put into practice in California:

> It is popularly supposed that the reservations of the nineteenth century were little more than concentration camps. It must be admitted that at their worst, and far too often, they showed a close degree of resemblance. On the other hand, the theory upon which they were based was relatively enlightened and represented the best that humanitarian sentiment could expect in an era when shooting, burning, hanging, and scalping were commonplace events. Behind their inception lay an official, legalistic doctrine not unlike what we see today in regional districts,

[23] Ibid., pp. 30–33.
[24] Ibid., p. 33.

Chief Chepah of the Monache tribe, photographed with his family in 1902. The Monaches lived in central California.

urban redevelopment, freeways, and other devices for improvement and "progress." The argument ran with the Indians, as it does now with the owners of condemned property, that, in the interest of the public welfare, they had been forcibly deprived of homes, food, and means of subsistence. In all equity these things should be replaced by something just as good.

The great vacant areas west of the Mississippi River seemed to provide sufficient raw land for full resettlement. The fact was recognized that the new occupants would have to be given help if they were to become established and support themselves under the American economic and agricultural system. Hence they were to be supplied with tools, with seed, and with building materials. The agents and other staff were charged with the responsibility for maintaining proper standards of public health and law enforcement as well as for instructing the tenants in the intricacies of American rural life. On paper, the system probably was as good as could have been devised under the existing conditions. Nevertheless, as applied to California, and as there administered, it was a complete failure for a generation and was notable for extraordinary abuses.

Perhaps the most critical reason for the collapse of the
earlier reservations was the peculiar political organization of
the California Indians, and the total disregard by white
officialdom of their ancient habitats, material culture, and
native languages. . . . California was unique in the United
States with respect to the structure of its indigenous society.
While, to the east, one found substantial tribes or
confederacies such as the Iroquois, Sioux, or Apache, along
the Pacific Coast were scattered dozens of little units, often
no more than single villages. . . . There was no superior
controlling class, . . . nor any significant intergroup
coordination. Each unit was confined to its own clearly
recognized home, with an adjacent territory for foraging of
not more than a few miles in extent. To tear out such a
tribelet, *in toto,* and transport it to a far place and strange
surroundings, inflicted a profound emotional injury.
Moreover, it was customary for the army and the Indian
Service to gather together the scraps and remnants of a
dozen different linguistic stocks and throw them together in
a confused mass at an undeveloped, unprepared
reservation. . . .

This unthinking displacement and reshuffling was carried
out in the most harsh and callous manner. The victims were
conducted under guard and were permitted to exist for days
without adequate clothing, food, or shelter, both en route
and after arrival at their destinations. Editorials frequently
appeared in the San Francisco newspapers deploring the
destitution of the Indians who were being brought from
interior points through the city for delivery at reservations
in the northern coast counties.

It is not surprising that those taken to reservations
attempted to escape as soon as it was physically possible.
Many contemporary press accounts and official reports attest
to the fact that hundreds were escaping and returning as
best they might to their ancient homes. Many of them were
recaptured, sometimes repeatedly, and taken back to the
reservations. Indeed, the extent of fugitivism reached such a
level that some of the new resettlement areas had to be
closed down permanently for sheer lack of occupants.

Once established upon the reservations, the Indians found

it very difficult to develop any settled economy or social
organization because of incessant attacks and harassment by
the neighboring white population. These people bitterly
resented the removal of good land for the use of the
despised Indians. Repeated instances are on record of
outright invasion and appropriation of sizeable tracts for
farming, as well as of unrestrained trespass for the ranging
of livestock. These measures graded into personal violence
and depredation, destruction of crops, burning of property,
and often illegal expulsion of the Indians from the vicinity.
It was the duty of the resident agents to protect their
domains from such insult and damage, but these
functionaries lacked the means and authority, and they were
often intimidated by threats of reprisal, or even secretly
shared the universal animosity against Indians on and off
the reservation.

The agents themselves were of inferior grade. The press
of the 1850's is replete with such and so many charges
against them that credibility is strained. They were
incessantly accused of neglecting their duties, of gross
immorality, of financial peculations of all sorts, and
actually of the murder of those who were placed under
their jurisdiction. . . .[25]

But somehow the Indians endured the deprivations,
indignities, and cultural shock of the reservations and—
through their own hard work and that of a few good Indian
agents and interested citizens—made them places where
a family could at least survive. In 1946, Congress passed
a piece of legislation called the Indian Claims Commission
Act. Under it, an Indian tribe could sue the government
for injuries inflicted upon it by the American people during
the last two hundred years. The California Indians filed
such a suit and, after lengthy hearings in 1954 and 1955,
were awarded a little over thirty million dollars. It was
estimated that thirty to forty thousand Californians of
Indian descent would be eligible to apply for portions of
the award.

[25] Ibid., pp. 37–40.

## SUGGESTED READINGS

Bingham, Edwin R., ed. *California Gold.* D. C. Heath.

Harte, Bret. *The Outcasts of Poker Flat and Other Stories.* New American Library, Signet Books.

Jackson, Helen Hunt. *Century of Dishonor: The Early Crusade for Indian Reform.* Edited by Andrew F. Rolle. Harper & Row, Torchbooks.

Kroeber, Theodora. *Ishi in Two Worlds: A Biography of the Last Wild Indian in North America.* University of California Press.

Kroeber, Theodora, and Heizer, Robert F. *Almost Ancestors: First Californians.* Ballantine Books.

Paul, Rodman W. *California Gold: The Beginning of Mining in the Far West.* University of Nebraska Press, Bison Books.

Paul, Rodman W. *Mining Frontiers of the Far West, 1848–1880.* Holt, Rinehart & Winston.

Pitt, Leonard. *The Decline of the Californios: A Social History of the Spanish-Speaking Californians.* University of California Press.

Potter, David M., ed. *The Trail to California: The Overland Journal of Vincent Geiger and Wakeman Bryarly.* Yale University Press.

Twain, Mark. *Roughing It.* Edited by Rodman W. Paul. Holt, Rinehart & Winston.

# THE CATTLEMEN

The term "cowboy" originated in the southern Appalachian Mountains about the time of the American Revolution. Until the 1820's, most of America's cattle were raised in Ohio and in the cow pens, pastures, and canebreaks of the South. Even after the war of 1812, thousands of head of cattle and pigs were driven in from Ohio to the feedlots and markets of Pennsylvania. But the American open-range beef cattle industry had its real beginnings in Texas, about 1840. After the Civil War, the cattle industry assumed the features familiar to most fans of western movies—the huge ranches, the large herds, and the long trail drives north to the "cow towns" connected by rail to the eastern markets. The first drive of Texas longhorns across the Red River to northern markets took place in 1866. In the next ten years, there was a great cattle boom, and the northern Great Plains—including parts of Wyoming, Colorado, Montana, and the Dakotas—were given over almost entirely to the grazing of large herds on open, unfenced, public lands. The open-range cattle industry ended in 1885 and 1886, when eighty-five percent of the herds died in a disastrous blizzard.

The longhorn cattle on the opposite page were painted by Frank Reaugh in 1899. Longhorns came in many colors—red, dun, brown, black, white, brindled, and spotted —and had an average horn span of four feet, although six feet was not uncommon.

## The Cowboy

In 1905, Owen Wister published his best-selling novel, *The Virginian.* Since that time, the American cowboy has been romanticized out of all recognition, especially in the hun-

137

dreds of B-grade westerns deriving largely from Wister and his strong, silent, courtly, and white-hatted hero. But there is no denying that the cowboy's life—like all lonely, dangerous, close-to-the-earth professions—was essentially a romantic one:

> Perhaps the strength and originality in [the cowboy's] speech are due to the solitude, and nearness of the stars, the bigness of the country, and the far horizons—all of which give him a chance to think clearly and go into the depths of his own mind. . . . Unlettered men rely greatly upon comparisons to natural objects with which they are familiar to express their ideas and feelings.[1]

Such was the observation of Ramon Adams, himself a cowboy and author of *Western Words,* perhaps the most complete compilation of terms and words used by the cowboy. Adams describes the cowboy as

> a man who followed the cows. A generation ago the East knew him as a bloody demon of disaster, reckless and rowdy, weighted down with weapons, and ever ready to use them. Today he is known as the hero of a wild west story, as the eternally hard-riding movie actor, as the "guitar pickin'" yodeler, or the gayly bedecked rodeo follower.
>
> The West, who knows him best, knows that he has always been "just a plain, everyday bow-legged human," carefree and courageous, fun-loving and loyal, uncomplaining and doing his best to live up to a tradition of which he is proud.[2]

The cowboy was courageous. He was often alone, and his environment was a physically dangerous one. Blizzards, the sun, horses, longhorns, other men—any of these could turn on him and take his life. As Walter Prescott Webb wrote,

[1] Ramon F. Adams, *Western Words: A Dictionary of the Range, Cow Camp and Trail* (Norman: University of Oklahoma Press, 1944), p. viii. Copyright 1944 by the University of Oklahoma Press.

[2] Ibid., pp. 41–42.

Courage became a fundamental and essential attribute in the [cowboy]. . . . The germ of courage had to be in him; but this germ being given, the life that he led developed it to a high degree. Where men are . . . in constant danger or even potential danger, they will not tolerate the coward.[3]

Courage alone did not guarantee survival, or even success as a cowboy; self-reliance and willingness to drop old methods and adopt new ones better fitted to his Great Plains environment were also characteristics of the cattleman.

That he was fun-loving hardly needs explanation. Long periods of routine, hard work, isolation, and boredom were compensated for by a few nights in town. These few nights gave the cowboy a reputation for being rowdy, perhaps lawless, and most certainly a spendthrift with his pay of thirty to sixty dollars a month. As Mari Sandoz observed in her *The Cattlemen,* the hardworking cowhand was

often rowdy when he hit town, spurring his horse and popping his pistol to scatter the anklers, the people afoot, to send them fleeing through the dusty street like a settler's hens before the hawk's approach. He was still sometimes a thief or a killer, as his boss might very well be, but any man who wasn't a worker, hardy, tough, and full of sand, wouldn't stick with the cow business long enough to pay for his saddle.[4]

The average cowboy was young. Anyone over thirty years of age on a ranch or a trail drive was considered an "old man." He was often an individual looking for excitement—or fleeing from trouble. He was not highly educated, and this may account for so few accounts of the cowboy's life written *by* a cowboy during the period of the open range. One such account does exist, however; *The*

[3] Walter Prescott Webb, *The Great Plains* (Waltham, Mass.: Blaisdell, 1959), p. 245. Copyright © 1959 by Walter Prescott Webb. Reprinted by permission of Xerox College Publishing. All rights reserved.

[4] Mari Sandoz, *The Cattlemen* (New York: Hastings House, 1958), p. 100. Copyright © 1958 by Hastings House.

*Log of a Cowboy* by Andy Adams is the most authentic piece of literature ever written about the cowboy.

The form of humor employed by a cowhand on a ranch or during a trail drive often differed from the crude or drunkenly brutal practical joking that cow-town merchants (called "paper-collar Comanches") associated with the cowboy. Adams related one instance in which the foreman of a trail drive appointed one of his cowboys, Joe Stallings, to be *segundo,* or foreman, in his absence. Joe good-naturedly took advantage of the situation by assigning the other men to the cook's duties, which included standing a night guard. (In return, the cook had promised to provide jam and jelly for the next Sunday.) Upon returning from night guard, one of the imposed-upon cowboys

> intentionally walked across Stallings' bed, and catching his spur in the tarpaulin, fell heavily across our *segundo.*
>
> "Excuse me," said John [the cowboy returning from night guard,] rising, "but I was just nosing around looking for the foreman. Oh, it's you, is it? I just wanted to ask if 4:30 wouldn't be plenty early to build up the fire. Wood's a little scarce, but I'll burn the prairies if you say so. That's all I wanted to know; you may lay down now and go to sleep."[5]

Concerning the cowboy's characteristic of loyalty, J. Frank Dobie, an authority on the American Southwest, observed: "Loyalty is more pronounced, it seems to me, in individuals not ambitious for themselves than in those who are. It is marked in certain hirelings without hope or intention of rising in the economic scale to be employers." Dobie illustrated this combination of loyalty and lack of personal ambition with the following anecdote:

> In 1882, Joe Erricson, a native of Sweden, nineteen years old, hired himself to help fence the far-spread S M S ranches in west Texas. In time he became range boss over seventy-five cowboys, twenty-five thousand cattle and five

---

[5] Andy Adams, *The Log of a Cowboy: A Narrative of the Old Trail Days* (Lincoln: University of Nebraska Press, 1964), pp. 234–235. © 1965. Reprinted by permission of the University of Nebraska Press.

hundred saddle horses. Then he married a lady who found ranch life far from attractive. He quit the land of grass and silences and moved with her to pavement and noises. Six months later he showed up in the office of A. J. Swenson, part owner and manager of the S M S's. "Andrew," he announced, "I'm lonesome." "Lonesome, Joe. For what?" "For the ranch. If you have a place for me, I'm coming back." A. J. Swenson put him in charge of the Spur Ranch of about half a million acres. There he lived and worked the remainder of his life. When he died in 1931 he had ridden S M S horses for nearly fifty years.

In August of that year he was confined to the house that was his home, but was still keeping up with ranch affairs. One morning he called a man in and told him to hitch his pair of bays to the buggy and drive him to where a herd of S M S cattle was being worked, a few miles away. When they arrived at the edge of the roundup grounds, he gave the driver a sign to stop. The buggy top was down. He rose to his feet, one hand on the dashboard, and stood in silence gazing at the cattle and the riders. Then he turned his head as if to look again at the Caprock in the hazy distance. Without a word he sank to the seat from which he had risen. He was dead.

Joe Erricson was loyal to the Swensons, loyal to his work, loyal to the S M S tradition. His loyalties seemed to depend upon following the life inside himself, the only kind of life he got satisfaction from  ranch life. He had to be true to himself.[6]

The cowboy was as uncomplaining as he was loyal. "Kickin' never gets you nowhere 'less you're a mule." The cowboy preferred to be optimistic about any situation no matter how bad it might appear. He seldom complained but chose to "swallow his trouble with his food."

The cowboy was often vain about his personal equipment and his dress. He would often opt for "a forty-dollar

---

[6] J. Frank Dobie, *Cow People* (Boston: Little, Brown, 1964), pp. 216–217. Copyright © 1964 by J. Frank Dobie. Reprinted by permission of Little, Brown and Company.

An American cowboy, photographed in 1887.

A Mexican vaquero, drawn by Frederic Remington.

saddle on a ten-dollar hoss." Though his equipment and clothing were ornate and exaggerated at times, they were also practical. A big, broad-brimmed hat served as an umbrella protecting the wearer from sun and weather. A neckerchief drawn over the face protected him from dust, and chaps or chaparreras protected his legs while riding through brush. High-heeled boots made riding easier and protected the ankles from constant chafing. Spurs were judged by some cowboys to be not only an occupational necessity but also a social necessity, especially when on foot in town.

Many authorities on the American West prefer the use of two terms in referring to the cattlemen of the West— cowboy for those men who worked cattle east of the Rocky Mountains and *vaquero* for those whose territory lay west of the Rockies. Americans anglicized this latter term to "buckaroo." But whether these cowboys, vaqueros, or buckaroos worked in Texas, Montana, or California, they faced much the same difficulties and dangers. Cowboys were Mexicans, Indians, Anglos, and Negroes. Just after the Civil War, more than five thousand black cowboys were herding cattle in the West.

Of American Negroes as cowboys, Philip Durham and Everett L. Jones have written:

> Now they are forgotten, but once they rode all the trails, driving millions of cattle before them. Some died in stampedes, some froze to death, some drowned. Some were too slow with guns, some too fast. But most of them lived through the long drives to Abilene, to Dodge City, to Ogallala. And many of them drove on to the farthest reaches of the northern range, to the Dakotas, Wyoming and Montana.
>
> They numbered thousands, among them many of the best riders, ropers and wranglers. They hunted wild horses and wolves, and a few of them hunted men. Some were villains, some were heroes. Some were called offensive names, and others were given almost equally offensive compliments. But even when one of them was praised as "the whitest man I've ever known," he was not white.[7]

Nat Love, a black cowboy.

An average trail drive numbering some 2,500 head of cattle would be handled by twelve to fifteen cowhands; and of this number, at least two or three drovers were usually black and often the cook as well.

## The Drover and the Vaquero

The cattle that the cowboys herded, the horses that they rode, much of the equipment that they used, and a large part of their terminology all were Spanish in origin. Coronado's expedition to the Southwest in 1540 brought the first cattle and horses to North America. During the next two and a half centuries, the establishment of Spanish missions and ranches in northern New Mexico, west Texas, southern Arizona, and the Pacific coast of California provided the nucleus of wild herds of longhorns and mustangs.

> The longhorn was . . . basically Spanish. Yet, when he entered upon the epoch of his continent-marking history, he

[7] Philip Durham and Everett L. Jones, *The Negro Cowboys* (New York: Dodd, Mead, 1965), p. 1. Copyright © 1965 by Philip Durham and Everett L. Jones. Reprinted by permission of Dodd, Mead, & Co. and Collins-Knowlton-Wing, Inc.

THE THOMAS GILCREASE INSTITUTE OF AMERICAN HISTORY AND ART

In this painting by James Walker, the vaquero is twisting the riata in turns or "dallies" around the saddle horn to increase his control over the lassoed horse.

was as Texan as his counterpart, the Texas cowboy. *Cavalier* means "horseman." The Texan had behind him the horse-riding tradition of the more literal than figurative "cavalier South." In the lower part of Texas he met the herd-owning Spanish *caballero*—which word also means "horseman." He met the Spaniard's *vaquero,* the mounted worker with cows. He met the ranching industry of the open range, appropriated it, and shortly thereafter began extending it beyond the limits of the wildest initial dream. The coming together, not in blood but in place and occupation, of this Anglo-American, this Spanish owner, and this Mexican vaquero produced the Texas cowboy—a blend, a type, new to the world. The cow that called forth both him and the industry he represented was the mother of the Texas Longhorn.[8]

[8] J. Frank Dobie, *The Longhorns* (New York: Grosset & Dunlap, 1941), p. xiv. Copyright © 1941 by J. Frank Dobie. Reprinted by permission of Grosset & Dunlap, Inc.

The Spanish word for cow is *vaca*, and a man who works with cows is a vaquero. Vaquero, as used in the Southwest, referred to any cowboy, but particularly Mexican cowboys. In the Northwest, vaquero became buckaroo; similarly, many Spanish terms were employed, though in slightly altered form, by men who adopted the techniques and equipment of the Spanish-American cultural heritage. Edward Larocque Tinker has examined the cowboy's vocabulary which, he notes,

> is still generously peppered, in the Southwest, with Spanish words. He wears a *sombrero* and *chaps* (*chaparreras*), his stirrups are protected by *tapacieros*, and his *lariat* (from *la riata*) has a *hondo* on the end, he rides a *bronco* when he works a *rodeo*, and disciplines it with a *quirt*. His saddle has *cinchas, latigos,* and *alforjas,* he calls his string of ponies a *remuda* and the equine stock of a ranch a *caballada*, which he often shortens to *cavvy*. He has twisted the word *mesteno* into *mustang,* the generic term for the descendants of Spanish horses, and *savvy,* a corruption of *sabe,* is understood by everyone. . . .[9]

A longhorn steer. After about 1880, ranchers started building up herds bred from Herefords, Aberdeen-Anguses, and other stock imported from England. These breeds were easier to manage, required less range, and produced better beef. Longhorns are seldom raised commercially today.

The cattle industry, which spread throughout the grasslands of the West following the Civil War, originated in southern Texas in the region of the Nueces River Valley. Semiwild longhorns, descendants of early Spanish cattle, thrived and multiplied in this region. The climate was mild; grass remained green throughout most of the year; sufficient water was available; occasional clumps of timber offered shade and protection. And the nomadic Plains Indians did not hunt that far south.

Veterans of the Civil War were attracted to this region beyond the settled towns and farms of east Texas. A man could become a rancher with little capital. The grass was free and so were the cattle. To establish ownership, he had only to brand them. To do this, he needed horses; and the mustang, the proud and spirited animal from which came the cow pony, also roamed free for the catching.

[9]Edward Larocque Tinker, *The Horsemen of the Americas and the Literature They Inspired* (New York: Hastings House, 1953), p. 96.

A herd of wild horses.

Frank Dobie describes the best of them as "tameless, and swift. . . . Their essence was the spirit of freedom."

Harry Sinclair Drago maintains in his *Great American Cattle Trails* that the longhorn and the mustang must be regarded as inseparable.

> The Longhorns have often been placed in the category of semidomesticated animals, an opinion seldom shared by men who depended on them for their livelihood and who, presumably, were best acquainted with them. The mustang gave man an ascendancy of a sort over the Longhorns; he could herd and drive them but he could not break their will. . . . The Longhorn was dominated by its ingrained compulsion for freedom, and it could not be bred out. . . . He could scratch a living where other cattle would have starved; his hoofs were hard and distance meant nothing to him when he was going to water—often thirty-five miles or more. In his semiwild state, he was a savage fighter, fearing nothing that walked on four legs. When man pitted the mustang against the Longhorn, it was a case of steel meeting steel, for in spirit they were two of a kind.[10]

## The Cow Town

Though his brand might be on thousands of head of longhorn cattle, a Texas rancher would realize no profit from them unless he found a market. A few attempts were made in 1866, immediately following the Civil War, to drive the cattle to railroads in Missouri; but these drives were generally unsuccessful. Farmers opposed the drovers, fearing the introduction of Texas fever or "blackleg" among their own cattle. Cattle thieves took their toll, and the timbered country reduced the herds considerably.

It was at this time, however, that railroads were crossing the Missouri River and pushing out onto the Great Plains. Cattle which brought only $3 to $5 per head in Texas would sell for as much as $40 or $50 in the North, where

---

[10] Harry Sinclair Drago, *Great American Cattle Trails* (New York: Dodd, Mead, 1965), pp. 80–81. Copyright © 1965 by Harry Sinclair Drago. Reprinted by permission of Dodd, Mead, & Co.

beef was scarce and cities were growing rapidly as a result of increased immigration and industrialization.

The ingenuity of Joseph G. McCoy, an Illinois cattleman, effected a union between northern markets, Texas cattle, and rail transportation to bring about the era of the long drive. McCoy conceived of the idea of establishing some accessible point where railroads and cattle trails could meet unmolested by angry farmers or cattle thieves. The location chosen for the meeting point between Texas drovers and eastern buyers was on the newly constructed Kansas Pacific Railroad at Abilene, Kansas. Abilene was far enough west to be away from settled areas and provided sufficient grassland to hold many cattle, and yet it was far enough east to allow shipment to the Illinois stockyards and slaughter houses. The first shipment of Texas cattle arrived in Chicago from Abilene on September 5, 1867. For the next two decades, Texas longhorns were driven north to the railroad towns in Kansas and Nebraska, the mining camps of Colorado and the Indian reservations of Montana.

By 1870, Abilene had grown from a dozen dirt-roofed log huts, whose only saloonkeeper sold prairie dogs to eastern tourists to provide himself an income, to a prosperous prairie city of four hotels, ten boarding houses, five drygoods and clothing stores, ten saloons, and numerous other businesses. Floyd Benjamin Streeter, in his *Prairie Trails and Cow Towns*, explains how Abilene was named:

Cattle being driven into a railroad car at Abilene. About 35,000 head of Texas longhorns were shipped east from Kansas in 1868; in 1869, this number jumped to more than 150,000.

> The town of Abilene was laid out in 1860 on land belonging to C. H. Thompson who had moved into the county from Leavenworth in the spring of that year. The name of the future cattle market was Biblical in origin, though this never would have been suspected after the cattle trade reached its height. When a name for the town was under consideration, Thompson asked Tim Hersey, his neighbor on the other side of Mud Creek, to suggest a name.
>
> "No," was the reply, "let my wife do it; she is a great reader."
>
> Mrs. Hersey knew her Bible from cover to cover. When

Cheyenne, Wyoming, in 1869.

the question of a name was referred to her, she turned to the third chapter of Luke, first Verse, and read, "Now in the fifteenth year of the reign of Tiberius Caesar, Pontius Pilate being governor of Judea . . . and Lysanias, tetrarch of Abilene." Looking up, she said, "Call the town 'Abilene.' It means 'City of the Plains,' and that exactly describes the location." [11]

Abilene, marking the terminus of the Chisolm Trail, was supplanted by other cow towns farther west—Dodge City and Ogallala on the Western Trail and Cheyenne on the Goodnight-Loving Trail. The farther west a cow town was located, the tougher became its reputation:

A drunken cowboy got aboard a Santa Fe train at Newton. When the conductor asked him for the fare, the cowpuncher handed him a handful of money.

"Where do you want to go?" asked the conductor.

"To Hell," replied the cowboy.

"Well, give me $2.50 and get off at Dodge." [12]

What was the relationship of the "cow towns" of the Great Plains to the brief success experienced by the cattlemen of the open range? Was the urban frontier of the Great Plains inspired primarily as a response to the cattleman's frontier or was this merely a profitable episode in the life of the town? In *The Cattle Towns,* an examination of five Kansas cattle trading centers, Robert Dykstra poses the question: What, in the final analysis, was the relationship of the Texas cattle trade to the successful town-building emphasis?

This is not a question easily or definitively answered. How a citizen judged whether the cattle trade had properly contributed to local prosperity and growth depended on his partisan viewpoint—that is, whether he was social reformer, farmer, or pure-and-simple businessman. It seems clear that the [prevailing general opinion] at the cattle town was

[11] Floyd Benjamin Streeter, *Prairie Trails and Cow Towns* (New York: Devin-Adair, 1963), p. 70. Copyright © 1962 by The Devin-Adair Company. Reprinted by permission.

[12] Ibid., p. 155.

nearly always that of its business community. At least until special circumstances intervened, this [general opinion of the community] consistently endorsed the cattle trade, and for good reasons. At the average frontier community the only substantial influx of capital came in the pockets of new settlers, or in the form of taxes on railroads and non-resident landholders. In light of this fact, not even the most lukewarm townsman could deny that the cattle trade's transients comprised an unusual resource. [Supporting this businesslike] endorsement was the feeling, even as far west as Dodge, that conventional agriculture would be the ultimate community economic base. Cattle trade profits were therefore to be made while the making was good; the future would take care of itself.[13]

## The Long Drive

The earlier cattle drives north from Texas were conducted by professional drovers who purchased cattle on credit and drove them north to the railroads. Later, ranchers either drove their own herds, or more often hired a competent trail boss. The long drive would begin early in the spring, when grass and water were available along the trail, and as soon as the herds could be rounded up from the open ranges. As the drovers gained experience, the trail herds became larger. It was found that about the same number of men could as easily handle a herd of 2,500 as it could a smaller one of 1,000. As trail drives became more routine, it was not unusual for herds to follow within a day of each other on the same trail or to be within sight of one another at many times, particularly at river crossings. And, as trail drives became longer, driving into the northern rangelands, it became necessary to identify the cattle with a special trail brand.

A trail-driving crew consisted of a foreman or a professional drover who directed the drive, approximately eight trail hands chosen for dependability and loyalty as much

[13]Robert Dykstra, *The Cattle Towns* (New York: Alfred A. Knopf, 1968), p. 359. Copyright © 1968. Reprinted by permission of Alfred A. Knopf, Inc.

as for their ability, one or two horse herders or wranglers who were placed in charge of the remuda or "cavvie yard" as the string of horses was called, and a cook. In *Vanguards of the Frontier,* Everett Dick points out that a good cook was a gold mine, because

> he would do more toward keeping up the morale of a trail crew than anyone else. He had to be not only a good cook but an expert bull-whacker or mule-skinner as well, for some wagons were pulled by oxen while horses furnished the motive power for others. The cook often was a hard character with a record of his own. He might be either Spanish or Negro with a notch or two on his gun. He was called the "old woman" by the crew, but he certainly was no lady if he were to be judged by his language.[14]

A cowboy standing guard as the herd settles down for the night.

A man's ranking was indicated by the position he was assigned with the herd as it strung out along the trail. The position of most responsibility was "point." Two men, one on each side of the herd, "pointed herd" as they rode abreast of the leaders; theirs was a position of importance especially in controlling a stampede. About a third of the way back on each side of the herd were the swing riders. These two men would be about fifty feet from each other—the width of the herd at that point. Two-thirds of the way back, there were two flank riders. The most undesirable position was that of "riding drag" or bringing up the rear of the herd. The three men of least experience, other than the wranglers, were assigned "drag" and it was in this position that a man ate the dust of the entire herd while attempting to drive the slower, lazier, more stubborn or lame cattle.

The job least respected among the more experienced trail hands was that of wrangler, usually assigned to the youngest member of the crew. Each cowboy was allotted at least five horses, and all the horses together comprised

[14]Everett Dick, *Vanguards of the Frontier: A Social History of the Northern Plains and Rocky Mountains from the Fur Traders to the Sod Busters* (Lincoln: University of Nebraska Press, 1941), p. 457. © 1941. Reprinted by permission of Everett Dick.

DENVER PUBLIC LIBRARY WESTERN COLLECTION

the remuda assigned to the wrangler's care. At night, the wrangler had to hobble the horses that were not being used in the night guard or being kept close by the trail hands for immediate use in an emergency. The best compliment given a wrangler was to say "he never lost a horse."

One of the first things a newly assembled trail crew did was to pick their mounts from the remuda. The foreman selected all his mounts first, perhaps as many as a dozen. Each hand was then allowed to pick one horse at a time by turns until only the least desirable ponies were left, usually pintos. An experienced cowboy knew that this freak of color in range-bred horses was the result of in-breeding which led to a physical and mental deterioration in the horse.

A cook working at his chuck wagon.

The chuck wagon completed the outfit. It was canvas-covered and usually a well-built four-wheeled wagon, though some crews used two-wheeled carts for chuck wagons. A water barrel was fastened inside the wagon bed and a spigot extended outside so that water could be easily obtained. A barrel of water would last the crew at least two days on the trail. A chuck box, mounted on back of the wagon, was divided into compartments to hold all the cook's utensils. His work table was a leaf lowered from the chuck box. Wood and dry cow dung were thrown into the "caboose," a cowhide tied by the four corners and hanging loose under the wagon. A box was built onto the front of the wagon to carry tools, pieces of rawhide, and all sorts of odds and ends which would come in handy during the drive.

The chuck wagon was the outfit's headquarters. It carried all the papers of the foreman, the hands' sleeping gear and few personal possessions, and a thirty-day supply of provisions. Supply points and the few towns on the trail provided the cook opportunities to replenish the provisions when necessary. The cook was the first man up in the morning. After breakfast, he drove the chuck wagon on ahead of the herd to a site designated by the foreman, and there fixed the noon meal. The same process was repeated for the evening meal.

Twenty miles per day was about the average distance covered on a drive. It was desirable, when beginning the drive, to move the cattle and remuda away from familiar range as soon as possible; the longer hours on the trail during the first few days helped to break the cattle to the drive.

There was actually no "driving" involved in a long drive. The herd trailed out behind the leaders—who usually led the entire distance—and moved of its own free will at about two or three miles per hour. The instructions given by the foreman of Andy Adams' crew at the beginning of a drive in 1882 provide an excellent example of what was expected of each man.

> "Boys, the secret of trailing cattle is never to let your herd know that they are under restraint. Let everything that is done be done voluntarily by the cattle. From the moment you let them off the bed ground in the morning until they are bedded at night, never let a cow take a step, except in the direction of its destination. In this manner you can loaf away the day, and cover from fifteen to twenty miles, and the herd in the mean time will enjoy all the freedom of an open range. Of course, it's long, tiresome hours to the men; but the condition of the herd and saddle stock demands sacrifices on our part, if any have to be made. And I want to caution you younger boys about your horses; there is such a thing as having ten horses in your string, and at the same time being afoot. You are well mounted, and on the condition of the remuda depends the success and safety of the herd. Accidents will happen to horses, but don't let it be your fault; keep your saddle blankets dry and clean, for no better word can be spoken of a man than that he is careful of his horses. Ordinarily a man might get along with six or eight horses, but in such emergencies as we are liable to meet, we have not a horse to spare, and a man afoot is useless." [15]

Though the foreman might not stand night guard duty as often as his men, he made up for it by riding almost twice as far as his men—he constantly circled the herd

[15] Adams, *Log of a Cowboy,* pp. 28–29.

as it grazed forward. The foreman would not leave the herd until it was bedded down at night, and he was often the man who awakened the cook the next morning. It was the foreman who led the herd from the bed ground just before dawn.

At dusk, the cattle were gathered in a large circle and allowed to graze before being moved to the bed ground. The foreman tried to select an area of old dry grass for the bed ground, preferably one that was elevated enough to catch any breezes. Cattle were bedded down only after being well watered and well grazed. Hunger and thirst increased the probability of stampedes.

A dark or humid night, a rainstorm and lightning, hungry and thirsty cattle, a sudden noise—any of these might cause a stampede. After a stampede, it was always several days before the cattle would settle down again and the men could relax their vigil. Frank Collinson, who began his cow-trailing career at the age of seventeen, has described a stampede in his *Life in the Saddle:*

. . . Sometimes on a clear night the cattle would be bedded down, when the air would suddenly become warm and still. Then distant thunder could be heard and phosphorous would shine on the long horns of the cattle and on the horses' ears. Then we knew a storm was brewing. Suddenly like a streak of lightning every steer jumped to its feet and was away on the run. The entire herd seemed to move like one huge animal.

In such instances the cowboys tried to keep in the lead so that the steers could eventually be turned in a circle. If the lightning and thunder and rain continued, the frightened animals would keep running for several miles.

Finally when they were herded there was water standing everywhere, and it was difficult or impossible to bed them again. Then the cowboys, cold and miserable, and often wet to the skin, stood guard the remainder of the night. Maybe one or two broke into song, but it took a brave lad to sing under such conditions.

The big job awaited us at the crack of dawn. We first counted the cattle, and if any were gone, we followed their

"Stampeded by Lightning," painted by Frederic Remington.

tracks on fresh horses. Maybe they were not far off—maybe they were twenty miles; but get them we had to do, even if they were half way back to the home range.[16]

A stampede might take its toll of men as well as of cattle; it then became the cook's duty to break out the shovel from the chuck wagon and dig a grave. But more often a stampede was just another incident to "story about" or to philosophize about.

Equally to be feared was a "dry drive." This would occur while driving the herd through a particularly arid stretch of the trail where water was available only at widely separated intervals. A dry drive might also be the result of a summer drought in a region normally offering abundant watering points. One such dry drive was described by Andy Adams:

. . . We had not been on the trail over two hours before the heat became almost unbearable to man and beast. Had it not been for the condition of the herd, all might yet have gone well; but over three days had now elapsed without

---

[16] Frank Collinson, *Life in the Saddle,* edited by Mary Whatley Clarke (Norman: University of Oklahoma Press, 1963), pp. 36–37. Copyright 1963 by the University of Oklahoma Press.

water for the cattle, and they became feverish and ungovernable. The lead cattle turned back several times, wandering aimlessly in any direction, and it was with considerable difficulty that the herd could be held on the trail. The rear overtook the lead, and the cattle gradually lost all semblance of a trail herd . . . [they] congregated into a mass of unmanageable animals, milling and lowing in their fever and thirst. . . . No sooner was the milling stopped than they would surge hither and yon, sometimes half a mile, as ungovernable as the waves of an ocean. After wasting several hours in this manner, they finally turned back over the trail, and the utmost efforts of every man in the outfit failed to check them. We threw our ropes in their faces, and when this failed, we resorted to shooting; but in defiance of the fusillade and the smoke they walked sullenly through the line of horsemen across their front. Six-shooters were discharged so close to the leaders' face as to singe their hair, yet, under a noonday sun, they disregarded this and every other device to turn them, and passed wholly out of our control. In a number of instances wild steers deliberately walked against our horses, and then for the first time a fact dawned on us that chilled the marrow in our bones,—*the herd was going blind.*[17]

The usual routine was monotonous. After long hours in the saddle under a hot sun, breathing dust, with no one to talk to except himself or the cattle, the drover welcomed the appearance of an occasional stranger. The stranger might be the foreman of a nearby trail herd come to discuss conditions along the trail—and to sample the cook's talents. Or he might be an Indian come to exact toll in the form of cattle for the right to cross reservation lands.

More often, the stranger was a "trail cutter" come to cut range cattle from the herd. As a trail herd made its way north, cattle other than those originally gathered for the drive would be absorbed into the herd. If these strays were not cut out by trail cutters, the honest foreman would keep an account of their brands; when he delivered the herd

---

[17] Adams, *Log of a Cowboy*, pp. 62–64.

and got paid for it, he would reimburse the rightful owners. Now and then cattle thieves operated in the guise of trail cutters; on such occasions a good foreman drew upon his knowledge of brands to detect false credentials.

Among the major natural obstacles encountered along the trails were the rivers: the Colorado, Brazos, Red, Canadian, Cimarron, Arkansas, and others. The crossing of one of these rivers was always a well-planned undertaking. At best, crossing several thousand head of cattle would be time-consuming; at worst, a crossing could involve cattle bogged in quicksand or carried away by strong currents. An experienced foreman sought as shallow a crossing as possible, one with a firm bottom, preferably rocky, and with gradual slopes on each bank. The cowboys preferred to keep the cattle from drinking water until they approached the river to be crossed. Hours and even days could be wasted just trying to get a few cattle to take the lead in crossing so that the remainder of the herd would follow. Once in the river, the cowboys had to keep the herd moving in order to prevent the cattle from milling, turning back in midstream, or scattering as they left the water at dozens of points up and down the river.

Broadway Street, Abilene, in 1875.

Eventually, however, the drive got to its destination—Abilene, Dodge City, Ogallala, or Cheyenne. After several months on the trail, the foreman or drover could at last turn the cattle over to the ranch owner, who was usually on hand to dicker with the buyers. To the cook, the end of the trail provided an opportunity to taste somebody else's grub for a change. The young horse wranglers looked forward to their first night in a cow town and were not usually disappointed. The experienced trail hands anticipated visiting a barber shop, a gambling hall, and a saloon—though not necessarily in that order.

> On reaching Dodge, we rode up to the Wright House, where [the foreman] met us and directed our cavalcade across the railroad to a livery stable. . . . We unsaddled and turned our horses into a large corral, and while we were in the office of the livery, surrendering our artillery, [the foreman] came in and handed each of us twenty-five dollars

in gold, warning us that when that was gone no more
would be advanced. On receipt of the money, we scattered
like partridges before a gunner. Within an hour or two, we
began to return to the stable by ones and twos, and were
stowing into our saddle pockets our purchases, which ran
from needles and thread to .45 cartridges, every mother's
son reflecting the art of the barber, [one of the cowboys]
had his blond mustaches blackened, waxed, and curled like
a French dancing master. . . .

After packing away our plunder, we sauntered around
town, drinking moderately, and visiting the various saloons
and gambling houses. . . .[18]

After the cattle and the remuda were sold and the men
had spent two-thirds of their pay on new clothes, boots,
and hats, it came time to head back to Texas and routine
ranch duties. As they waited for the next long drive north,
the cowboys might sort out their memories of the last one.
Like most people, cowboys remembered the few good—or
bad—moments, and forgot the monotony, boredom, and
dreary discomforts that made up most of the drive. A
cowboy might remember, as did Andy Adams, that

in the stillness of those splendid July nights we could
hear the point men chatting across the lead in front, while
in the rear, the rattling of our heavily loaded wagon and
the whistling of the horse wrangler to his charges reached
our ears. The swing men were scattered so far apart there
was no chance for conversation amongst us, but every once
in a while a song would be started, and as it surged up and
down the line, every voice, good, bad, and indifferent,
joined in.[19]

## The End of the Open Range

The first northern ranches were started along the settlers'
trails leading westward over the Rockies. These road
ranches supplied Oregon and California-bound emigrants

[18] Ibid., pp. 198–199.
[19] Ibid., pp. 313–314.

with fresh stock. At such ranches, one fat and well-conditioned steer might be exchanged for two trail-worn ones, and thus herds were quickly built up. A milk cow brought from a midwestern farm would be traded for needed provisions by her owner who despaired of ever reaching Oregon with the cow still alive, but who was in need of flour. Thus were begun in the 1840's and 1850's the ranches of the northern Great Plains and valleys of the Rocky Mountains. These ranches were further stocked, in the 1870's and 1880's, with longhorns driven up from Texas. These early ranchers of Wyoming, Colorado, and Montana were usually old mountain men who, after the decline of the fur trade, were reluctant to leave the country in which they had trapped and traded for twenty years.

John Iliff, the first of the cattle kings of the northern ranges, got his start from the stock of gold seekers heading toward the mines of Colorado beginning in 1858–59. He built his herd from purchases of longhorns brought up the Goodnight-Loving and Western cattle trails from Texas. By 1861, Iliff was supplying the mining towns with beef from a herd grazing a range which extended for more than seventy-five miles up and down the South Platte River.

Longhorns driven up the Bozeman Trail provided the base for herds in southwestern Montana and a source of beef for the mining towns near Bozeman and Helena. Many Texas cowboys remained in these northern ranching regions, lured by unoccupied rangelands and the demand for experienced cowhands.

The range and ranch cattle industry spread throughout the Great Plains and by the 1880's occupied nearly all the grasslands of that vast area. Walter Prescott Webb has identified five steps in the development of the Great Plains cattle industry:

> The first step was made when the Spaniards and Mexicans established their ranches in the Nueces country of southern Texas, where natural conditions produced a hardy breed of cattle that could grow wild; the second step occurred when the Texans took over these herds and learned to handle them in the only way they could have been handled—on

horseback; the third step was taken when the cattle were driven forward to market; the fourth came when a permanent depot was set up at Abilene which enabled trail-driving to become standardized; the fifth took place when the overflow from the trail went west to the free grass of the Great Plains.[20]

The process of establishing a ranch on the northern ranges was described to the National Stock Growers' Convention in Chicago in 1886 by a successful Wyoming rancher.

> Except for the money to purchase the cattle, investment was slight enough. A homestead entry of 160 acres along some stream was selected as the basis for operations. If there was wild hay on the land, forage for the riding stock was assured. Ranch houses and corrals might come later, but many an early cattleman spent the first season or two in a dugout cut in the hillside near the creek with a similar one close by for sheltering his horses in the worst storms. Beef from his herd, bacon, beans, and coffee brought by pack horse from the nearest settlement, constituted the bill of fare.[21]

From approximately 1870 until 1885, the Great Plains was a region of open range, an empire of grass. In 1875, the *Live Stock Journal* of Buffalo, New York, proclaimed that "cotton was once crowned king but grass is now. . . . If grass is King, the Rocky Mountain region is its throne and fortunate indeed are those who possess it." But, for the most part, the rancher did not possess it.

The range, here merely open and unfenced grasslands, was *used* by the rancher, not *owned* by him. Each rancher possessed what was recognized by his neighbors as "range rights." Contrary to the understanding of many an eastern

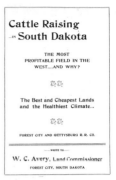

This poster urging easterners to take up cattle-raising in South Dakota was published by a railroad company which stood to make money by selling land and freight service to the would-be ranchers.

---

[20] Webb, *Great Plains*, p. 224.

[21] Ernest Staples Osgood, *The Day of the Cattleman* (Chicago: University of Chicago Press, 1957), p. 49. Copyright © 1929 by the University of Minnesota, renewed 1957 by Ernest Staples Osgood. Reprinted by permission. All rights reserved.

Ranchers, cowboys, and cooks gathered for a roundup near the Belle Fourche River in northeastern Wyoming in 1887.

tenderfoot or foreign investor in western cattle, range rights did not constitute legal ownership of portions of rangelands. When the farmers pushed out onto the grasslands and took up homesteads of 160 acres—or in the more arid regions at a later date, 320 acres—these homesteads were recognized as the sole legally owned portions of the grasslands. The rest remained public domain, which the government could and did give away to those who promised to live on it. Many ranchers, utilizing tactics of the farmer-enemy, homesteaded 160 acres along the stream where the ranch headquarters were located and had their cowboys take up more homesteads which the rancher then purchased.

The rancher's range rights had meant his right to a portion of a stream and all the rangeland back from that stream to the divide which marked the boundary between one stream valley and the next. Claims upon a distance of frontage along a stream therefore entitled a rancher to the rangeland back of the stream, giving him access to the two basic requirements—grass and water. No attempt was made by the ranchers to fence off portions of rangelands.

Range cattle grazed freely, intermingling with stock of other herds. Cowboys might occasionally, as a neighborly act, throw cattle back across the divide onto their home range, but the roundup in the spring would separate the cattle for the purpose of branding and marking calves. The full roundup would catch any strays missed in the spring.

A single rancher did not conduct his own roundup, but participated with his neighbors in a roundup of an entire district involving the ranges of a number of ranchers. Roundups required cooperative efforts and organization. The cattlemen of a district would meet to select one of their number as a general superintendent of the roundup; this was an experienced rancher in whose judgment the other ranchers had confidence. The superintendent's authority and instructions were respected by the ranchers and cowboys. Every rancher whose range was included in the roundup contributed something according to the size of his outfit—chuck wagons, food, horse remudas, gear and equipment.

A cowboy cutting out a cow and calf for branding.

Each range in the district to be covered by the roundup was worked in succession. Cowboys fanned out over a range and worked all the cattle toward the center, where the size of the herd grew larger as did the number of brands represented. The man whose range was being worked was given the first "cut." All the cows which bore his brand were cut out of the assembled herd, and the calves that followed were branded and marked. As the roundup proceeded onto the next range, he would hold his cattle in a separate herd. Until the introduction of barbed wire in the mid-1870's, making possible the erection of corrals, cowboys had to guard the herds day and night.

Though it was possible to succeed by going it alone, the cattleman was eventually forced to seek the cooperation of his fellow ranchers. In every western state, some form of cattlemen's organization came into existence. In his book *The Day of the Cattleman,* Ernest Staples Osgood lists three common aims of the cattle community:

. . . First, to preserve the individual's ownership in his herd and its increase; second, to afford protection to the

A calf being branded. The scars left by the hot irons were permanent, but by adding new scars a rustler could often alter a brand beyond recognition.

A poster showing the registered brands in Elbert County, Colorado.

individual's herd; and third, to control the grazing of the public domain in order to prevent overcrowding.[22]

As a member of a group, the cattleman could protect his property—his cattle—and what he often considered to be his property—his range. A uniform system of branding, requiring the registration of brands, helped to protect the rancher from thieves. A cattlemen's protective association could hire brand inspectors to check the legitimacy of brands as stock was brought to markets and shipping points. The association hired detectives to apprehend cattle thieves. Herds brought up from Texas were inspected for disease, particularly Texas fever, and these herds were in some instances prevented from entering northern ranges. The cattlemen's organizations could secure favorable railroad rates for shipping cattle to eastern markets, bargain with Indian agents for grazing privileges on reservation lands, or influence law-making bodies to pass legislation favorable to the cattle industry. Working cooperatively, the cattlemen protected valuable rangelands from grass fires and punished those guilty of setting them.

His study of the rise and development of cattlemen's organizations has prompted Professor Osgood to observe:

> . . . One can watch the characteristic frontier individualism succumb to the equally characteristic frontier need for group effort, the evolution of custom into law, and the appearance of certain institutions, which became part of the economic and social structure of the Far West.[23]

The most difficult problem facing the cattleman was that of controlling the grazing on public-domain lands which did not belong to him, but on which he relied for grazing his own stock. This problem, along with such factors as the introduction of barbed wire, homesteading on the public domain, overstocking of the ranges, and the severe weather conditions of the mid-1880's, led to the passing of the rancher's open-range frontier.

[22] Ibid., p. 115.
[23] Ibid., p. 117.

Speculation by eastern investors caused more cattle to be introduced to the western rangelands than they could support. Such articles as the following, published in the *Breeder's Gazette* in 1883, were partly responsible for the overgrazing.

### How Cattlemen Grow Rich

A good sized steer, when it is fit for the butcher market will bring from $45 to $60. The same animal at its birth was worth but $5.00. He was run on the plains and cropped the grass from the public domain for four or five years, and now, with scarcely any expense to his owner, is worth forty dollars more than when he started on his pilgrimage. A thousand of these animals are kept nearly as cheaply as a single one, so with a thousand as a starter and with an investment of but $5,000 in the start, in four years the stock raiser has made from $40,000 to $45,000, allow $5,000 for his current expenses which he has been going on and he still has $35,000 and even $45,000 for a net profit. That is all there is of the problem and that is why our cattlemen grow rich.[24]

*The Beef Bonanza, or How to Get Rich on the Plains,* one of a number of books and articles that stimulated the rapid growth of the cattle industry in the 1880's.

When disaster came, it was the big eastern investor and the foreign speculator who suffered the greatest financial losses, and the resulting withdrawal of capital from the cattle industry brought the boom to an end.

Wintering cattle on the open range, rather than providing them with hay or other forage, had always been a gamble. If the previous summer feeding had been poor due to drought or overstocked ranges, the cattle would lack the vitality necessary to survive even an average winter on the open range. And the northern ranges were flooded with cattle in the summer of 1885. In addition to the burden of native stock, the grasslands had to support hundreds of thousands of eastern cattle unused to rustling forage on their own along windswept ridges. That summer, President Cleveland had ordered the removal of 200,000 head of cattle from the Cheyenne-Arapaho reservation lands in

[24]Ibid., pp. 85–86.

Indian Territory. Their owners, who had experienced a severely dry summer, sent the cattle to northern ranges to winter. Even a normal winter resulted in losses of five to ten percent of the herds, but the winter of 1885–1886 was one of the severest in the history of the Great Plains.

In the spring of 1886 cattlemen reckoned their winter losses at eighty-five percent of their herds. And to such a loss was added the prospect of declining cattle prices. In their attempt to get out of the cattle business, southwestern cattlemen had flooded the market with their herds. Cattle were bringing the lowest prices in the history of the open range. A few Montana and Wyoming cattlemen drove small herds of young stock to the agricultural areas of those territories where small ranchers had feed to spare, or they shipped them to farmers in eastern Nebraska and Iowa. Such actions foreshadowed the changes which were to take place in the cattle industry.

The summer of 1885 had been hot and dry; grass was thin, and the remaining cattle were in poor condition to face the coming winter. Professor Osgood, utilizing newspaper accounts of the time, described that dreadful winter of 1885–1886:

> In the latter part of November, there was a heavy fall of snow, so heavy that in many places the cattle could not get down to the grass. Gloomy reports began to come in from all sections. Those who had put up hay fed all they could; the rest, whose cattle were all out on the ranges, prayed for a chinook [a warm wind that blows from the coast of Oregon to the northeast]. It came, early in January, booming up from the southwest, melting the snow and blowing the exposed ridges bare. Men took heart, they might get through without disaster. But the odds were against them for from the twenty-eighth of January to the thirtieth, the Northwest was swept by a blizzard such as the ranges had never before experienced. Down from the north came a terrific wind before which the cattle drifted aimlessly or sought shelter in the coulees [creek beds]. A merciless cold locked up every bit of the poor grazing that remained. Men were forced to keep to the ranch houses for weeks as the bitter

cold and the high winds scourged the range. They dared not think of the tragedy that was being enacted outside. Un-acclimated "dogies" and young stock from Iowa and Wisconsin huddled in the quaking aspens and cottonwoods to die. Dry cows [cows not nursing young] and steers, whose resistance was greater, lingered on. One morning the inhabitants of the outskirts of Great Falls looked out through the swirl of snow to see the gaunt, reeling figures of the leaders of a herd of five thousand that had drifted down to the frozen Missouri from the north. Inhabitants of ranch houses tried not to hear the noises that came from beyond the corrals. The longing for another chinook that never arrived became the yearning for a miracle. Old-timers, who were hardened to range losses, were in a state of absolute panic. . . . The disaster was complete.[25]

Those portions of the open range not occupied by farmers with their windmills and barbed wire remained open for another decade or two as remnants of a passing frontier. But cattlemen realized that they could not rely upon the open range—their stock had to be fed through the winter. Herds that had survived the disasters of 1885 and 1886 were drastically reduced. As the ranges recovered, cattlemen fenced them into summer and winter pastures and installed windmills to pump water to those sections on which they grew hay to be cut and stored for winter feeding. In the decade 1880–1890 the acreage set aside for the cultivation of hay increased more than tenfold, marking the decline of the open-range cattle industry and the passing of the cowboy as a frontier figure.

Old-time cowboys looked back nostalgically to the time when a cowboy had been, essentially, a man who worked with cows:

Cowboys don't have as soft a time as they did. I remember when we sat around the fire the winter through and didn't do a lick of work for five or six months of the year, except to chop a little wood to build a fire to keep warm by. Now we go on the general roundup, then the calf roundup, then

[25]Ibid., pp. 220–221.

comes haying—something that the old-time cowboy never
dreamed of—then the beef roundup and the fall calf
roundup and gathering bulls and weak cows, and after all
this, a winter of feeding hay. I tell you times have changed.
You didn't hear the sound of a mowing machine in this
country ten years ago. We didn't have any hay and the man
who thinks he is going to strike a soft job now in a cow
camp is woefully left.[26]

## The Cattleman and the Grasslands

It is interesting to note that the cattleman—especially the
owner of a large spread—was frequently assigned a
"heavy" or villainous role in many western movies of the
1930's, 1940's, and even 1950's. The big rancher was often
portrayed as a sort of old-line capitalist who had built up
his enterprise in a bygone day, and was now resisting—
usually by foul means—the small-potato but nevertheless
rightful aspirations of the farmers and homesteaders, who
wanted to turn the vast and "wasted" spaces of the prairies
into a patchwork of prosperous small businesses. The
farmers and the homesteaders—so the scripts went—at first
got bullied and killed by the wicked rancher and his hired
gun-slinging goons, but eventually they won. They won
because their side represented the future, law-and-order,
cooperative rather than individualistic enterprise, and because they usually had a better though more polite gun-
slinging goon of the *Virginian* type backing them up.

In the 1870's and after, farmers and homesteaders *did*
turn much of the shortgrass plains into farmland. But this
was not a triumph of small enterprise or of the free spirit,
American style. This rush to farm the plains was inspired
largely by war-boomed agricultural prices, and by a vastly
improved farming technology. It was, if anything, a triumph of human greed. And it was, in any case, an ecological disaster: these farmed-over plains became Dust Bowls.

The ranchers were right. Much of these drier plains and
prairies simply did not receive enough rainfall to be viable
farmlands. The soil could not be exposed to the sun and

[26]Ibid., p. 289.

to the vast winds—it would simply blow away. Although beef cattle are by no means ideally suited to the grasslands habitat, they are better for it than the plow. And so today, parts of these former grasslands are slowly and painfully being returned to what belongs there—a thick, earth-preserving blanket of grass.

## SUGGESTED READINGS

Adams, Andy. *The Log of a Cowboy: A Narrative of the Old Trail Days.* University of Nebraska Press, Bison Books.

Blasingame, Ike. *Dakota Cowboy: My Life in the Old Days.* University of Nebraska Press, Bison Books.

Bronson, Edgar B. *Reminiscences of a Ranchman.* University of Nebraska Press, Bison Books.

Dick, Everett. *Vanguards of the Frontier: A Social History of the Northern Plains and Rocky Mountains from the Fur Traders to the Sod Busters.* University of Nebraska Press, Bison Books.

Dobie, J. Frank. *The Longhorns.* Grosset & Dunlap, Universal Library.

Durham, Philip, and Jones, Everett L. *Adventures of the Negro Cowboys.* Bantam, Pathfinder Books.

Dykstra, Robert. *The Cattle Towns.* Atheneum.

Osgood, Ernest Staples. *The Day of the Cattleman.* University of Chicago Press, Phoenix Books.

Smith, Henry Nash. *Virgin Land: The American West as Symbol and Myth.* Random House, Vintage Books.

A South Dakota homestead on a fine spring day, painted by Harvey Dunn. The brief spring, with its prairie flowers, must have been especially welcome to the pioneer woman and her daughters. Most of the year the plains climate was harsh, with raging blizzards in winter and searing heat in summer.

# THE PIONEER

# SETTLERS

The mountain men, the prospectors, and the cattlemen all pushed the frontier westward, exploring new territories and uncovering new possibilities. But without the pioneer settlers who came after them, the frontier would have remained just that—a wilderness in which only a few brave men and women dared to live, far from the comforts and civilized customs of their native states. The mountain men, the prospectors, and the cattlemen were relatively few and they moved from place to place, following the game, the lucky strikes, or the good grass. The pioneer settlers came in great numbers, rooted themselves in the land, and built up around them communities not too different from those they had left behind. The earlier frontiersmen opened up the frontier; the pioneer settlers made it their own and made it American.

Very often history books discuss the settlement of the West primarily in terms of its political effects on the East or on the United States as a whole. They talk about the West's role in the shifting sectional alliances that were part of the struggle between North and South for political control of the nation. They talk about the grand notion of "manifest destiny," and about how the steady movement westward influenced the nation's foreign policy during the nineteenth century. They talk about the economic prob-

169

lems of the farmers of the Great Plains, and about how those problems led to a political movement that eventually altered the laws and affected the thinking of the entire nation. These things are important, of course, but they have been discussed fully in other books in this series. In this chapter we will concentrate on one aspect of the settlement of the West that is sometimes overlooked—the pioneer settlers themselves and their experiences in the Old Northwest, the Oregon Territory, and the Great Plains, the three principal farming frontiers.

### The Old Northwest

To the north of the Ohio River, stretching from Pennsylvania on the east to the Mississippi River on the west, lies a region known in American history as the Old Northwest. Under the Ordinance of 1787, this territory became the first colony of the United States of America. Troubled conditions in the eastern and southern states, together with the attractiveness of the Northwest country itself, led thousands of Americans to leave their settled homes and to begin new lives in the western wilderness. Following the War of 1812, successive waves of a great migration poured into the region.

Running from the fringe of the plantation South to the Canadian border, the Old Northwest was a center of fusion for population elements from all corners of the American states as well as from Europe. Its colonial background was both British and French, and its borders contained some of the most formidable aboriginal warriors in the world—the Winnebago, the Sauk, and the Fox. Its soil ranged from fertile prairie and flood plains to sand dunes and rock. In addition to its rich mineral deposits and vast resources of timber and water, the region contained an abundance of wildlife that made it the birthplace of the American fur trade. Here in the Old Northwest, uniquely American experiments in settlement and government took place—and established a pattern which emerged again and again as the great migration of pioneer settlers proceeded westward.

The historian Ray Allen Billington has suggested that

IN THE COLLECTION OF THE CORCORAN GALLERY OF ART

Emigrants making camp for the night along the trail to the Old Northwest.

the first major flow of immigrants into the Old Northwest came from the South. The chief reason for the southern exodus, according to Billington, was the rapid expansion of the plantation system, which engulfed the western Carolinas, Georgia, and eastern Tennessee during the postwar years. Many small farmers were forced to sell out to the large landholders. Those who managed to keep their farms soon found that they could not compete with the big plantations, with their hundreds or even thousands of acres and their slave labor. Many independent farmers opposed slavery for humanitarian as well as economic reasons, and nearly all of them disliked the rigid class distinctions fostered by the plantation system. The combination of these forces, social and economic, drove thousands of back-country southerners across the Ohio.

Despite their common dislike of the plantation system, there were marked social and economic differences among the southern migrants themselves. Some had been proud and prosperous; others had been barely scratching out a living before the plantations came. The historian R. C. Buley has described one North Carolina family who arrived in the Northwest by boat, bringing with them a team of young horses, a buggy, four farm wagons, a year's supply of groceries, and a number of luxury household goods including a piano. Their intention was to bring as much comfort to the wilderness as possible. Others were less fortunate. A contemporary writer recorded his observations of another couple from the same state:

> Behind the rest, some distance in the rear, comes the lonesome looking couple from Old North Carolina. They had evidently, from their appearance, ventured their all, such as it was, upon the enterprise. An old one-horse cart, with two high creaking wheels, and an old store box for a body—drawn by a lean pony of the preceding generation, constituted their mode of conveyance. A bed, a spinning wheel, a pair of cards [for cleaning and compressing cotton fibers before they were spun into thread], a bag of dye stuff, and a few hanks of colored cotton, with six sickly looking children, made up their stock in trade. As they moved slowly along, man walking before, and the wife behind, the cart, their lean pony occasionally stopping to crop the tall grass which stood by the way, it was evident to all who saw them, that they had long since arrived at that term of life which the magistrate alluded to, who married them, when he said "better for worse." [1]

The second major group of immigrants came from the New England area, and they too were mostly small farmers who had been driven from their land. In their case, the driving force was the factory system, which spread rapidly throughout the Northeast after about 1810. Among the earliest and most successful of the factories were textile mills. To meet the mills' demand for wool, many landowners enlarged their farms and turned the fields into pasture land. The "sheep craze," as Billington called it,

[1] Adapted from a quotation in R. C. Buley, *The Old Northwest,* 2 vols. (Bloomington: Indiana University Press, 1950), 1:27.

swept through New England between the years 1825 and 1840, and those who lost their farms to the large land-owners were left with the choice of going to work in one of the mills or moving west.

Farmers who survived the sheep craze faced other problems. Traditionally, New England's farmers had been highly self-sufficient, growing nearly all of their own food and making or trading locally for the few manufactured goods—guns, household utensils, farm equipment—that they required. By luring craftsmen away from the villages to the larger towns, and by producing goods that were often better and cheaper to buy and repair than handmade ones, the factories led small farmers to abandon their self-sufficient operations. To buy the new mass-produced goods they needed cash, and to get the cash they began to specialize. Instead of raising nine or ten different crops and several kinds of livestock, a farmer would devote all his time, energy, and land to producing a single crop like wheat. This did bring the farmer more cash, but it also meant that he had to spend more—his farm no longer supplied him and his family with all the vegetables and meat they needed, or with wool for clothing, hides for shoes and harnesses, or tallow for soap and candles. And it was not long before the farmer's cash yields began to decrease—the thin, rocky, worn-out New England soil was unable to bear the strain of intensive monocrop agriculture.

Stephen Bonga, a free black man, was one of the early settlers in northern Wisconsin.

The development of the Old Northwest, the opening of the Erie Canal in 1825, and the invention of the steamboat, which came into common use on the Great Lakes in the 1830's, compounded the problems of the New England farmers. Grain could be produced more cheaply in the Northwest, where the landholdings were larger and where the soil was fresh and fertile. By 1845, it cost only twenty-five cents to ship a bushel of wheat from Chicago to Buffalo by steamboat, and from Buffalo to New York City by barge on the Erie Canal. A million and a half bushels of wheat were passing through Buffalo every year. Faced with competition on this scale, the New England farmer had little choice but to move, and the best direction in which to move seemed to be west.

The Yankee pioneer was described by the same observer who noted the progress of the poverty-stricken couple from North Carolina. The New Englander provided an interesting contrast:

> First in order, as he is always first when speculation is concerned, comes the hardy, enterprising New Englander. Of all the emigrants to the West, Brother Jonathan alone knows where he is going to—the cheapest mode of travel, and what he is going to do when he gets there; he alone has read the preemption laws [laws concerning settlers' claims to public land], and knows what sum he must take with him, or notions in the way of trade, to secure a home in the wilderness. Already, before he gets there, he converses fluently about ranges, townships, and sections [public lands were divided into 640-acre tracts called sections; a settler could buy a quarter-section of 160 acres for as little as $1.25 an acre], has ascertained the number of acres in each sub-division, the amount reserved for schools, and is ready on his arrival to avail himself of his new position.[2]

Not all the pioneers were farmers, of course. Some were businessmen who expected to make fortunes in land speculation, some were artisans and craftsmen unwilling to trade their independence for factory jobs in the East, some were European immigrants, others were doctors, lawyers, teachers, storekeepers. Together, their conestoga wagons loaded down with household goods, they moved westward in ever-increasing numbers. Those from the Northeast came over the Catskill and Genesee turnpikes or the National and Wilderness roads, while those from the South passed through the Cumberland Gap, the Saluda Gap, or Ward's Gap. The most fortunate came by water—from the north by way of the Erie Canal and the Great Lakes, or from the east by way of the Ohio, Miami, Scioto, and Wabash rivers. A traveler on the National Road was moved to remark: "Old America seems to be breaking up and moving westward. We are seldom out of sight as we travel on

---

[2] Quoted in ibid., p. 47.

this grand track, towards the Ohio, of family groups before and behind us."[3]

In the Northwest, the differences among the travelers would begin to disappear. The wealthy and the dispossessed, the businessman, the craftsman, and the farmer, the Yankee, the southerner, and the foreigner would live side by side. They would help each other, they would elect each other to office, they would intermarry. As R. C. Buley has observed:

> In the hardships and necessary co-operations of frontier
> life the good qualities were brought out as well as the bad,
> and "narrow-nosed Yankee" and "shiftless Kaintuck"
> learned to recognize the useful traits of each other.[4]

Westward-bound travelers on the National Road. The building is a toll house operated by the government.

When they arrived in the wilderness, the settlers were confronted with the most basic problems of existence—food, shelter, and survival. A pioneer woman described the last stages of her journey to her new home in Indiana:

> On the 16th day of February, 1825, I, in company with
> Mr. Odell's family, left Wayne county, Indiana, to emigrate
> to the Wabash country. Our journey lasted fourteen days.
> We had rain every day, except two, during our trip. The
> men would cut brush on which to lay our beds, to sleep.
> Our clothes would be wet upon our backs in the mornin,
> sometimes. The country from White River to the Wabash
> was an unbroken wilderness, uninhabited, with the
> exception of a few Indians at Thorntown. We got along
> tolerably well, until we got this side of Thorntown, when our
> wagon broke down. The next morning I got on the horse,
> with my babe in my lap. Sometimes it rained, and then it
> snowed, as fast as it could come down. I was on the horse
> from sunrise until dark, with a child in my arm, two years
> old. You may be sure that I was very much fatigued.
> The next day my husband came with our goods. On the
> day following he was taken sick and kept down about six

---

[3] Quoted in Ray Allen Billington, *Westward Expansion: A History of the American Frontier* (New York: Macmillan Co., 1960), p. 295.

[4] Buley, *The Old Northwest,* 1:48.

Settlers building a log cabin pause to talk to a hunter on his way home with his kill.

weeks. We thought he would die. We had no doctor, nor any medicine. . . .

I was confined [in childbirth] the 21st day of August, and could procure a nurse but for two days, when I had to get up and perform my work as best I could. . . . Another family came to the neighborhood, who had settled on Deer Creek, who all got sick and lost a child. They wanted me to wash for them, as they had no washing done for six weeks. I told them I would try; and I did try, and performed as large a day's work as ever I did, when my babe was but three weeks old.

The next December my husband went up to Deer Creek, and built a cabin. February 15, 1826, we started for our new home. The weather was very cold, and the snow about a foot deep. We stopped at John Carey's, and got some fire—we had no matches those times. We drove up to the cabin; I crawled under the wall, scraped away the snow, and kindled a fire, while the men sawed out a door. The snow was about shoe-top deep in the house. We threw down some clapboards, and on them we placed our beds. We slept inside, and the hogs outside.

The next morning the mud was as deep in our cabin as the snow had been the evening before. The weather was cold. We built a log-heap in our new cabin, but still we almost froze.

My husband would hew puncheons [split logs] all day, and chink our cabin at night. We were nearly three miles from our nearest neighbor. We brought corn-meal with us, sufficient, as we thought, to last until after planting; but it gave out, and I had to pound corn in an iron pot, with an iron wedge driven into the end of a hand-spike, and sift it through a basket-lid. We used the finest of the meal for breakfast, and the coarse for dinner and supper. We got our corn planted about the first of June, and then went to mill in a pirogue [dugout canoe], down the Wabash. . . .

I was taken sick about the first of July, and both our children. I shook forty days with the ague. We then got some quinine, which stopped it for ten days. . . .

I never saw a woman, except one, for three months.[5]

Yet this woman was more fortunate than most. She had been able to stay in a small settlement with friends while her husband constructed a sturdy log cabin. Most families went together to the homestead site. There the family's first chore was to erect a temporary shelter of some sort. Usually this shelter took the form of a three-sided dwelling variously referred to as a "lean-to," "pole-shed," or "half-faced camp." It consisted of two sturdy poles placed in the ground about fourteen feet apart and a roof that slanted from the top of the poles all the way to the ground on the north side. On the south side, which was left open, a log fire was kept burning night and day. The sides and roof of the shelter were covered with branches, brush, dried grass, and clay mud; the interior was lined with the skins and pelts of any animals—deer, bears, wolves—that the settlers had been lucky enough to kill. In the two far inside

[5] Adapted from a quotation in Robert W. Richmond and Robert W. Mardock, eds., *A Nation Moving West: Readings in the History of the American Frontier* (Lincoln: University of Nebraska Press, 1966), pp. 24–26. © 1966. Reprinted by permission of the University of Nebraska Press.

corners, just under the sloping roof, were beds of dry leaves.

In the year 1816, one family migrated from Kentucky to the Buckhorn Valley of southern Indiana. When they settled near Little Pigeon Creek, they had nothing but the land on which they stood, for even the team and wagon that carried them had been rented. The first labor of that family—which consisted of Tom Lincoln, his wife Nancy, his daughter Sarah, and his seven-year-old son Abraham—was to build an open-faced shelter exactly like the one described above. They lived in the shelter for a full year before building a cabin.

When a settler decided that it was time to build a log cabin, he and his family sometimes had to do the work alone. More often, however, cabin-raising was a cooperative effort in which neighbors from several miles around participated. Usually the owner of the prospective cabin felled the ash, beech, or maple logs in advance, cut them to the proper size (most cabins were ten feet by twenty feet), and dragged them to the site. On the day of the cabin-raising, the workers leveled the ground, split and notched the logs, made frames for the windows, door, and chimney, and cut planks for the roof. After the walls were in place, spaces between the logs were chinked in to make the structure weatherproof, and holes were cut for the windows, door, and fireplace. The workers might also build the stone chimney and fireplace and finish the roof with rough shingles, or the owner might do these things by himself later. All of the work was accomplished in less than a day "under the inspiration of liberal drafts of hard liquor and anticipation of sporting and gastronomic feats to come," as R. C. Buley remarked, for after the work was done there would be a party with plenty to drink, plenty of food prepared by the settlers' wives and daughters, and more often than not singing, dancing, and contests in which strength and skill could be demonstrated. The log cabins were primitive, but they served the settlers well, and they have served the nation since as a symbol of the settlers' accomplishments. They were, as one writer romantically expressed it, "rude tenements, taunted and jeered at by

The settlers on this heavily wooded land had more than enough timber to build two cabins and a split-rail fence. The tree stumps must be uprooted before they can begin planting.

an aristocratic party—yet still the citadels of our young republic—the low but mighty towers of our nation."[6]

Like the cabin, the furniture and many of the household utensils were made from materials supplied by the settlers' own land. A bed, for example, was constructed by placing two poles in the floor near a wall of the cabin. Horizontal rails connected the poles with the cabin wall and with each other to make a frame. A hammocklike net to support the mattress was woven of strands of rope, strips of deer hide, or strings of twisted elm bark; the mattress itself might be a conventional one stuffed with feathers or cornhusks, or it might consist of layers of bearskins. Nearly every cabin had a sturdy hickory broom, and many of the eating utensils were made from the durable exterior of gourds.

The most useful and universal of all frontier tools was the ax. With it the pioneer built his cabin, cleared his land, cut firewood to keep warm, created furniture, household utensils, and farm implements, and even—on rare festive occasions—"edged her up a bit and shaved with her," as Ray Allen Billington noted. A wide variety of styles was available (Baltimore or Yankee pattern, single- or double-bitted, concave or ridged, jumped, new patent or home-made, double-portioned, light or heavy, and so on), and the advantages and disadvantages of each style were carefully evaluated and discussed. A man might travel a hundred miles from home to secure the ax of his choice. Great pride was taken in the skillful use of the ax—it was a skill valued second only to marksmanship.

The first settlers in the Old Northwest found that their traps and flintlocks could supply them with an abundance of food in the form of deer, bears, squirrels, ducks, geese, partridges, quail, passenger pigeons, and wild turkeys. A week's supply of game food could be easily accumulated in half a day. In the nearby streams, the settlers could net or spear barrels full of wall-eyed pike and bass. Most families kept a cow or two for milk, butter, and cheese, and cultivated a kitchen garden containing corn, pumpkins, beans, potatoes, carrots, and other vegetables. A hive

Since axes, hand saws, oxen or mules, and fire comprised a frontier family's basic tools, building a shelter and preparing the land for crops and pasture was arduous work.

---

[6] Buley, *The Old Northwest,* 1:144.

filled with wild honey was always a valuable find. Salt was perhaps the scarcest of all necessary commodities. After discovering a natural salt-lick, a pioneer woman would have to boil approximately one hundred gallons of water in order to accumulate one bushel of salt.

The activities of frontier life were endless and varied, yet they followed something of a prescribed pattern from season to season. Spring was the time for plowing the fields, sowing the crops, planting a garden, and—as the sap was beginning to rise—for making maple sugar and syrup. In the early summer the crops had to be cultivated, and by the late summer it was time for the harvest. The fall of the year brought a flurry of activity including corn husking, soap and candle making, butchering, and the annual preparation of cider and apple butter. In their spare time members of the family hunted game, split firewood, added an extra room or porch to the cabin, made their own clothes, canned fruits and vegetables, and repaired farm tools.

In addition to the hard work required by the normal routine of life in the wilderness, the pioneers faced other challenges. Illness was a constant danger, as were Indian attacks. The "public lands" on which the pioneers had settled were, of course, Indian lands, and—after they discovered that government treaties protecting their territories were useless when white men began moving in—the Indians of the Old Northwest fought bravely for their homes. For forty-five years, from 1795 to 1840, the Miamis fought battle after battle to protect their beautiful Ohio River Valley, but finally there were no Miamis left to carry on the fight. In Illinois, an alliance of bands from the Sauk, Fox, Winnebago, Pottawotamie, and Kickapoo tribes terrorized the pioneer settlements until 1832, when their leader, Black Hawk, was captured. As settlers continued to pour into the Old Northwest, the odds against the Indian warriors eventually became too great. The woodland tribes—or what was left of them—began to flee westward, into the territory of the Plains Indians.

It would be impossible to describe every hardship, every chore, every danger, and every annoyance with which the pioneer settler was forced to deal. But perhaps the discus-

Black Hawk, painted by George Catlin.

sion of one tiny problem would serve to magnify the more serious hardships. Consider, then, R. C. Buley's vivid description of the most common of pests—the housefly.

> Screens were lacking, manure piles were plentiful, and soon after settlements developed in any region, the housefly became a pest to be taken for granted. Swarms of them infested the cow barn or milk house, got into the milk and cream and even the butter. They overran the kitchen and filled the house. Dried fruit was frequently so bespecked as to be almost black. At mealtimes a fly switch of branches and leaves or a duster of narrow-cut paper strips was kept at hand to enable one of the children to "mind the flies." Babies slept with clusters of flies parading over their mouths. A few fastidious persons used cheese cloth or netting for protection, but flies were commonly accepted and regarded as much less dangerous than the night air. As a traveler described the situation during the summer:
> "The house is no sooner entered than you hear a continued hum, and the room is almost darkened by myriads of houseflies, which, in Illinois, are never seen out of doors, and which, when there are sick people in bed, require the constant attention of some assistant to drive them off, otherwise, if the patient were a child, or very weak, I believe they would soon suffocate him. Molasses, sugar, preserved fruit, bread, everything on the table, is loaded with them, and the very operation of fanning them off drives numbers of them into the molasses and other things of an adhesive nature. It is not safe to open your mouth. It is evident, too, on examining the molasses, that the small red ant has been purloining it, and has left a number of his unfortunate companions enveloped in its mass; whilst ever and anon a cockroach makes a dash at the table, and in nine cases out of ten, succeeds in scampering across over meat dishes and everything that comes in the way, and that too in spite of the bitter blows aimed at him with knife and spoon, he is 'so t'nation spry.'" [7]

[7] Ibid., pp. 233–234.

In looking back over their lives, the pioneers of the Old Northwest often romanticized "the good old days," glossing over the isolation and ignorance, the discomfort and deprivation, that were part of the frontier experience. Wrote one old pioneer:

> I recall my pioneer days as the happiest of my life. Coarse food and rough diet were the regimen of those days, but every cabin was a tent of refuge and relief from want. There were no instances of heaped up wealth, or pauper tramps. There existed . . . a general spirit of charity and free giving. . . . The condition of oppression and want was but the occasional tares [weeds] in a general harvest of sweet anticipations, ever existing pleasure and happiness.[8]

Of course, exaggeration in the reverse also occurred. Many an old pioneer's recollections of battling bears, wolves, and wild Indians bore more relationship to fiction than to fact.

### The Oregon Trail

As the pioneer settlers discovered that the Old Northwest and the Mississippi Valley were becoming crowded, they pressed farther westward in search of new trails, new lands, and new opportunities. In 1800 the region west of the Mississippi had been only a blank on the map. In 1880 it was occupied by more than eleven million citizens of the United States, and the nation's "manifest destiny" to extend from the Atlantic to the Pacific had been accomplished.

Ray Allen Billington has identified the new areas of settlement and described the people who pioneered those areas in his book *Westward Expansion:*

> The pioneer farmers who followed the traders into the far west came largely from the Mississippi Valley frontier. There, in the tier of states bordering the Father of Waters, lives a hardier crew of frontiersmen than could be found elsewhere in the United States. Rich in experience but poor in cash, toughened by a rough-and-tumble environment

[8] Quoted in ibid., p. 139.

"The Oregon Trail" by Albert Bierstadt, a German immigrant who traveled in the American West in 1858.

where each man's revolver or bowie knife made the law, indoctrinated with a restlessness inherited from generations of pioneering forefathers, they made ideal colonizers. Between 1825 and 1845 they elbowed their way into Texas, peopled the lush valleys of Oregon, settled the forbidding wastes of the Great Basin, and muscled into Spanish California in such numbers the Mexican War only climaxed an annexation movement well underway.[9]

A number of factors combined to bring about the great emigration to Oregon: a prolonged period of hard times in the East following the panic of 1837, a flood of alluring propaganda in the form of exaggerated travelers' descriptions of the Willamette Valley and encouraging reports circulated by the federal government, and higher prices for farm produce on the Pacific markets. All of these things tended to draw men in the direction of the Columbia River.

A study of the pioneers' westward movement over the Oregon Trail reveals, among other things, the physical environment of the West, the diverse types of people who

[9] Billington, *Westward Expansion,* p. 466.

settled there, and the alternating impact of heritage and environment. Jesse Applegate, an emigrant who endured the hardships of trail life, remarked of his fellow travelers:

> No other race of men with the means at their command would undertake so great a journey, none save these could successfully perform it, with no previous preparation, relying only on the fertility of their own invention to devise the means to overcome each danger and difficulty as it arose. They have undertaken to perform with slow-moving oxen a journey of two thousand miles. The way lies over trackless wastes, wide and deep rivers, ragged and lofty mountains, and is beset with hostile savages. Yet, whether it were a deep river with no tree upon its banks, a rugged defile where even a loose horse could not pass, a hill too steep for him to climb, or a threatened attack of an enemy, they are always found ready and equal to the occasion, and always conquerors. May we not call them men of destiny? They are people changed in no essential particulars from their ancestors, who have followed closely on the footsteps of the receding savage, from the Atlantic seaboard to the great Valley of the Mississippi. . . .[10]

The young women in this 1859 drawing must have had a great deal of courage to attempt the long, hard trip to Oregon with only two oxen and an awkward two-wheeled cart. Most emigrants had sturdy four-wheeled wagons and six or eight oxen.

The great migration began with a flood of westward-bound emigrants converging on the frontier town of Independence, Missouri—the eastern terminus of the Santa Fe and Oregon trails. During the month of May, wagonloads of people assembled for the overland trek at this widely known center of trade. The pioneer's first encounter with Independence was a "violent shock of strangeness"—a condition that would characterize the entire emigration. The historian Bernard De Voto described the town best:

> All conditions of mankind were there, in all costumes: Shawnee and Kansa from the Territory [the Indian Territory, Oklahoma] and wanderers of other tribes, blanketed, painted, wearing their Presidential medals; Mexicans in bells, slashed pantaloons, and primary colors

---

[10] Quoted in Robert V. Hine and Edwin R. Bingham, *The Frontier Experience* (Belmont, Calif.: Wadsworth, 1963), p. 99.

speaking a strange tongue and smoking shuck-rolled cigarettes [cigarettes rolled in corn husks]; mountain men in buckskins preparing for the summer trade or offering their services to the emigrant trains; the case-hardened bull-whackers [wagon drivers] of the Santa Fe trail in boots and bowie knives, coming in after wintering at the other end or preparing to go out; rivermen and roustabouts, Negro stevedores, soldiers from Fort Leavenworth, a miscellany of transients. . . .

From now on the habits within whose net a man lives would be twisted apart and disrupted, and the most powerful tension of pioneering began here at the jumping-off. Here was a confusion of tongues, a multitude of strange businesses, a horde of strangers—and beyond was the unknown hazard. For all their exuberance and expectation, doubt of that unknown fermented in the movers and they were already bewildered. They moved gaping from wheelwright's to blacksmith's, from tavern to outfitter's, harassed by drovers and merchants trying to sell them equipment, derided by the freighters, oppressed by homesickness, drinking too much forty-rod [cheap liquor], forming combinations and breaking them up, fighting a good deal, raging at the rain and spongy earth, most of them depressed, some of them giving up and going ingloriously home.[11]

One traveler described Independence as a "great Babel upon the border of the wilderness." A more famous observer, the nineteenth-century historian Francis Parkman, recorded his impressions of the wild and enterprising town in 1846:

The town was crowded. A multitude of shops had sprung up to furnish the emigrants and Santa Fe traders with necessaries for their journey; and there was an incessant hammering and banging from a dozen blacksmiths' sheds, where the heavy wagons were being repaired, and the horse

[11]Bernard De Voto, *The Year of Decision: 1846* (Boston: Houghton Mifflin, 1942), pp. 141–142.

and oxen shod. The streets were thronged with men, horses and mules.[12]

In Independence, the pioneer made his final preparations for the journey west. Because supplies would be available only at two or three forts widely spaced along the trail, each family had to buy enough provisions to last for several weeks at least, and provisions for several months were desirable. The usual emigrant wagon had a capacity of no more than two to three thousand pounds, so careful consideration was given to the weight as well as the cost of supplies. An average wagonload included the following items:

| Food for One | Utensils | Spare Parts |
|---|---|---|
| Bacon—150 lbs. | 2 Iron Kettles | Chain Links |
| Coffee—25 lbs. | Frying Pan | Doubletrees & |
| Flour—15 lbs. | Coffee pot | whippletrees |
| Sugar—25 lbs. | Bake pan | [wooden bars |
| Salt | Butcher knives | used in the |
| Pepper | Knives, forks, | harness rig] |
| Saleratus | spoons, Cups | Ox Yoke |
| [baking soda] | Gutta-percha | Harness parts |
| Beans & Rice | bucket [gutta- | Horseshoes & |
| Vinegar & Spices | percha was a | Ox shoes |
| | hard, rubberlike | Tar bucket of |
| | substance made | grease |
| | from the sap of | Rope |
| | certain trees] | Nails |
| | Medicines | Buckskin |
| | Matches | Ammunition |
| | Soap | Trinkets for |
| | Spade, Ax, Hammer | Indians |
| | Rifle & Revolver | (Mirrors, |
| | | Ribbons, |
| | | Tobacco, etc.)[13] |

[12]Francis Parkman, *The Oregon Trail* (New York: New American Library, 1964), p. 16.

[13]Frederica Coons, *The Trail to Oregon* (Portland, Ore.: Binfords & Mort, 1954), pp. 6–7. Reprinted by permission of the author.

The pioneer's biggest and most important purchase was the livestock that would pull his wagon to Oregon. Although oxen were slower than mules, they were more frequently selected because they were stronger, less expensive, and not desired by the Indians. Young animals that had been acclimated by at least a year's residence in the plains environment were the best buys. The typical pioneer bought six or eight oxen at $25 to $50 a yoke, or pair. (Freight wagons traveling the Santa Fe Trail were much larger than the emigrant wagons, with capacities of two to five tons, and required from ten to twenty oxen to pull them.) Even though the emigrants were careful, many got stuck with bad stock which died on the trail.

After purchasing his stock, securing the necessary supplies, and repairing his wagon, the pioneer's next step was to join a wagon train. Wagon trains contained from twenty-five to well over a hundred wagons, with sixty being the average number. The wagons themselves varied widely in size and sported canvas tops in a rainbow of colors. The average train of sixty wagons housed upwards of two hundred men, women, and children, and opinions on the character of these emigrants have not been uniform. Francis Parkman wrote:

> Among them are some of the vilest outcasts in the country. I have often perplexed myself to divine the various motives that give impulse to this strange migration; but whatever they may be, whether an insane hope of a better condition in life, or a desire of shaking off restraints of law and society, or mere restlessness, certain it is that multitudes bitterly repent the journey, and after they have reached the land of promise are happy enough to escape from it.[14]

Yet a traveler from Virginia offered quite a different perspective when he wrote that the majority of the emigrants were "plain, honest, substantial, intelligent, enterprising, virtuous. . . . They were indeed much superior to those who usually settle in a new country."[15]

A pack mule. In Missouri during the 1840's, good mules sold for $200 to $400 a yoke, prices that few emigrants could afford. Faster than oxen and tougher than horses, mules were used primarily by the government and by the most prosperous freighting companies.

[14] Parkman, *The Oregon Trail*, p. 17.
[15] Quoted in De Voto, *Year of Decision*, p. 147.

Most probably the emigrants were a mixed lot, some good and some bad, but it might be noted that it was far more difficult and expensive to make the two-thousand-mile trip from Missouri to Oregon than it had been to travel five hundred miles from the eastern foothills into the Old Northwest. Many people simply could not afford the thousand dollars required to equip and supply themselves for the journey. "Moving west" was no longer the easiest recourse for those who had failed at farming or business in the East or South. The only way a very poor man could go was to hire on as a bull-whacker, or wagon driver, on one of the big freight trains. The bulk of the emigrants were farmers who owned moderate amounts of property, although each wagon train also contained a sampling of professional men and craftsmen—lawyers, clergymen, teachers, doctors, carpenters, blacksmiths, gunsmiths, stonemasons. In addition, people from nearly every country in northern Europe could be found along the Oregon Trail. On the whole, the evidence suggests that the Oregon migration was drawn from more stable elements than the previous migrations into the Old Northwest.

Before moving out, the members of a wagon train had one final chore. They had to agree upon a set of rules and a method of decision-making to govern their organization and behavior on the trail. The process involved a considerable amount of argumentation and electioneering. The travelers were free men on the move, taking the law with them and making it over to suit their needs. Peter Burnett, a pioneer who traveled to Oregon in 1843, described the organizing process:

An emigrant waiting for the wagon train to pull out, painted by Olaf Seltzer.

> The emigrants were from various places, unacquainted with each other, and there were among them many persons emulous of distinction, and anxious to wear the honors of the company. A great difference of opinion existed as to the proper mode of organization, and many strange propositions were made. I was much amused at some of them. . . . A red-faced old gentleman from east Tennessee state, high up on Big Pidgeon, near Kit Bullard's Mill, whose name was Dulany, generally styled "Captain," most

THE THOMAS GILCREASE INSTITUTE OF AMERICAN HISTORY AND ART

seriously proposed that the meeting should adopt the criminal laws of Missouri or Tennessee, for the government of the company. This proposition he supported by an able speech, and several speeches were made in reply. Some one privately suggested that we should also take along a penitentiary, if Captain Dulany's proposition should pass.[16]

Finally the travelers arrived at a set of rules acceptable to all. The following plan of government was probably fairly typical:

### Wagon Train Constitution

*Resolved,* Whereas we deem it necessary for the government of all societies, either civil or military, to adopt certain rules and regulations for their government, for the purpose of keeping good order and promoting civil and military discipline. In order to insure union and safety, we deem it necessary to adopt the following rules and regulations for the government of the said company:—

*RULE 1.* Every male person of the age of sixteen, or upward, shall be considered a legal voter in all affairs relating to the company.

*RULE 2.* There shall be nine men elected by a majority of the company, who shall form a council, whose duty it shall be to settle all disputes arising between individuals, and to try and pass sentence on all persons for any act for which they may be guilty, which is subversive of good order and military discipline. They shall take especial cognizance of all sentinels and members of the guard, who may be guilty of neglect of duty, or sleeping on post. Such persons shall be tried and sentence passed upon them at the discretion of the council. A majority of two thirds of the council shall decide all questions. If the captain disapprove of the decision of the council, he shall state to them his reasons, when they shall again pass upon the question, and if the same decision is again made by the same majority, it shall be final.

---

[16] Quoted in Hine and Bingham, *The Frontier Experience,* p. 96.

*RULE 3.* There shall be a captain elected who shall have supreme military command of the company. It shall be the duty of the captain to maintain good order and strict discipline, and as far as practicable, to enforce all rules and regulations adopted by the company. Any man who shall be guilty of disobedience of orders shall be tried and sentenced at the discretion of the council, which may extend to expulsion from the company. The captain shall appoint the necessary number of duty sergeants, one of whom shall take charge of every guard, and who shall hold their offices at the pleasure of the captain.

*RULE 4.* There shall be an orderly sergeant elected by the company, whose duty it shall be to keep a regular roll, arranged in alphabetical order, of every person subject to guard duty in the company; and shall make out his guard details by commencing at the top of the roll and proceeding to the bottom, thus giving every man an equal tour of guard duty. He shall also give the member of every guard notice when he is detailed for duty. He shall also parade every guard, call the roll, and inspect the same at the time of mounting. He shall also visit the guard at least once every night, and see that the guard are doing strict military duty, and may at any time give them the necessary instructions respecting their duty, and shall regularly make report to the captain every morning, and be considered second in command.

*RULE 5.* The captain, orderly sergeant, and members of the council shall hold their offices at the pleasure of the company, and it shall be the duty of the council, upon the application of one third or more of the company, to order a new election for either captain, orderly sergeant, or new member or members of the council, or for all of them, as the case may be.

*RULE 6.* The election of officers shall not take place until the company meet at Kansas River.

*RULE 7.* No family shall be allowed to take more than three loose cattle to every male member of the family of the age of sixteen and upward.[17]

---

[17] Quoted in ibid., pp. 97–98.

In addition to the captain, orderly sergeant or vice-captain, and council members, most wagon trains elected a secretary, a treasurer, a variety of committee chairmen, and sometimes a judge. The authority of all these officers was entirely theoretical. The members of the train nearly always reserved the rights to object and to debate. As a result, many wagon trains arrived in Oregon with a set of officers and a system of organization quite different from those they had selected in Independence. Some captains of trains were good and some were poor, but most were adequate and learned as they drove.

At last the trains were ready to begin their arduous journey. Most trains left in April or early May, as soon as the grass began to turn green. The earlier a train left, the more grass there would be along the trail for the stock. An early departure also helped ensure a safe passage through the mountains before snowfall.

Accounts differ as to the amount of discipline the emigrants would accept once they were actually on the trail. Contrasting the organization of the wagon trains on the Oregon Trail with the near-military discipline of the big freight caravans that traveled in columns of two or four along the Santa Fe Trail, Bernard De Voto has concluded that the average wagon train was "an uncohesive assemblage of individualists."

A bull-whacker, or teamster, on one of the freight trains that traveled the Santa Fe Trail, painted by Olaf Seltzer.

, , , A captain who wanted to camp here rather than there had to make his point by parliamentary procedure and the art of oratory. It remained the precious right of a free American who could always quit his job if he didn't like the boss, to camp somewhere else at his whim or pleasure—and to establish his priority with his fists if some other freeborn American happened to like the cottonwood where he had parked his wagon. Moreover, why should anyone take his appointed dust when he could turn off the trail? Why should he stand guard on the herd of loose cattle, if he had no cattle in it? . . . They combined readily but with little cohesiveness and subdued themselves to the necessities of travel only after disasters had schooled them. They strung out along the trail aimlessly, at senseless intervals and over as wide a space as the country permitted. So they traveled fewer miles in any day than they might have, traveled them with greater difficulty than they needed to, and wore themselves and the stock down more than was wise. They formed the corral badly, with too great labor and loss of time, or not at all. They quarreled over place and precedence that did not matter. They postponed decisions in order to debate and air the minority view, when they should have accepted any decision that could be acted on. Ready enough to help one another through any emergency or difficulty, they were unwilling to discipline themselves to an orderly and sensible routine.[18]

Jesse Applegate, perhaps the most often quoted authority on the Oregon Trail, recorded his experiences as a member of one of the earliest wagon trains to cross the continent. His account does not support De Voto's conclusions, although it might be noted that Applegate was reminiscing thirty-three years after the trip. Applegate's comments are valuable not only for their description of trail discipline and the daily routine of trail life, but also because they reveal something of the character of the emigrants themselves.

The migration of a large body of men, women and children across the continent to Oregon was, in the year 1843, strictly an experiment; not only in respect to the members, but to the outfit of the migrating party. . . . It is four o'clock A.M.; the sentinels on duty have discharged their rifles—the signal that the hours of sleep are over—and every wagon and tent is pouring forth its night tenants, and slow-kindling smoke begins largely to rise and float away in the morning air. . . . By 5 o'clock the herders begin to contract the great, moving circle, and the well-trained animals move slowly towards camp, clipping here and there a thistle or a tempting bunch of grass on the way. In about an hour five thousand animals are close up to the encampment, and the teamsters are busy selecting their teams and driving them inside the corral to be yoked. The corral is a circle one hundred yards

[18] De Voto, *Year of Decision,* p. 154.

deep, formed with wagons connected strongly with each other; the wagon in the rear being connected with the wagon in front by its tongue and ox chains. . . .

. . . From 6 to 7 o'clock is a busy time: breakfast is to be eaten, the tents struck, the wagons loaded and the teams yoked and brought up in readiness to be attached to their respective wagons. All know when, at 7 o'clock, the signal to march sounds, that those not ready to take their proper places in the line of march must fall into the dusty rear for the day.

There are sixty wagons. They have been divided into fifteen divisions or platoons of four wagons each, and each platoon is entitled to lead in its turn. The leading platoon today will be the rear one tomorrow. . . .

It is on the stroke of seven; the rush to and fro, the cracking of whips, the loud command to oxen, and what seemed to be the inextricable confusion of the last ten minutes has ceased. The clear notes of a trumpet sound in the front; the pilot and his guards mount their horses; the leading divisions of the wagons move out of the encampment, and take up the line of march; the rest fall into their places with the precision of clock work, until the spot so lately full of life sinks back into that solitude that seems to reign over the broad plain. . . . The wagons form a line three quarters of a mile in length; some of the teamsters ride upon the front of their wagons, some walk beside their teams; scattered along the line companies of women and children are taking exercise on foot. The pilot, by measuring the ground and timing the speed of the wagons and the walk of the horses, has determined the rate of each, so as to enable him to select the nooning place, as nearly as the requisite grass and water can be had at the end of five hours' travel of the wagons. . . . He and his pioneers are at the nooning place an hour in advance of the wagons, which time is spent in preparing convenient watering places for the animals. . . . As the teams are not unyoked, but simply turned loose from the wagons, a corral is not formed at noon, but the wagons are drawn up in columns, four abreast the leading wagon of each platoon on the left. . . .

The desire for cheap, abundant, and fertile farmlands lured succeeding generations of Americans westward across the continent.

Today an extra session of the council is being held to settle a dispute. . . . It is now one o'clock; the bugle has sounded and the caravan has resumed its westward journey. It is in the same order, but the evening is far less animated than the morning march; a drowsiness has fallen apparently on man and beast; teamsters drop asleep on their perches and even when walking by their teams, and the words of command are now addressed to the slowly creeping oxen in the soft tenor of women or the piping treble of children, while the snores of the teamsters make a droning accompaniment. . . . The sun is now getting low in the west and at length the painstaking pilot is standing ready to conduct the train in the circle which he has previously measured and marked out, which is to form the invariable fortification for the night. . . . Within ten minutes from the time the leading wagon halted, the barricade is formed, the teams unyoked and driven out to pasture. Every one is busy preparing fires of buffalo chips to cook the evening meal, pitching tents and otherwise preparing for the night. . . . All able to bear arms in the party have been formed into three companies, and each of these into four watches; every third night it is the duty of one of these companies to keep watch and ward over the camp, and it is so arranged that each watch takes its turn of guard duty through the different watches of the night. . . . They begin at 8 o'clock P.M., and end at 4 o'clock A.M.

[The evening] meal is just over, and the corral now free from the intrusion of cattle or horses, groups of children are scattered over it. . . . Before a tent near the river a violin makes lively music, and some youths and maidens have improvised a dance upon the green. . . . It has been a prosperous day; more than twenty miles have been accomplished of the great journey. . . . But time passes; the watch is set for the night, the council of old men has broken up and each has returned to his own quarters . . . the violin is silent and the dancers have dispersed. . . . All is hushed and repose from the fatigue of the day. . . .[19]

[19] Quoted in Hine and Bingham, *The Frontier Experience,* pp. 98–103.

Perhaps the wagon train's daily activities were not as orderly as Applegate's account suggests, but nevertheless a certain routine was repeated day after day over two thousand miles of alien and hostile land. In the beginning, the trail which covered this vast distance was so vaguely marked in some places that only experienced guides could lead the settlers through. After a few trains had made the trip, however, it became clearly marked—and sometimes grimly marked with the graves of emigrants and the whitening bones of oxen.

The trail followed the line of least resistance, staying close to creeks and rivers to assure the travelers of grass and water. Oxen pulled the wagons along this trail at a rate of two miles per hour. Depending on a wide variety of hazards, a wagon train traveled anywhere from ten to twenty miles per day.

From Independence to a point forty miles west, the Santa Fe and Oregon trails followed the same route, moving along the south bank of the Kansas River, passing through the Shawnee mission, and finally arriving at the famous sign, "Road to Oregon," which marked the trails' junction. The Oregon Trail crossed the Kansas River at Papan's Ferry and continued northwest past Fort Leavenworth and on to Alcove Springs.

At Alcove Springs, the emigrants were near a good fording area on the Big Blue River, a hundred and seventy-five miles from Independence. Some rivers along the trail were too deep to ford, and then the settlers would build a crude raft from nearby cottonwood trees and put it back and forth across the stream. When timber was not available, the travelers simply filled the cracks in their wagon boxes and used them as boats. The stock had to swim across.

After crossing the Big Blue at Alcove Springs, the trail angled northwest along the valley of the Little Blue, into "Newbrasky," and eventually reached Fort Kearney. At Fort Kearney, where the Mormon and Oregon trails united, the emigrants were three hundred miles from Independence and in need of fresh supplies. Some travelers— those who had not shopped carefully in Independence—

were also forced to replace supplies that they had expected to last the entire trip. One traveler noted:

> We discovered that we had been imposed upon . . . in the purchase of our bacon, for it began to exhibit more signs of life than we had bargained for. It became necessary to scrape and smoke it, in order to get rid of its tendency to walk in insect form.[20]

From Fort Kearney west the trail followed the valley of the Platte River for nearly a thousand miles. The travelers had anxiously awaited their first view of the great river, but upon sighting it they were not always impressed. Francis Parkman remarked:

> At length . . . the long expected Valley of the Platte lay before us. We all drew rein, and sat joyfully looking down upon the prospect. It was right welcome; strange, too, and striking to the imagination, and yet it had not one picturesque or beautiful feature; nor had it any of the features of grandeur, other than its vast extent, its solitude, and its wildness. . . . Here and there, the Platte divided into a dozen thread-like slices . . . an occasional clump of wood rising in the midst like a shadowy island. . . . Its low banks, for the most part without a bush or a tree, are of loose sand, with which the stream is so charged that it grates on the teeth in drinking. . . .[21]

By this time most of the emigrants were accustomed to life on the trail, but past Fort Kearney that life became gradually more difficult to endure. The climate, consisting of heat waves, violent thunderstorms, and northerly winds of exceptional velocity, was almost intolerable. One settler recalled, "Oxen might die of heat beside streams made impassable by yesterday's rain while the owner sniffed from a cold produced by day before yesterday's norther."[22] Sudden and prolonged gusts of wind flattened the tents and wagons and produced dust storms so severe that when they ended people were unrecognizable—and some had

[20] Quoted in Coons, *The Trail to Oregon,* p. 18.
[21] Parkman, *The Oregon Trail,* pp. 55–56.
[22] Quoted in De Voto, *Year of Decision,* p. 144.

choked to death. Such a storm was often followed by a torrential downpour which resulted in flooding conditions, stampeded stock, and mired wagons.

But the settlers' most constant enemy was the heat. It cracked their lips, peeled their cheeks, and turned their skins almost black. The dry air would shrink the wagon wheels, and without warning a spoke would pull out, a wheel would roll off, and the wagon would stall. The same brittleness could cause a wagon tongue to snap in two.

In addition to the natural hazards of the weather, the pioneers were now in continual danger of Indian attacks. At first, the Indians' reaction to the overland migration had been one of awe, as the Belgian missionary Pierre-Jean De Smet observed:

> Our Indian companions who had never seen but the narrow hunting-paths by which they transport themselves and their sledges, were filled with admiration on seeing this noble highway which is as smooth as a barn floor swept by the winds, and not a blade of grass can shoot up on it on account of the continual passing. They conceived a high idea of the countless White Nation, as they expressed it. They fancied that all had gone over that road, and that an immense void must exist in the land of the rising sun. . . . They styled the route the Great Medicine Road of the Whites.[23]

That feeling of awe soon vanished, however, particularly among the Pawnees, who were expert horse thieves. Young warriors often raided the wagon trains at night, sometimes to steal livestock and sometimes simply to give the travelers a good scare. Later, as the travelers kept coming and it became clear that there were still many more in the land to the east, larger war parties mounted more serious attacks. The pioneers lived in constant fear of the Indians and seldom wandered far from their wagons.

Buffalo were another menace to the trains. The herds were immense and could easily overrun a camp, particu-

[23] Quoted in Hiram Chittenden and Alfred Richardson, *The Life, Letters and Travels of Father Pierre Jean De Smet* (New York: F. P. Harper, 1905), p. 121.

CULVER PICTURES, INC.

This herd of stampeding buffalo at Yellowstone National Park is probably much smaller than those faced by the Oregon travelers, but the photograph suggests the size and speed of the animals.

larly when stampeded by the Indians for that purpose. A traveler provided the following description of a buffalo stampede:

> As the gathering cloud came nearer on the opposite side of the valley . . . the ground seemed to fairly tremble . . . when a gust of wind from down river lifted the cloud for awhile, and we beheld a compact black mass, extending beyond farther than we could see and coming in unbroken masses from the rear. The quaking of the earth and the rumble of the torrent continued for a long time, many estimating the herd to be from four to eight miles long and of unknown width. Surely many, many thousands of those animals.[24]

One wagon train was held up from before noon until sundown while such a herd crossed in front of them. Still, there were compensations. The buffalo were a source of fresh meat, which could be dried and preserved as jerky. The hides gave the travelers warm blankets, and the dried manure or buffalo chips served as "prairie coal" for the campfires.

[24] Quoted in Coons, *The Trail to Oregon,* p. 54.

Aside from the buffalo, wild game food was rather scarce and consisted of prairie chickens, jackrabbits, wild turkeys, and perhaps a coyote or rattlesnake. As a result of the travelers' poor diets, together with the bad cooking, dirty utensils, improperly preserved food, and impure drinking water, repeated epidemics of dysentery and diarrhea besieged the trains. The most dreaded of trail diseases was cholera. In the year 1852 alone, it took the lives of five thousand emigrants along the trail. Regardless of the year, everyone who kept a diary noted the abundance of fresh graves. One woman compiled the following list through eight days of travel:

> June 14—passed seven new-made graves.
>    16—passed eleven new graves.
>    17—passed six new graves.
>    18—we have passed twenty-one new graves today.
>    19—passed thirteen graves today.
>    20—passed ten graves.
>    22—passed seven graves. If we should go by the camping grounds, we should see five times as many graves as we do.[25]

At the junction of the North and South Platte rivers, the emigrants were faced with the decision of fording the river at that point, traveling another sixty miles southwest to an alternate crossing, or traveling yet another twenty miles to the Julesburg or Upper California crossing. No matter what the choice, the crossing was always dangerous. With quicksand, swift currents, mired stock, and other hazards to deal with, a traveler might need from one to two hours to get his wagon across.

In western Nebraska, the trail brought the settlers to Ash Hollow—a real test of their ingenuity. There the roadway ended abruptly on a high hill and the wagons had to be let down into the hollow below by use of a system of ropes and pulleys called a windlass. Once in the hollow, however, the travelers found themselves in the most pleasant camping area they had seen since they left Alcove Springs.

[25] Quoted in ibid., p. 50.

Beyond was alkali country where sudden gales of wind produced blindness in both men and stock. Most water holes were dry; those that weren't held water that was unfit to drink. Oxen bloated on the foul water, their hooves swelled and festered in the alkali and rocks, and as the grass diminished many grew gaunt and died.

Despite the endless hardships, the process of life—marriage, birth, and death—continued as the wagons crossed the plains. Bernard De Voto described it best:

> The guests formed a procession behind a fiddler and
> conducted Mr. and Mrs. Mootrey to the nuptial tent. A
> mile away they saw faint sparks moving by twos in another
> procession, torches lighting the dead boy's body to its desert
> grave. A mile or so in the opposite direction still a third
> train was camped, and there at the same moment a dozen
> desert-worn women were ministering to one of their
> sisterhood who writhed and screamed under a dusty wagon
> cover . . . and in due time her child was born.[26]

As the wagons moved westward, the loads seemed to grow heavier and the distance they could travel in a day grew shorter. Consequently the settlers began disposing of excess weight. The trail became strewn with ornate pieces of furniture, ancestral relics, household goods, and a variety of utensils. The trail litter represented some of the optimism the emigrants had felt when their journey began; it also represented a portion of their family heritage which an overpowering environment dictated they leave behind. The trail began to work its changes on the characters of the travelers.

> . . . Drenched blankets, cold breakfasts after rainy nights,
> long hours without water, exhaustion from the labor of
> double-teaming through a swamp or across quicksands or
> up a slope, from ferrying a swollen river till midnight,
> from being roused to chase a strayed ox across the prairie
> two hours before dawn, from constant shifting of the load
> to make the going better. Add the ordinary hazards of

[26] De Voto, *Year of Decision,* p. 163.

the day's march: a sick ox, a balky mule, the snapping of
a wagon tongue, capsizing at a ford or overturning on a
slope, the endless necessity of helping others who had
fallen. . . . Add the endless apprehension about your
stock, the ox which might die, every day's threat that the
animals on which your travel depended might be killed
by disease or accident or Indians, leaving you stranded in
the waste. Such things worked a constant attrition on the
nerves . . . add to them a bad storm or some neighbor's
obstinacy that reacted to the common loss. The sunniest
grew surly and any pinprick could be a mortal insult. The
enforced companionship of the trail began to breed
hatred. . . . The very width and openness of the country
was an anxiety . . . the strongest personality diminished.
There was no place to hide in, and always there was the
sun to hide from . . . the little line of wagons was pygmy
motion in immensity, the mind became a speck. A speck
always quivering with an unidentified dread which few
could face and which the weaker ones could not control.
The elements of human personality were under
pressure. . . . Some survived it unchanged or strengthened
in their identity; some suffered from it, inflicting it on
their families, for the rest of their lives. And it grew as
the trip went on. Worse country lay ahead and the
drained mind was less able to meet it.[27]

A wagon train ap-
proaching Chimney
Rock.

At intervals between Ash Hollow and Scotts Bluff, a
number of enormous rock formations marked the trail. The
first of these formations were known as Jail Rock and
Courthouse Rock. Perhaps the most famous of all the
landmarks along the trail was Chimney Rock, which was
described in 1832 by Captain Benjamin Bonneville:

. . . At this place was a singular phenomenon, which is
among the curiosities of the country. It is called the
Chimney. The lower part is a conical mound rising out of
the naked plain; from the summit shoots up a shaft or
column, about one hundred and twenty feet in height, from
which it derives its name. The height of the whole . . . is a

[27] Ibid., pp. 159–160.

hundred and seventy five yards . . . and may be seen at the distance of upwards of thirty miles.[28]

From far out on the plains, the wagon-train scouts could see the spire. To them it heralded progress and signaled that the second phase of their long journey was about to begin. It also meant some relief from the harsh drought, for at the base was a good campsite with a spring.

From Chimney Rock, the earlier trains traveled through Robidoux Pass to avoid the rugged bluffs near the river. Later trains, however, discovered a route through the bluffs, and thereafter Mitchell Pass or Scotts Bluff became the most popular crossing point. The trail from Mitchell Pass, all the way to Fort Laramie, followed along between bluffs on the south and the Platte River on the north.

Fort Laramie came as a welcome relief to the trail-weary travelers. These were the first buildings they had seen since leaving the Shawnee mission in eastern Kansas. At Fort Laramie the emigrants rested for a few days, writing letters home, repairing their wagons, buying fresh supplies from Sutler's store, and having their stock reshod. Many travelers traded their oxen for mules, which were better for crossing the mountainous terrain that awaited them.

One day out of Fort Laramie, the emigrants camped at Registar Cliff, where many of them carved their names for future travelers to read. The next important objective on the trail was an enormous rock, measuring one mile in circumference at its base, in southcentral Wyoming. At that point the wagon trains were 838 miles from Independence, Missouri. They usually arrived at the rock in early July, and because so many of the trains camped near there on July 4, it was given the name Independence Rock.

After carving their names into Independence Rock, the emigrants continued their journey across the Sweetwater River, past Devil's Gate, and on through South Pass. At South Pass they were just halfway to Oregon and the worst part of the trip was still ahead of them.

---

[28]Quoted in *Chimney Rock* (Washington, D.C.: National Park Service, U.S. Department of the Interior, 1966), p. 1.

The trail angled southwest from the pass, and the travelers were faced with the decision of using the Sublette cut-off or going on south to Fort Bridger. Most of the travelers selected the latter route. The infamous Donner party was among many, however, who chose the cut-off. At Fort Bridger, 1,070 miles from where they started, the emigrants stopped to replenish their supplies for the remainder of the trip. The fort was established in 1843 by the widely known trapper and trader, Jim Bridger, who described it in a letter:

> I have established a small fort with a blacksmith shop and a supply of iron in the road of the emigrants on Blacks Fork of Green River which promises fairly. They, in coming out, are generally well supplied with money, but by the time they get there are in want of all kinds of supplies. Horses, provisions, smith work, etc., bring ready cash from them, and should I receive the goods hereby ordered will do a considerable business in that way with them.[29]

From Fort Bridger, the trail turned north by the oasis of Soda Springs and then on to Fort Hall. There was an abundance of both water and grass on this section of the trail. It was also the section which contained various cut-off routes leading to the Humboldt River and on to California. Many emigrants made the decision to splinter off in that direction.

At Fort Hall the trail joined the Snake River and followed it for three hundred miles all the way to Oregon. It was a barren stretch of land filled with little but sand, alkali, dust, and wind. After leaving Fort Boise, near the Oregon border, the settlers had to cross the Blue Mountains to reach the Columbia River. This was one of the most treacherous parts of the trip, and the journey of fifty miles consumed four days of travel. Some of the emigrants went all the way to Fort Walla Walla while others chose the Umatilla cut-off.

Upon reaching the Columbia River, the remaining three hundred miles was very often traveled in forty-foot-long

[29] Quoted in Coons, *The Trail to Oregon*, p. 114.

canoe-shaped boats called *bateaux*. In contrast to the slow progress of the wagon trains, this last three hundred miles by water required only five days of travel. Still, some of the settlers chose to finish the trip by wagon rather than sell livestock and other possessions that could not be accommodated on the boats.

At last, in the month of October, the journey was over. Although they were tired and strained after six months of trail life, the emigrants had to draw upon all of their ingenuity and endurance to adapt themselves to a new environment and create a civilized place to live. Some were very discouraged:

> If there are any persons in Sangamon [County, Illinois] who speak of crossing the Rocky Mountains to this country, tell them my advice is to stay at home. There you are well off. You can enjoy all the comforts of life—live under a good government and have peace and plenty around you—a country whose soil is not surpassed by any in the world, having good seasons and yielding timely crops. Here everything is on the other extreme: the government is tyrannical, the weather unseasonable, poor crops, and the necessaries of life not to be had except at the most extortionate prices, and frequently not then. . . .[30]

The majority, however, were more optimistic:

> We . . . lost twenty head of cattle and four horses in getting to Oregon, which besides various other losses, would have brought us, Oregon prices about $1,500. We hope, however, to soon make it up if health and life are spared. . . . Country around presents some handsome scenery, as well as good soil. Well watered and covered with a luxurious growth of all wild products.[31]

On the whole, the more optimistic point of view was justified. In the Pacific Northwest, the emigrants found much the same conditions that had attracted so many settlers to the Old Northwest—fresh, fertile soil, plenty of

[30] Quoted in De Voto, *Year of Decision,* p. 125.
[31] Quoted in Coons, *The Trail to Oregon,* p. 160.

timber and water, and an abundance of wildlife—and they had the added advantage of milder winters, which meant that their growing seasons would be longer and their lives more comfortable.

## The Settlement of the Great Plains

On a map of the United States drawn during the mid-1800's, the land area extending from the Missouri River to the Rocky Mountains and from the Texas Panhandle to the Canadian border was labeled the "Great American Desert." This area was legally opened to settlement by the passage of the bitterly debated Kansas-Nebraska Act in 1854, but the real settlement boom followed the enactment of the Homestead Act in 1862. There had been many land acts before 1862—so many as to be confusing to pioneer settlers and later students alike—but all of these acts had required the pioneers to buy the land on which they settled. Under the Land Act of 1804, a pioneer who settled on surveyed public lands was required to register with a federal land office and then to buy a minimum of 160 acres (a tract known as a quarter-section) for a minimum price of $1.64 an acre. If he chose to pay the full amount at once he received an eight-percent discount, but the law allowed him four full years to pay and most settlers took advantage of the credit provision. The Land Act of 1820 reduced the minimum price per acre to $1.25 and abolished the credit system. Thereafter the settler had to pay promptly in cash or risk losing the land he had improved to speculators or other nonresident purchasers, although later a series of acts called preemption laws did give him some protection. By today's standards, $200 for 160 acres of land would be very cheap indeed, but in the nineteenth century it was a sizable amount for a poor man to acquire, particularly when added to the cost of the livestock, equipment, and supplies required for the journey west. So the Homestead Act of 1862, which guaranteed settlers free legal title to 160 acres after they had occupied the land for five years, was a strong stimulus to emigration. Settlers moved into the newly opened Kansas and Nebraska territories by the thousands. The farming frontier—which had begun east of the Appalachians a century before, extended into the Old Northwest, and then traveled the overland trail to the Pacific Northwest—gradually began to fill the void it had passed over.

Everett Dick, an historian, described this new breed of pioneer:

> The first permanent settlers on the prairies were those adventurous ones who feared neither the dangers of Indian attacks nor the privations of life in a region remote from civilization. They formed a frail, thin line of settlement along the overland trails. . . . This development was a new thing in the history of the frontier. It is true that settlement often followed rivers but never before had settlement pushed out across a barren area. . . .[32]

Among the settlers on the Great Plains were a number of black families. The family above homesteaded in Nebraska in the 1880's.

The Great Plains region presented an environment much different from previous frontiers. The blistering heat of summer and the raging blizzards of winter, the seasons of drought and the deluges of rain, the spring tornados and the breathless summer nights—together these things created an exhausting challenge.

The pioneers found very little that was familiar to them. Timber for homes, sheds, or split-rail fences was almost nonexistent. Rainfall was erratic and few streams ran all year round, so water had to be taken from deep wells. Normal farming operations were futile because of the tough prairie sod. In order to succeed, the frontiersman had to devise new methods or purchase newly developed farm implements. The human ingenuity required to conquer this hostile environment produced innovations which were altogether strange to the traditional farmer—barbed wire, windmills, and sod buildings.

As the farming frontier approached the fringes of the cattle kingdom, there was an increased demand for efficient fencing material. Farmers had to have fences of one kind

---

[32]Everett Dick, *The Sod-House Frontier, 1854–1890* (Lincoln, Neb.: Johnsen Publishing Co., 1954), p. 102. © 1954. Reprinted by courtesy of Johnsen Publishing Co.

or another to prevent livestock and trespassers from ruining their crops. The stone fences of New England had given way to rail fences in the Old Northwest, but the split-rail fence proved highly impractical on the Great Plains. A 160-acre homestead which cost its owner twenty dollars in registration fees might cost a thousand dollars to fence when the purchase price of the lumber and the shipping fees were added up.

Hundreds of inventors took out patents on new types of cheap fencing, but one solution proved superior to all the rest. It was devised by Joseph Farwell Glidden, a farmer near DeKalb, Illinois. His idea was best described by Ray Allen Billington:

> Faced with the problem of enclosing his own six-hundred-acre farm, Glidden devised a practical fence by twisting together two strands of wire in such a way they would hold pointed wire barbs at short intervals. After convincing himself the "barbed wire" fence could be produced cheaply, he patented his invention on November 24, 1874, rented a small factory in De Kalb, hired a crew of boys to string the barbs on the twisted strands, and began manufacturing his product as the Barb Fence Company.[33]

An 1882 advertisement for barbed wire and other farm supplies.

Joseph Glidden was not the first person to design barbed wire, patents having been issued as early as 1801. The difference in Glidden's product was that it could be mass produced by using machines, thus making it available at a price most people could afford. Nearly 3,000,000 pounds of barbed wire were sold in 1876, and by 1880 the figure had soared to 80,000,000 pounds. The price of the wire dropped from twenty dollars per hundred pounds in 1870 to less than four dollars in 1890. The historian Walter Prescott Webb remarked:

> It was barbed wire, and not railroads or the homestead law that made it possible for the farmers to resume, or at least accelerate, their march across the prairies onto the plains. . . . The invention of barbed wire revolutionized

---

[33] Billington, *Westward Expansion,* p. 691.

land values and opened up to the homesteader the fertile Prairie Plains.[34]

Cattle grazing on the far side of a barbed wire fence.

The strongest resistance to barbed wire came from the cattle ranchers, who were accustomed to treating most of the territory between Texas and Wyoming as open range. When the farmers began fencing in the rangeland, the cattlemen complained that they were being threatened with extinction. The cattle drovers referred to the new wire fencing as "the Devil's Rope," "the Devil's Necklace," or "the Devil's Hatband." The drovers' hostility stemmed from some genuine grievances. The new fences blocked their trails, sealing them off from vital water supplies and sheltered camping grounds. Cattle were frequently injured on the wire. Many of the cattlemen resorted to wire cutting, a practice that resulted in what some historians have called the "Barbed Wire War."

Water was as essential to plains agriculture as good fencing. The pioneers soon discovered that methods which had proven successful on earlier frontiers, such as the open well, would not work on the Great Plains. Most settlers resorted to expensive well-drilling machines to reach the deep subsurface pools. Well drillers charged from $1.25 to $2 a foot to drill a well, and in the plains country a well might be anywhere from fifty to five hundred feet deep. After reaching the water, the settlers were still faced with the problem of raising it to the surface. With an average wind velocity of twelve to fourteen miles per hour sweeping the plains, the logical solution was to devise a windmill. The cost of a manufactured windmill ranged from $100 to $150, so many settlers decided to build their own.

Windmills varied in construction and appearance with the owner's imagination, skill, and available building materials. The prairie settlers found their materials for windmill construction in the gears, cogs, and levers of broken-down farm machinery, and in scrap lumber, canvas from

[34] Walter Prescott Webb, *The Great Plains* (Waltham, Mass.: Blaisdell, 1959), pp. 316–317. Copyright © 1959 by Walter Prescott Webb. Reprinted by permission of Xerox College Publishing. All rights reserved.

old tarpaulins, packing boxes, and flattened tin cans. The farmers gave descriptive names to these creations, names such as "jumbo," "go-devil," "battle-axe," and "merry-go-round." Homemade mills were objects of considerable pride. Walter Webb observed, "The windmill is like a flag marking the spot where a small victory had been won in the fight for water in an arid land."[35]

Another of the settler's pressing needs was, of course, housing. Upon locating his homestead, the settler prepared a temporary shelter by excavating a dugout in the side of a hill or in a ravine. The family lived in the wagon box while the father used the team and wagon frame to haul brush, grass, and sod.

In 1872 an old settler named Oscar Babcock estimated the cost of constructing a dugout fourteen feet square:

A homemade windmill in Nebraska.

| | |
|---|---|
| One window | $1.25 |
| 18 feet of lumber for front door | .54 |
| Latch and hanging (no lock) | .50 |
| Length of pipe to go through roof | .30 |
| 3 lbs. nails to make door, etc. | .19½ |
| Total | $2.78½ [36] |

Months later, the pioneers would erect a more permanent structure called a sod house. The process of construction was described by Charles S. Reed, who helped build several "soddies" as a young boy:

> The first step was to "break" the ground, which was done by turning the sod over with a "breaking plow." . . . The moldboard of a breaking plow consisted of three curved rods that turned the sod over grass side down, instead of a solid metal plate. . . . Pieces of sod used in building were usually about three inches thick, twelve inches wide, and thirty inches long. . . .
>
> The mechanics of building a sod house were fairly simple, but required good workmanship to put up a good

[35] Quoted in Donald Danker, "Nebraska's Homemade Windmills," *The American West* 3, no. 1 (1966): 15.

[36] Quoted in Dick, *The Sod-House Frontier*, p. 112.

one. . . . The first tier of sod was laid grass side down on the virgin ground site. If the building space was not level, the lower corners were built up by sod so that the upper tiers of sod in the wall would be level. . . .

In erecting a wall, the slabs of sod were crisscrossed so that the joints would be broken all the way up the wall. Thus each layer of sod (all of which were laid grass side down) was laid into the wall differently from the layer below it. . . .

If you kept the walls straight, it was pretty easy going until you reached the top of an opening where a window or door was to be. A door opening was provided by just not laying any sod in the door area, and a window opening was provided by running the solid wall only up to the bottom of the window and then leaving an open area the size of a window. The top of a window or door opening required special care. It was necessary to place some flat boards across the top of the window or door opening to support the wall that had to be on top. . . .

The most important thing about a sod house was its roof. The common sod house had a gable roof. . . . In my country, getting a good ridge pole long enough to reach from the top of one outside end wall to the other end of the house, or even to a sod cross partition, was quite a job. In the early days, such a piece of timber was . . . always a long tree trimmed down. If the builders were lucky enough to have flat boards, one end of the board was nailed to the top center of the ridge pole and then extended down over the side walls about two feet. Then paper (tar paper if they could afford it) was placed on top of the sheeting boards and then sod (grass side up) was closely fitted together so as to form a slanting roof down to the end of the eaves. This made as good a roof as you could build unless you could afford wooden shingles. . . .

Flooring varied. In most of the earliest soddies the ground on the inside of the house would be leveled and swept free of any dust, and then the hard dirt surface would be covered by homemade rag carpets or often used bare. Most of the sod houses I remember, however, had at least rough board floors.

Men building a sod house in western Nebraska, about 1890.

NEBRASKA STATE HISTORICAL SOCIETY

NEBRASKA STATE HISTORICAL SOCIETY

Above, three brothers—George, Jacob, and Marcus Perry—entertain guests at their sod house near Merna, Nebraska, in 1886. Below, the homestead of Peter M. Barnes near Clear Creek, Nebraska, in 1887.

NEBRASKA STATE HISTORICAL SOCIETY

Sometimes the interior would be just the plain ends of the sod smoothed off. However, most people tried to improve this, and would cover the inside walls with paper, cloth or plaster. The plaster . . . was a mixture of sand and clay troweled onto the sod wall. . . . People who were lucky enough to afford cement would put it into the plaster mix, and this made fairly permanent plaster. Generally speaking, the outside walls were left plain, but a few people plastered the outside. Some that could not afford to plaster the wall on the outside with cement would put a fine mesh wire over the outside walls.

Most people visualize life in a soddy as being very dirty, but actually a sod house could be kept quite clean. A good sod house was always comfortable. . . . Sod houses were durable too. . . .[37]

Life in a sod house wasn't always pleasant. During rainstorms, for example, the roof became soggy and rivulets of water dripped all over the house. The roof continued to drip for several days after the rain had ended, and the floor became a quagmire. Women recalled having an umbrella held over them while they cooked or were sick in bed. Occasionally, the whole roof would cave in from the excess weight of saturation. Even in dry weather, dirt and grass continually fell from the ceiling. The average life of a sod house was six to seven years.

Still, the sod house was not without its advantages. It was cool in summer, warm in winter, rarely blew over in the high winds, and was in no danger of destruction by prairie fires. In addition, the construction of a sod house was very inexpensive, a fact attested to by Howard Ruede, a Kansas homesteader, in 1877:

. . . I made out an estimate of the cost of our house. This does not include what was paid for in work: Ridgepole and hauling (including two loads of firewood) $1.50; rafters and straw, 50¢; 2 lb. nails, 15¢; hinges 20¢; window 75¢; total cash paid $4.05. Then there was $4 worth of lumber, which

A settler inside his sod house near Wausa, Nebraska.

NEBRASKA STATE HISTORICAL SOCIETY

[37] Quoted in Richmond and Mardock, *A Nation Moving West,* pp. 306–308.

was paid for in work, and $1.50 for hauling the firewood,
50¢, makes $10.05 for a place to live in and firewood
enough to last all summer. . . .[38]

The plains environment made life exceptionally difficult
because every season brought new hardships. Winters
could be especially severe, with fierce blizzards and temperatures that remained below zero for weeks. Women's
feet froze during the course of normal household chores.
Water froze in the glasses at mealtimes. The fact that two
to three inches of snow blew through the cracks into a sod
house in one night was not considered remarkable. Hogs,
cattle, chickens, and horses were frequently moved into the
one-room soddies with the people for mutual survival.
When fuel became scarce, the settlers were sometimes
forced to chop up their furniture to burn.

Fuel was as difficult to obtain as water. Many of the
pioneers depended upon dried buffalo chips or cow manure. In the fall of the year these fuels were gathered by
the wagonload and stacked up for winter. A farmer was
fortunate indeed when a trail drive bedded down for the
night near his property, because it meant that he would
have a winter's supply of fuel. As the herds of buffalo and
cattle disappeared, the farmers used either the woody
stalks of sunflowers or twisted bundles of grass. Special
stoves called "Hay-Burners" were widely sold in the 1870's.

Raging spring floods added to the settlers' hardships,
especially among those who had settled near streams which
had appeared to be nearly dry in summer. In the spring,
after the heavy snows began to melt, these streams swelled
to a boiling menace, sweeping away houses, barns, fences,
livestock, implements, and anything else that stood in their
paths.

The summer months normally brought searing heat
waves which parched the soil and burned the crops. For
weeks at a time the temperature did not fall below 100
degrees. Although it wasn't a joking matter, plains pioneers

[38] Howard Ruede, *Sod-House Days, 1877–1878* (New York: Cooper
Square, 1966), p. 27.

NEBRASKA STATE HISTORICAL SOCIETY

A farmer, Swain Finch, trying to protect his corn from a swarm of locusts during the plague of 1874.

often remarked in jest that sinners were buried in overcoats to protect them from sudden changes in temperature. The monotony of the summer heat was occasionally broken by a devastating tornado, a pounding hail storm, or a choking dust storm.

The settlers' diets seldom varied. Day after day the menu consisted only of corn. In 1862, the *Nebraska Farmer* published a list of thirty-three different recipes for cooking corn. The prairie environment contained few fruits or berries and very little wild game, so most of the homesteaders were forced to rely upon the productivity of their own gardens.

From 1874 to 1877, in addition to all their other summer hardships, the plainsmen had to endure plagues of grasshoppers, or locusts as they are called when they mass together. The insects filled the sky like enormous clouds, and when they settled they pelted houses like hailstones and alighted on trees in such great numbers that their weight broke off large limbs. They ate everything —cornstalks, grain, garden vegetables (including those that grew underground, like carrots and potatoes), the leaves and bark of trees, pitchfork and plow handles, lumber off houses, clothes, and even horses' harnesses. When the insects left, the whole country was a scene of ruin and desolation. Many settlers were forced to accept relief from either the territorial or United States government. Others packed up what remained and left the plains forever.

One of the greatest terrors of the plains farmers was the prairie fire, which occurred most frequently in autumn. A campfire, the discharge of a gun, a spark, a bolt of lightning—any one of these was enough to start a blaze in the dry fall grass. The fire moved across the plains destroying stock, stacks of hay, winter range, barns, and occasionally a human life. Fires often lasted as long as six weeks. Plains inhabitants who were accidentally caught in such a fire had to start a backfire or quickly get into a dugout in order to save their lives. The fire left a strange darkness, as reported by one Kansas pioneer:

Montana ranchers mixing bran, crude arsenic, molasses, lemon juice, and water in canvas wagon covers. The poisoned bait was used to attract and kill locusts.

> The darkness that follows the going out of a prairie fire is something portentous. From being the center of a lurid glare you are suddenly plunged into the bottom of a bucket of pitch. Nothing reflects any light, and there is nothing to steer by. You don't know where you are nor where the house is; everything is black. Your throat is full of ashes and you can hardly breathe. . . . You may feel as if you were the last survivor in a horrible world of cinders and blackness.[39]

The plains environment was especially unkind to women. Many women, accustomed to the less demanding chores of housekeeping in the East, burst into tears at the first sight of their new homes. Most of them, however, had enough courage to stay. To the valor of these women, Everett Dick paid high tribute:

> These solitary women, longing to catch a glimpse of one of their own sex, swept their eyes over the boundless prairie

[39] Quoted in Dick, *The Sod-House Frontier*, p. 219.

A pioneer woman standing at the door of her home in Custer County, Nebraska.

NEBRASKA STATE HISTORICAL SOCIETY

and thought of their old home in the East. They stared and stared out across space with nothing to halt their gaze over the monotonous expanse. Sometimes the burning prairie got to staring back at them and they lost their courage. They saw their complexion fade as the skin became dry and leathery in the continual wind. Their hair grew lifeless and dry, their shoulders early bent, and they became stooped as they tramped round and round the hot cookstove preparing the three regular, though skimpy meals a day. There was little incentive to primp and care for one's person. Few bothered much about brush and comb. Hollow-eyed, tired, and discouraged in the face of summer heat, drought, and poverty, they came to care little about how they looked. As has been noted some begged their husbands to hitch up the team, turn the wagon tongue eastward and leave the accursed plains, which they declared were never meant for human habitation.

But by no means were all the women crushed and defeated by the rude frontier. Many a member of the sunbonnet sex bore her loneliness, disappointment, and heartaches without a complaint, and encouraged her husband to stick it out in the face of failure, frustration, and utter rout. Valorously she rallied the broken forces and assailed the common enemy once more. Brushing aside the unbidden tears, she maintained her position by the side of her hardy helpmate, and together, unflinchingly they waged a winning struggle against the odds of poverty, defeat and loneliness.[40]

But life on the Great Plains was not entirely dismal. Although most of the prairie homesteaders lived on the edge of poverty, they still maintained their hospitality and neighborliness, even to strangers. The Sunday visit was one of the most common social events on the prairie. Families would spend the entire day together, sharing food and conversation, and helping to dispel each other's loneliness.

Though careless in dress, crude in manners, and coarse in language, the homesteaders held a loyal concern for

[40] Ibid., pp. 234–235.

each other. The very nature of the frontier created a community spirit. Neighbors frequently came together because of someone's misfortune. They joined in the spring plowing, a house-raising, or a husking bee.

Dancing was perhaps the most enjoyed of all amusements. Any occasion warranted a dance—a holiday, a wedding, a birthday, the opening of a new store, or the close of a successful harvest. For the most part, dances were gala affairs even in communities that were not fortunate enough to have musicians. A dance might be held with only a single mouth harp to provide the music. In Nebraska, a dance was reported in the local newspaper as having had a big drum, a little drum, a fiddle, a pitchfork for a triangle, a keg of beer for company, and considerable noise for variety. Masquerade and calico balls were very popular in the frontier towns. Several town councils proposed the construction of dancing schools before they did high schools.

For other types of social entertainment, the pioneers enjoyed playing checkers, dominoes, and an infinite variety of card games. Fourth of July picnics and barbecues were popular and often featured the sports of baseball, croquet, mumblety-peg, keno, wrestling, foot racing, marksmanship, horse racing, broad jumping, and high jumping. These sports, however, should not be thought of in modern terms. The high-jump area consisted of a string held between two cornstalks or posts, while horse racing was usually a contest between two old plow horses. Baseball games were played without the assistance of backstops, masks, or gloves. The players used only a bat fashioned from a board or fence post and a ball made of a roll of yarn, twine, or string which was covered with a piece of leather from an old boot. They played the game with two to four bases, depending on available materials. The game was filled with action and the scores were generally high. In 1871, the Milford, Nebraska, Blue Belts were leading in their game, after four hours of play, by a score of 97 to 25.

Traveling revivals, medicine shows, and circuses occasionally broke the monotony of prairie life. For the most part, however, the settlers' entertainment was homemade.

Small farming communities often could not afford to support a full-time minister. This "circuit preacher," drawn in 1867 by A. H. Waud, traveled from place to place holding services, presiding over weddings and funerals, and advising his far-flung congregation.

There was a great informality in prairie government. The selection of a county seat often erupted into a "county seat war" among communities that were hardly more than dry spots on the plains. Observing that three small Nebraska towns were all competing for the honor of becoming the center of their county's government, one writer remarked, "Republican City and Melrose each had a store, hitching post, and a clothes line, while Alma had only her buffalo skull."[41]

Elections were frequent and often heated. They were usually held under a shade tree or in a settler's dugout. Voters were occasionally asked to line up behind their candidate and then to vote by filing past the election official. After casting their votes, many returned to the line to vote again. One man was observed voting five times. When questioned, he replied that he had voted once for himself and then had cast four proxy votes for his friends who would have voted for his candidate except that they were out of the territory.

Meetings of the state legislatures were often exciting events. In 1862, the quarrels grew so violent in the Dakota legislature that the governor was forced to send an armed detachment of twenty cavalrymen with fixed bayonets into the House of Representatives to preserve order. During such meetings, members could be observed whittling, sleeping, sitting on top of their desks, or just walking around. One man was seen eating hard-boiled eggs with a jackknife. It was not at all uncommon to adjourn the meeting to a nearby saloon.

The political campaigns were equally exciting. In the midst of loud music, excessive drinking, and violent fist fights, a candidate would mount a heap of barnyard refuse and deliver a fiery speech. Crude though they were, these were the beginnings of government on the Great Plains.

Although the plains environment bordered on the intolerable, settlers homesteaded there in unprecedented numbers. Ray Allen Billington reported:

[41] Ibid., p. 460.

A larger domain was settled in the last three decades of the century than in all America's past; 407,000,000 acres were occupied and 189,000,000 improved between 1607 and 1870; 430,000,000 acres peopled and 225,000,000 placed under cultivation between 1870 and 1900. Surveying that breath-taking advance, the director of the census announced in 1890 that the country's "unsettled area has been so broken into by isolated bodies of settlement that there can hardly be said to be a frontier line."[42]

That settlers could succeed in the plains environment in such numbers was largely due to the inventive genius of such men as James Oliver and Cyrus McCormick. These men were representative of the inventors who produced the farm implements which conquered the plains—iron and steel plows, grain drills, reapers, disk and toothed harrows, cultivators, binders, listers, headers, threshing machines, and combines. In 1890, the United States Commission of Labor published figures showing how much time and money a farmer could save, on one acre of produce, by using mechanized equipment:

McCORMICK'S PATENT VIRGINIA REAPER.

D. W. BROWN, OF ASHLAND, OHIO,

An early handbill advertising the McCormick reaper.

| Crop | Time Worked | | Labor Cost | |
|------|------|------|------|------|
| | Hand | Machine | Hand | Machine |
| Wheat | 61 hours | 3 hours | $3.55 | $.0.66 |
| Corn | 39 hours | 15 hours | 3.62 | 1.51 |
| Oats | 66 hours | 7 hours | 3.73 | 1.07 |
| Loose Hay | 21 hours | 4 hours | 1.75 | 0.42 |
| Baled Hay | 35 hours | 12 hours | 3.06 | 1.29[43] |

The new technology was not an unmixed blessing, however. Before he could begin increasing his yields and cutting his costs, a farmer first had to buy the machines—and the machines were expensive. Although most farmers managed to acquire one or two pieces of modern equipment, few could afford to take full advantage of the new inventions without going heavily into debt. Even one or

[42] Billington, *Westward Expansion,* p. 705.
[43] Quoted in ibid., p. 697.

two pieces of equipment might mean a mortgage on the farm. And of course there were many to whom the Agricultural Revolution was worse than meaningless, for it meant only that they would fall further behind their more prosperous neighbors. A man could homestead on the plains for as little as a ten-dollar filing fee and a promise to build a suitable habitation within a year. Many of the settlers who came had a difficult time accumulating the ten dollars. They couldn't begin to pay for fencing materials or a good well, let alone expensive farm machinery.

Some poor emigrants made the long trip west only to find that they could not even acquire decent land on which to farm. In many areas, land speculators had made a mockery of the Homestead Act. The small farmer who arrived expecting to get a good homestead often discovered that he had to accept inferior land because the speculators had consolidated the choice lands into tracts to be sold at exorbitant prices. Speculators accumulated the land by circumventing the requirement of a suitable habitation. Some built miniature houses; others rented portable cabins on wheels for five dollars apiece. The system of inspection was totally inadequate, and thousands of acres passed into the hands of speculators for fifty cents an acre, and were in turn sold to the farmers at a cost of five to ten dollars per acre.

Harvesting on a highly mechanized farm, about 1898.

TITLE INSURANCE AND TRUST COMPANY

Subjected to the privations of a harsh environment and indebted to the banks, the equipment manufacturers, and the land speculators, the sod-house farmers somehow withstood it all—and could even recall their experiences with a bit of pleasure. An old pioneer, recalling the settling of the West, thoughtfully remarked, "By Damn, wouldn't it be fun to tear it down and start all over again!"

## SUGGESTED READINGS

Black Hawk. *Black Hawk: An Autobiography.* University of Illinois Press, Illini Books.

Brown, Dee. *Gentle Tamers: Women in the Old Wild West.* University of Nebraska Press, Bison Books.

Fite, Gilbert. *The Farmer's Frontier, 1865–1900.* Holt, Rinehart & Winston.

Gates, Paul W. *The Farmer's Age.* Harper & Row, Torchbooks.

Kraenzel, Carl F. *The Great Plains in Transition.* University of Oklahoma Press.

McGlashan, Charles F. *The History of the Donner Party: A Tragedy of the Sierra.* Stanford University Press.

Paden, Irene. *The Wake of the Prairie Schooner.* Southern Illinois University Press, Acturus Books.

Parkman, Francis. *The Oregon Trail.* New American Library, Signet Books.

Richmond, Robert W., and Mardock, Robert W., eds. *A Nation Moving West: Readings in the History of the American Frontier.* University of Nebraska Press, Bison Books.

Shannon, Fred A. *American Farmers' Movements.* Van Nostrand Reinhold, Anvil Books.

Shannon, Fred A. *The Farmer's Last Frontier, 1860–1897.* Harper & Row, Torchbooks.

Stewart, Elinore P. *Letters of a Woman Homesteader.* University of Nebraska Press, Bison Books.

Webb, Walter Prescott. *The Great Plains.* Grosset & Dunlap, Universal Library.

## CHAPTER SEVEN

# THE PROPRIETORS

Although it may sound strange to speak of an "urban frontier," there was in fact a continual wave of town founding and urban development in the American West. Studies of the nation's westward expansion often give the impression that the movement was wholly rural. In his discussions of the frontier, Frederick Jackson Turner assigned subordinate roles to the western towns, suggesting that they were simply outgrowths of the trapping, mining, ranching, and farming frontiers. But another historian, Richard Wade, has offered quite a different view:

> The towns were the spearheads of the frontier. Planted far in advance of the line of settlement, they held the West for the approaching population. Indeed, in 1763, when the British threw the Proclamation Line along the Appalachians to stop the flow of settlers, a French merchant company prepared to survey the streets of St. Louis, a thousand miles through the wilderness. . . . The establishment of towns preceded the breaking of soil in the transmontane west.[1]

While it is true that the farms, the ranches, and the mines were the foundations of the frontier economy, it is also

The scene on the opposite page—a row of shops, a dusty street, a shipment of goods delivered by rail or freight wagon—was typical of the proprietors' frontier during the second half of the nineteenth century.

[1]Richard Wade, *The Urban Frontier: The Rise of Western Cities, 1780–1830.* (Cambridge: Harvard University Press, 1959), p. 1.

true that those farms, ranches, and mines could not have been established or maintained without centers of trade where the pioneers could sell their products and buy needed supplies. Some of these settlements, like Pittsburgh, Cincinnati, Louisville, and St. Louis on the earlier frontier, and Chicago, Kansas City, Omaha, Denver, and San Francisco on the later one, grew up into cities, and these cities in turn served the smaller towns and villages as essential centers of supply and distribution.

The town and the country together made up the frontier economy. And if the country provided the town with its reason for being, the town provided the country with a civilized community where comfort and culture as well as supplies and marketplaces could be found. While countrymen struggled with the land, townsmen struggled to establish hotels, livery stables, banks, warehouses, newspapers, schools, theaters, libraries, churches, and governments. The frontier town dwellers were also pioneers, in every sense of the word.

A survey of a number of western cities, including Kansas City, Santa Fe, Denver, Omaha, Seattle, and San Francisco, reveals very similar and in some cases almost identical histories of development. For this reason, an in-depth study of a single city, rather than shorter sketches of several cities, will be used to explore the nature of the urban frontier. The city of Denver was selected for this study because it is perhaps most representative of all the frontier settlements that grew up into cities during the late nineteenth century. Denver is located at the center of the region known as the Great West, the region bounded by the Mississippi River on the east and the Pacific Ocean on the west and by Canada on the north and the Rio Grande on the south. In that location, the "Queen City of the Plains" was continually in touch with the growing and changing westward movement.

### The Origins of Denver

Occasional probes of the uncharted Rocky Mountain wilderness had been made by some of the frontier's most famous explorers, including Zebulon Pike and John C.

John C. Frémont explored this portion of the Rockies in 1842. The snow-capped mountain in the background is Frémont's Peak, 13,730 feet high.

Frémont, who was led by the mountain man Kit Carson. Accounts of these explorations encouraged other groups of adventurers to move into the region. The mountain men came first, followed by the prospectors. It was the latter group that founded what was to become the city of Denver.

Numerous trading parties and lone travelers told of rich mineral deposits in the Pikes Peak area. The publication of those stories built up increasing interest in the region, and during the summer of 1858 the first prospecting parties began to arrive. The William Green Russell party came all the way from Georgia, made a placer strike near present-day Englewood, Colorado, and, after exhausting it, moved north. News of the party's success trickled into Kansas, and from Lawrence came the group which established the first permanent settlement in the region. On September 6, 1858, this group organized the Montana Town Company and assigned a civil engineer to survey and lay out Montana City. A dispute over location resulted in part of the Lawrence party's breaking away, moving farther north, and, on September 24, organizing the St. Charles Town Association.

Kit Carson, photographed on a visit to Washington, D.C., in 1847.

Considerable attention was given to the selection of a proper site for the latter settlement. The experience of town proprietorship had taught these men to locate on a major traffic artery. St. Charles was consequently established near the Platte River–Cherry Creek junction, which was also the intersection of a trapper's trace and military trail from Fort Bridger to New Mexico.

Late in October the Russell party returned from the north and decided to found a settlement of their own on the south side of Cherry Creek, opposite St. Charles. On November 1, the constitution of the Auraria Town Company was formally adopted.

Two weeks later, a Kansas prospecting party under the leadership of General William Larimer, an experienced banker, railroad builder, politician, and city founder, arrived at the rivers' junction. The Larimer group immediately jumped the St. Charles land claim and on November 22, 1858, established the Denver City Company.

It was probably inevitable that trouble should emerge between the neighboring settlements of Auraria and Denver. Even during times of hardship, the promoters of the two communities advertised their civic pride to the point of absurdity. Bitter rivalry resulted and the two settlements contested each other's claims to population supremacy, the first white birth, the first bank, the first school, and the first anything that seemed to be what a proper town ought to have. The rivalry was reflected in a letter written in the spring of 1859 by an enthusiastic resident of Denver City:

Them Southern desperadoes from Georgia that located their city on the west side of Cherry Creek have reached the end of their rope. They have lied about our townsite . . . wherever they had a chance to wag a tongue or write a letter. But their doom is sealed already and Denver is the city of the present and the future. We have thirty-eight beautiful and substantial buildings in our town now, while them contumacious villains has but eighty. Theirs are huts and hovels and shanties that you wouldn't drive a cow into for shelter, while ours are to be called palaces by comparison. We have named our city after Gov. Denver, as fine a gentleman as ever set foot on the soil of Kansas, while them braggarts have gone to the poetry book for a name—and they'll go to the devil for a history. . . . They think because they have got the newspaper and the express office that Denver City is done for. If you hear any of their lies back in the States, contradict them. . . . They are making a great hullabaloo because they have got the first board roof . . . a good mud roof ain't a thing to be despised in a dry country like this. If they are well made, there is no particular danger of them washing down on a family. . . . 'Tisn't as if pioneers were sporting velvet carpets and satin upholstery that a little stream of muddy water running down here and there would spoil. . . . No, sir, friend Witter, Denver City is the bobtail hoss that I have bet all my money on and you and me will live to see marble palaces lining its streets. . . . Now Larimer and me and the rest of us fellows want you to come out this summer and put your shoulders to the wheel with us and you'll make a fortune. . . . The plains are covered with posies now and the mountains are a sight you will never see anywhere else out of Paradise. Everybody is well—nobody gets sick here, not even over in Auraria, where you'd think people would want to die just to get away from it.[2]

Occasionally the rivalry erupted into violence, and in every dispute the first question asked was, "Are you a Denver man or an Aurarian?" The feud was finally resolved when Golden City, some ten miles west of Denver, revealed its ambitions of becoming territorial capital, thereby creating a need for consolidation of the two Cherry Creek settlements. Neither settlement was much by itself, but together the two made up a presentable town to serve as the capital. The unification was officially completed in December, 1859, when the territorial legislature granted the new town a charter and a joint election was held for mayor.

At the time of unification the settlement consisted of cabins roughly built out of materials that were readily

[2] Quoted in Nolie Mumey, *A History of the Early Settlement of Denver* (Glendale, Calif.: Arthur H. Clark, 1942), pp. 190–194.

available to men more interested in panning for gold than in building houses. These materials were normally cottonwood logs, mud, and prairie sod.

The people who composed the early settlement came from all walks of life and had moved west for many different reasons. Some had been bankrupted by the depression of 1857 and some had broken laws in the East, but others had been successful businessmen, craftsmen, and professional men. Nearly all of them, however, had come hoping to strike it rich in one way or another. Historians have not always agreed on the prevailing character of Denver's early population. Jerome Smiley expressed one point of view in *The History of Denver,* published in 1901:

The proprietor of a frontier store, warming his feet at the stove as he waits for customers.

To assert or imply that as a whole the mass was composed of bankrupts, criminals, gamblers and loafers, is stupid, ignorant nonsense, formulated from the stories it was once common to relate of many places in the west. . . . As to loafers, this country was probably the most uninviting region in the world for them. The truth is that while many had been bankrupted, and many others impoverished by the collapse in 1857, in the main the men who came here in the pioneer times were of average honesty, and of more than average enthusiasm and heedlessness. They were inspired by no worse motive than one to better their worldly condition. . . .

But many other Denver historians, including contemporaries of the period, have drawn a picture of lawlessness, thievery, murder on a daily schedule, rampant prostitution, and universal gambling. One eyewitness to the extent of the community's gambling habits allegedly saw the probate judge of the county lose thirty Denver lots in less than ten minutes in a public saloon on a Sunday morning. Shortly afterward he observed the county sheriff pawning his revolver for twenty dollars to spend in betting at faro. The historian Stanley Zamonski estimated that one-tenth of the population lived on the profits of prostitution. Robert L. Perkin, another historian, quoted a contemporary citizen as stating that the other nine-tenths of the population lived on the profits of gambling. If these accounts are assumed to be even partially accurate, they must cast some suspicion on Smiley's complimentary description.

The origins of the city of Denver were not unlike those of many other western towns, towns that were fated to boom fantastically only to wither and disappear into oblivion. Denver City successfully avoided that fate because of the quality and experience of her early leaders. The men who founded the community were experienced city founders. They selected the most favorable location, organized formal town companies, and even had a civil engineer survey and stake out their settlements. These leaders were more interested in founding a city than in searching for gold; they made their profits selling plots of land through the town companies. Their optimism and their knowledge of what causes a city to succeed or fail was reflected in a speech delivered by William Larimer during the winter of 1858 following the creation of the Denver City Company:

The first permanent house in Denver, built in November, 1858, at the corner of Wynkoop and Twelfth Streets.

> We are satisfied with our prospects here and intend to stay until this country is fully explored. . . . The late financial panic which has prostrated every branch of trade will bring an influx of enterprising people. . . . A railroad is coming. The Pacific Railroad has planned to build through the West. And even without a branch at this point we can tap it at the crossing of the North and South Platte. . . . The whole country is demanding that this road be built. The West is demanding it. Denver City demands it. . . . Manifest Destiny has shaped its end. We have laid the foundation for a city, an outlet for this gold bonanza and for the Rocky Mountain Region.[3]

## The Economic Base of Denver

Although the gold strike made by the Russell party in 1858 had not been extensive, the Denver City Company circulated reports of rich gold discoveries in the Rocky Mountains in order to lure settlers to the region. When large

[3] Quoted in Stanley Zamonski and Teddy Keller, *The Fifty-Niners* (Chicago: Swallow Press, Sage Books, 1961), p. 18.

numbers of these settlers started returning to their homes in the East, frustrated by months of unsuccessful prospecting, the company seemed headed for disaster. Then, in the spring of 1859, rich gold deposits really were discovered in the Rocky Mountains, and the Colorado gold rush began in earnest. Denver City, with its strategic junction of rivers and trails, became the gold country's principal center of trade. By March, 1859, the population had swelled to six hundred people.

When the gold rush began, the Cherry Creek community already had a general merchandise store, a hardware store, a jewelry store, a blacksmith's shop, and a carpenter's shop. The settlement's first saloon had opened on Christmas Day, 1858, and when the gold seekers arrived in the spring there was also a hotel, a bakery, and a drugstore. The town's first bank and a federal mint began operations in July, 1860, making Denver Colorado's most important center of capital.

The supplies needed to feed, clothe, and equip the new settlers severely strained the region's already overburdened transportation facilities. There were no railroads west of the Missouri River, and everything had to be freighted in by wagon. On May 7, 1859, the first stagecoach arrived in Denver; ten days later, the first Leavenworth-to-Pikes Peak express coach completed its nineteen-day trip across the plains.

The major objective of Denver City's leaders throughout the 1860's was to secure a position on the route of the transcontinental railroad. In November, 1866, the Union Pacific announced its decision to build across the plains of Wyoming, by-passing Denver. The city was stunned, but some of its more determined citizens, led by John Evans, raised enough money to finance the Denver-Pacific Railroad, which joined the main line at Cheyenne on June 22, 1870. During its first month of operation, the railroad carried over a thousand passengers and thirteen million pounds of freight to Denver. The city began to grow as never before. In 1870 the population was 4,759; in 1880 it was 35,629.

The 1860's also brought significant changes in Denver's

The "fifty-niners" who swarmed into Colorado during the early days of the gold rush considered themselves lucky to find a dry sawdust bed on a saloon floor.

first principal industry, gold mining. Placer mining—in which "free" or pure gold was recovered from the beds and banks of streams—had become unproductive as early as 1860. Gold seekers were forced to turn to tunnel mining, which required more expensive equipment, was considerably slower, and yielded more gold-containing ore than free gold. At first tunnel mining was unproductive, too. Although assays proved that the ore contained gold, smelting techniques were not advanced enough to extract the gold efficiently. Then, in January, 1868, the region's first practical smelter was fired at Black Hawk, Colorado. Hard-rock mining became big business, too big for the individual prospector, who either had to leave the gold fields, try to survive on the dwindling rewards of placer mining, or accept a job for wages with one of the large mining companies. From 1858 to 1870, Colorado's mines had produced $33 million in gold. The output climbed steadily thereafter, reaching a high of $235 million in the first decade of the twentieth century.

The area's first major silver discovery was made in 1864.

For the next thirty years, silver mining was even more profitable than gold mining. Silver mining more than any other single activity was responsible for bringing wealth to Denver.

The city became largely self-sustaining. A number of settlers went into agriculture, and those with large landholdings usually made a great deal of money. Cattle raising flourished on the prairies and in the mountains until the middle 1880's. Denver served as the market for both cattle and sheep and became the big cow town of the region, developing stockyards and packing houses.

A variety of things composed the economic base of Denver, and each had its turn emerging as the dominant economic force. An accurate economic description of Denver during its first decade would be to say that it was the marketing, distributing, and coinage center of the Pikes Peak region.

### Problems in Early Denver

A frontier judge, painted by Olaf Seltzer, an artist from Denmark who settled in Montana and became well known for his sketches of western life.

One of the most pressing urban problems in Denver City was its high rate of crime. It had developed a coast-to-coast reputation as a wide-open town. Part of the problem can be attributed to the unusually rapid increase in population. Most of the city's new residents during the gold-rush period were determined to get rich quick, and some of them were not too particular about how they did it.

Saloons, among the first established business houses in the community, were the source of much of the lawlessness. Because few evenings passed in these saloons without a gun fight, the musicians lined the low enclosures surrounding the bandstands with sheet iron. Stanley Zamonski reported that a good orchestra, at the first shot, could vanish behind the armored enclosure and then come up into the gunsmoke playing without losing a beat.

Most of the inhabitants relied on weapons to arbitrate disputes. The first fifteen people buried in the town cemetery died of gunshot wounds. If a fair fight resulted in death, no questions were asked. If the killing was obviously murder, the victim's friends usually apprehended the killer and hanged him.

The general character of law and order in early Denver City was described in a letter written October 4, 1859, by Libeus Barney:

Some time since, a barber, and a butcher got into a quarrel in Auraria, the latter knocking the former down, and on his recovery, the knight of the razor drew a knife, and with desperation inflicted five separate wounds in the abdomen of his antagonist. The barber was arrested, tried for murder, but the remarkable evidence that usually attends the defense in similar cases, was not wanting in this, and the *justifiable homicide* now parades the streets free as the winds. . . . At Golden City, last month, a gambler, while on a spree, was flourishing his bowie knife and revolver, threatening to take the life of anyone who should have the presumption to obstruct his pathway. He had his career suddenly brought to a close by an infuriated mob, who seized, bound, tied and hung the desperado all within the short time of twenty minutes; believing the adage that "an ounce of preventative is worth a pound of cure." There is scarcely a day revolves, but some one crime or another is committed; theft, robbery or murder.[4]

A frontier sheriff, painted by Olaf Seltzer. Unlike most sheriffs of the period, this one is not wearing a "peacemaker"—the Colt .45 revolver that was favored by both lawmen and outlaws from 1873 until the turn of the century.

Law and order finally arrived in May, 1861, with the first territorial governor, William Gilpin. Gilpin had a system of courts functioning by July. In September, the territorial legislature enacted a civil and criminal code which, among other provisions, established penalties for counterfeiting gold dust and coins.

Because so many of its buildings were made of wood, Denver was extremely vulnerable to fire. Despite the dangers, the inhabitants were often careless with fire. They casually burned off forests around mountain diggings, left their campfires smoldering for days, set prairie fires to clear brush, and stored gunpowder in shacks. Finally, on July 15, 1862, the city council decided to organize a volunteer hook and ladder company and several bucket brigades. However, the cart and buckets were still on order and the

[4] Libeus Barney, *Letters of the Pikes Peak Gold Rush* (San Jose, Calif.: Talisman Press, 1959), pp. 47–48.

fire department was only on paper when a fire on April 19, 1863, destroyed property worth $350,000. The "Great Fire of '63" became the dividing line between architectural eras. Denver rebuilt largely with brick and began to take on an urban appearance. Fire hydrants were installed in April, 1871.

Flooding was another danger that was compounded by the carelessness of the town's inhabitants. Many of the business houses built so close to the rivers that they were forced to put down pilings to get a firm foundation. On three occasions, in 1864, 1878, and 1885, Cherry Creek flooded and washed out everything close to its banks.

Street maintenance was a more constant, if less drastic, problem. Denver's planners did have the foresight to make the streets eighty feet wide, so that traffic was not unduly congested. They did not make any provision for paving, however, and the streets were always either muddy or dusty. Pedestrians had to be especially alert for galloping horses, manure, rubbish, and criminals. These hazards were worse at night because there were no street lights until 1871, when gas lights were installed. Wandering livestock was an additional street hazard. As late as 1880, marksmen were shooting wild antelope on the main street of the community.

Still another problem was the water supply. The first residents of Denver drank directly from the rivers. Later, well water was sold by the bottle or bucket, and this continued to be a profitable business even after the citizens began to dig their own wells. But surface wells and bottled water could not keep up with Denver's growing population. In January, 1872, the Denver City Water Company piped the first water into Denver homes from the underground flow of Cherry Creek. Later in 1872, Denver homes began to get indoor plumbing.

### Sand Creek

For two years, from 1864 to 1865, Denver also had an Indian problem. In 1851, in a treaty signed at Fort Laramie, leaders of the Cheyenne, Arapaho, and Sioux tribes agreed to allow the United States government to build roads and military posts in their territory. Although the Indians did not relinquish any claims to the territory itself—Denver City was built on what was legally Cheyenne and Arapaho land—they were reluctant to enforce their ownership even after the gold rush brought hundreds of white settlers who began turning their hunting grounds into ranches and damming their streams to look for gold. Black Kettle and White Antelope of the Cheyennes and Little Raven of the Arapahoes knew what resistance had cost other tribes to the east, and they were willing to make room for the whites rather than risk war.

The Indian leaders' peace-keeping tactics worked successfully until early in 1864, when the new territorial governor, William Evans, and the district's military commander, Colonel John M. Chivington, raised a large army of volunteers for reasons that were not made explicit at the time but were understood to concern the Indians. More than a few Colorado settlers joined to avoid being drafted into the regular Union army, which would have sent them into the South to fight the Confederates. There followed several clashes between army troops and Indians, all of them provoked, the soldiers claimed, by the Indians. The Cheyennes and Arapahoes were also blamed for a number of wagon-train raids to the north that were actually the work of the Sioux. In the summer of 1864, Governor Evans declared that a state of war existed between the Indians and the territorial government. He ordered all friendly Indians to report to a reservation near Fort Lyon. Indians not at the reservation were to be considered hostile, and civilian groups as well as army units were authorized "to kill and destroy as enemies of the country wherever they may be found, all such hostile Indians."

A Cheyenne woman.

The killing and destroying had already begun when news of the governor's proclamation reached the Cheyenne and Arapaho leaders, who were scattered across Colorado and western Kansas in summer hunting parties. Although they could not imagine how they would survive if they were not free to follow the buffalo, most members of the two tribes agreed to report to the reservation. The problem was getting there. With the help of a sympathetic army officer, Major Edward W. Wynkoop, seven Indian leaders traveled four hundred miles to Denver to request a safe conduct for their people. When they arrived in late September they found that the governor did not want to see them, and it took Wynkoop some time to persuade him to change his mind. At the meeting, Black Kettle told Evans:

> . . . Major Wynkoop proposed that we come to see you. We have come with our eyes shut, following his handful of men, like coming through fire. All we ask is that we may have peace with the whites. We want to hold you by the hand. You are our father. We have been traveling through a cloud. The sky has been dark ever since the war began. These braves who are with me are willing to do what I say. We want to take good tidings home to our people, that they may sleep in peace. I want you to give all these chiefs of the soldiers here to understand that we are for peace, and that we have made peace, that we may not be mistaken by them for enemies. I have not come here with a little wolf bark, but have come to talk plain with you. We must live near the buffalo or starve. When we came here we came free, without any apprehension, to see you, and when I go home and tell my people that I have taken your hand, and the hands of all the chiefs here in Denver, they will feel well, and so will all the different tribes of Indians on the plains, after we have eaten and drunk with them.[5]

Evans responded by accusing the Cheyennes and Arapahoes of forming an alliance with the Sioux, and he refused to make a peace treaty with the delegation. He did, however, arrange for the safety of those who wished to go to Fort Lyon.

For a short time things were peaceful. The Indians established their main camp on the reservation at Sand Creek, about forty miles north of Fort Lyon. The Indian leaders often visited the fort, which was commanded by their friend, Major Wynkoop. Game was scarce on the

[5] Quoted in Dee Brown, *Bury My Heart at Wounded Knee: An Indian History of the American West* (New York: Bantam Books, 1972), p. 80.

Above, soldiers kneel in the snow to fire. Below, defeated Cheyennes flee on foot to the camps of the Sioux. Both scenes were painted by Frederic Remington.

reservation that winter, and Wynkoop began issuing army rations to the camp. This action did not meet with the approval of army officials. Wynkoop was reprimanded for "letting the Indians run things at Fort Lyon" and also for having escorted the delegation of chiefs to Denver without authorization.

On November 5, 1864, Wynkoop was replaced by Major Scott J. Anthony. Anthony spoke peaceful words to the Indians and gave them permission to send hunting parties outside the reservation until he could obtain more rations from the government. A few weeks later he requested additional troops for the fort. The reinforcements, led by Colonel Chivington himself, arrived within twenty-four hours. Just before dawn on November 29, seven hundred soldiers, armed with rifles and a battery of four cannons, rode to the camp at Sand Creek. The Indians later reported that 105 women and children and 28 men, including White Antelope, were killed in the massacre that followed; most of the men, they said, were away hunting buffalo. In his official report, Chivington stated that his soldiers had killed from four hundred to five hundred warriors. The soldiers took seven captives, although one of them, the son of a white trader, was killed in custody.

About four hundred Indians managed to hide or run from the camp in time to save their lives, and eventually they joined the hunting parties who had been away from the camp at the time of the massacre. The leaders who had advocated peace were either dead or discredited. Black Kettle and Little Raven, accompanied only by a few relatives and old men, fled south of the Arkansas River to the land of the Kiowas. The majority of the survivors went north to join the Sioux in their war against the whites. In January, 1865, the alliance of Cheyenne, Arapaho, and Sioux warriors raided settlements and wagon trains all along the South Platte River, killing and scalping settlers, ripping up miles of telegraph wires, and destroying freight shipments. Cut off from the outside world and short of food and supplies, the residents of Denver were panic-stricken; many believed that the city itself would be attacked. But the Indians, knowing that the army was closing in, moved north across the Platte, into the Powder River country of the powerful Teton and Oglala Sioux. The army did not attempt to follow them there.

Although the Indians had been driven from the settled parts of Colorado, the question of the ownership of the land remained. If the land belonged to the Cheyennes and Arapahoes, then the United States had no right to sell it or give it away to homesteaders. Titles to mines, ranches, businesses, and other property worth millions of dollars could conceivably be invalidated. In the summer of 1865, a delegation of white officials sought out Black Kettle and Little Raven in the land of the Kiowas. They offered to make a treaty of peace if the Cheyennes and Arapahoes would waive all claims to land in Colorado. When Little Raven protested that his people could not give up the lands where their ancestors had lived and were buried, one of the officials, James Steele, said to him:

> We all fully realize that it is hard for any people to leave their homes and graves of their ancestors, but, unfortunately for you, gold has been discovered in your country, and a crowd of white people have gone there to live, and a great many of these people are the worst enemies of the Indians—men who do not care for their interests, and who would not stop at any crime to enrich themselves. These men are now in your country—in all parts of it—and there is no portion where you can live and maintain yourselves but what you will come in contact with them. The consequences of this state of things are that you are in constant danger of being imposed upon, and you have to resort to arms in self-defense. Under the circumstances, there is, in the opinion of the commission, no part of the former country large enough where you can live in peace.[6]

This was, for once, plain talk. Black Kettle replied:

> Our forefathers, when alive, lived all over this country; they did not know about doing wrong; since then they have died, and gone I don't know where. We have all lost our

[6] Quoted in ibid., pp. 97–98.

way. . . . Our Great Father sent you here with his words to us, and we take hold of them. Although the troops have struck us, we throw it all behind and are glad to meet you in peace and friendship. What you have come here for, and what the President has sent you for, I don't object to, but say yes to it. . . . The white people can go wherever they please and they will not be disturbed by us, and I want you to let them know. . . . We are different nations, but it seems as if we were but one people, whites and all. . . . Again I take you by the hand, and I feel happy. These people that are with us are glad to think that we have peace once more, and can sleep soundly, and that we can live.[7]

On October 14, 1865, the treaty was signed. The Cheyennes and Arapahoes, represented by Black Kettle and Little Raven, agreed to surrender all their lands and to remain south of the Arkansas River with the Kiowas. The United States government agreed not to kill them so long as they kept their word. After two brief years of bloodshed, the white pioneer settlers had become the sole proprietors of Colorado.

## Social and Cultural Life in Denver

The family above was typical of early-day Coloradoan pioneers.

DENVER PUBLIC LIBRARY

Culture and learning followed the prospectors to the Denver City settlement within a year. In the early fall of 1859, the settlement's first book store was opened. By November a circulating library was in operation. Denver's first church, lodge, and charitable organization, the Ladies' Aid Society, were all functioning by 1859. In the cultural history of Denver City the date October 3, 1859, is auspicious. Early that day, Professor O. J. Goldrick opened the settlement's first school. That same evening saw the town's first theatrical opening night. Colonel Thorne's theatrical troupe came south from Laramie, Wyoming, and opened *The Maid in Croissey* in Apollo Hall. The opening was described in a letter written the following day:

Last night was ushered in an event of paramount interest to Pike's Peakers. Mr. Charles Thom [sic] the far-famed

[7] Quoted in ibid., p. 98.

itinerant theatrical showman, with a company of eleven performers, made their debut at "Apollo Hall," before a large, though not very remarkable select audience. Admittance, one dollar; comfortable accommodations for three hundred and fifty; receipts, 400, which tells well for the patronage, if not for the appreciation of art in this semi-barbarous region.[8]

Within a week, frontier show-business promoters offered competition from the neighboring settlement of Auraria. Cibola Hall was refurbished and a large number of would-be thespians were hired from the gold fields. Insulted, Colonel Thorne left Denver, but theater was there to stay. It thrived during the following years with the opening of the Denver Theater in November, 1860, and finally reached a peak with the construction of the Tabor Grand Opera House in the 1880's. The life and legend of the silver-rich Tabor family was recently made the subject of an opera, *The Ballad of Baby Doe.*

The Union School founded by O. J. Goldrick was the forerunner of the first public schools of 1862, though it was not until 1872 that Denver built its first schoolhouse. Attention was also given to higher education in Denver. Early in 1863, a seminary was proposed, and on September 10 the *Rocky Mountain News* carried the following item: "The University building is being pushed forward rapidly and when finished will compare most favorably with any similar structure west of St. Louis." The building was completed by Christmas and the school opened in 1864. In 1880 it became known as the University of Denver.

Probably the greatest stimulant to Denver culture was the arrival of the railroad in 1870. Along with thousands of immigrants, it brought a number of celebrities—writers, politicians, ministers—to the region, and these visitors left marked effects on thinking Denverites. The railroad also brought new styles, ideas, and trends which slowly began to alter some of the provincial aspects of Denver society.

At the very heart of Denver's early history was the *Rocky Mountain News.* The paper survived the fire of '63, the

[8] Barney, *Letters,* p. 50.

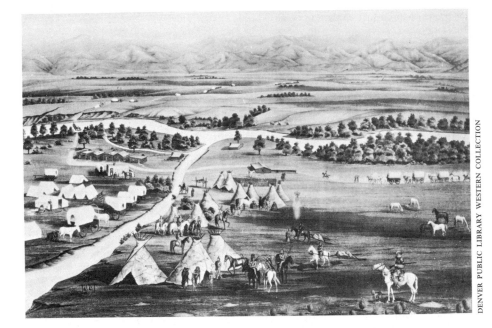

Above, a drawing of the Denver settlement as it appeared in 1859. Below, a large freight caravan, photographed in Denver in the late 1860's or early 1870's.

flood of '64, and countless competitors, and through it all supported almost every civic achievement Denver attained. It advertised the gold strikes, advocated territorial status and later statehood, supported the railroad connection with Cheyenne, aided the development of higher education, and pushed for a whole series of urban improvements. From 1867 to 1876, thirty-two newspapers were founded in Denver, but all of them eventually failed and only the *News* remained. The *Rocky Mountain News* was the single most important unifying element in the settlement and it grew in proportion with the town.

During the early years Denver's social structure was not very rigidly defined. It wasn't until the middle 1870's and the 1880's that the city became socially stratified. During this later period the silver kings began to build their elaborate mansions. Society editors were always interested in the activities of "the Sacred Thirty-Six," led by Mrs. Crawford Hill. The wives of some of Denver's wealthiest silver kings, including Baby Doe Tabor, Mrs. J. J. "Molly" Brown (whose life was the subject of the Broadway musical *The Unsinkable Molly Brown*), and the Baroness Louise von Richthofen discovered that they were socially unacceptable to "the Sacred Thirty-Six." The husbands of these exclusive ladies had to reorganize their clubs to drop "undesirables."

Even in the wide-open atmosphere of Denver City's earliest years, social acceptance was never extended to racial minorities. The first black residents were slaves who had arrived with the Russell party from Georgia in 1858. Although the territorial by-laws allowed blacks to vote after the Emancipation Proclamation, they were not permitted to serve on juries or to attend public schools. In 1865 a black school was established in Denver, and Coles Hall became the center of the community's black activities. In 1868 a lodge of black Masons was organized. A few of Denver's blacks were independent craftsmen and business proprietors, but most were forced to accept more menial occupations.

The condition of the Chinese in Denver and throughout the West was even worse. As aliens they had virtually no rights, and many state and territorial legislatures passed discriminatory laws requiring them to pay special taxes, prohibiting them from owning land, or ordering them to refrain from seeking employment in certain occupations, such as mining. The following editorial, which appeared in a newspaper in the Rocky Mountain area in 1882, would not have been considered extreme by its readers:

> The Chinese are the least desired immigrants who have ever sought the United States . . . the almond-eyed Mongolian with his pigtail, his heathenism, his filthy habits, his thrift and careful accumulation of savings to be sent back to the flowery kingdom.
>
> The most we can do is to insist that he is a heathen, a devourer of soup made from the fragrant juice of the rat, filthy, disagreeable, and undesirable generally, an incumbrance that we do not know how to get rid of, but whose tribe we have determined shall not increase in this part of the world.[9]

By 1880 there were 238 Chinese in Denver, laborers who had stayed on after the completion of the transcontinental railroad. "Chink Alley," the slum section in which they lived, was the scene of an ugly race riot—really a raid by some of the city's white inhabitants—in that year. Several Chinese were killed, but the raid failed in its purpose. The Chinese did not leave the city.

### A Comparative View

It is interesting to compare the growth of Denver with that of earlier frontier communities. In *Cities in the Wilderness,* Carl Bridenbaugh traces the urban development of five colonial settlements—Boston, Newport, Philadelphia, New York, and Charleston—between 1625 and 1742. While the founders of Boston, Newport, and Philadelphia were motivated by religious reasons to start settlements, those of New York and Charleston were guided by commercial interests. And, with the exception of Philadelphia, none

[9]Quoted in Duane A. Smith, *Rocky Mountain Mining Camps: The Urban Frontier* (Bloomington: Indiana University Press, 1967), p. 31.

of these early communities was planned or grew rapidly. Between 1630 and 1742, the fastest growing towns in British America were Boston, Philadelphia, and New York, which attained populations of about 16,000, 13,000, and 11,000 respectively.

In *The Urban Frontier,* Richard Wade explores the growth of Pittsburgh, Cincinnati, Lexington, Louisville, and St. Louis. All of these communities were established between the Allegheny Mountains and the Mississippi River during the second half of the eighteenth century. Unlike most colonial urban centers of the 1600's and early 1700's, the trans-Allegheny communities were founded by wealthy land speculators and professional town-builders. Two of these communities—Cincinnati and St. Louis—were not yet one hundred years old in 1860 when their populations had swollen to 160,000 and 100,000 respectively. Also at this date the population of seven other cities—New Orleans, Chicago, Baltimore, New York, Brooklyn, Boston, and Philadelphia—had grown beyond the 100,000 mark.

American frontier communities founded on the Great Plains and in the West during the second half of the nineteenth century more closely resembled the trans-Allegheny communities than those of colonial times. These western frontier communities were established largely by land speculators and professional town-builders, and those communities that became cities did so rapidly—more rapidly, in fact, than those of the earlier frontiers. Denver, for example, attained a population of 105,000 during its first thirty years.

The accelerated growth of frontier cities was made possible by the development of the steam engine and the resultant industrial revolution and expanding technologies that followed, especially those of transportation and communication. The urban centers of colonial times grew slowly because they were dependent on sailing ships, stage coaches, and saddle horses for transportation and communication. The advent of the steam engine and the appearance of steamboats and then railroads during the early and mid-1800's hastened the development of the trans-Allegheny frontier. But only the railroad because it freed man of his dependence on canals and navigable waterways for cheap transportation, made possible the rapid growth of urban centers on the Great Plains and in many parts of the West. The railroad deserves as much credit for developing these last frontiers as the now legendary Colt six-shooter and the Winchester repeating rifle do for taming them.

The more rapid development of each succeeding frontier also was noticeable in areas besides population growth and transportation. Fifty years had passed before the first colonial city acquired fire-fighting equipment and began building with brick. These same feats were achieved by trans-Allegheny communities in about twenty-five years, and by Denver in only five years. The first colonial newspaper, the Boston *News-Letter,* was not published until 1704, or seventy-four years after Boston was established. Newspapers appeared in the trans-Allegheny frontier within fifteen years of settlement. The *Rocky Mountain News* was published in Denver six months after the first settlers arrived. In the colonial communities, sixty years elapsed before their twenty-four-foot-wide thoroughfares were identified with street signs and lighted at night. Denver performed these civic responsibilities for its eighty-foot-wide streets within thirteen years.

Denver, unlike many other settlements, was founded with the stated intention of creating a city and was fortunate in being led by experienced and civic-minded founders. Although the details might differ, the general outline of Denver's history is similar to the histories of other cities founded on the Great Plains and in the West during the late 1800's. Stanley Zamonski summed up the achievement of Denver's early proprietors:

> They had given birth, at the foot of the Rockies, to a lusty, squawling, infant city. The howling baby had teethed on a six-shooter and nursed on a whiskey bottle, and had learned to crawl over floods and under flying bullets. . . . Already the child could stand on wobby legs.[10]

[10]Zamonski and Keller. *The Fifty-Niners,* pp. 269–270.

## SUGGESTED READINGS

Bancroft, Caroline. *Silver Queen: The Fabulous Story of Baby Doe Tabor.* Johnson Publishing Co.

Bancroft, Caroline. *The Unsinkable Mrs. Brown.* Johnson Publishing Co.

Bridenbaugh, Carl. *Cities in the Wilderness: Urban Life in America, 1625-1742.* G. P. Putnam's Sons, Capricorn Books.

Feitz, Leland. *Cripple Creek: A Quick History of the World's Greatest Gold Camp.* Golden Bell.

Glaab, Charles N. *The American City: A Documentary History.* Dorsey Press.

Green, Constance M. *American Cities in the Growth of the Nation.* Harper & Row, Colophon Books.

Mumford, Lewis. *The City in History: Its Origins, Its Transformations, and Its Prospects.* Harcourt Brace Jovanovich, Harbinger Books.

Riegel, Robert E. *The Story of the Western Railroads: From 1852 Through the Reign of the Giants.* University of Nebraska Press, Bison Books.

Wade, Richard. *The Urban Frontier: Pioneer Life in Early Pittsburgh, Cincinnati, Lexington, Louisville, and St. Louis.* University of Chicago Press, Phoenix Books.

# BIBLIOGRAPHY

## Chapter One

Babcock, C. Merton, ed. *The American Frontier: A Social and Literary Record.* New York: Holt, Rinehart & Winston, 1965.

Billington, Ray Allen. *America's Frontier Heritage.* New York: Holt, Rinehart & Winston, 1967.

Billington, Ray Allen. *Frederick Jackson Turner.* New York: Oxford University Press, 1973.

Billington, Ray Allen. *Westward Expansion: A History of the American Frontier.* New York: Macmillan Co., 1960.

Clark, Thomas D. *Frontier America: The Story of the Westward Movement.* 2nd ed. New York: Charles Scribner's Sons, 1969.

Craven, Avery. "Frederick Jackson Turner." In *Marcus W. Jernegan Essays in American Historiography,* edited by William T. Hutchinson. New York: Russell & Russell, 1958.

Curti, Merle E. *The Making of an American Community: A Case Study of Democracy in a Frontier County.* Stanford, Calif.: Stanford University Press, 1969.

Hacker, Louis M. "Sections or Classes." *The Nation,* 26 July 1933.

Hofstadter, Richard. "Turner and the Frontier Myth." *The American Scholar* 18, no. 4 (1949).

Hofstadter, Richard, and Lipset, Seymour M., eds. *Turner and the Sociology of the Frontier.* New York: Basic Books, 1968.

Jacobs, Wilbur. "Frederick Jackson Turner." *The American West* 1, no. 1 (1964).

Jacobs, Wilbur. *The Historical World of Frederick Jackson Turner.* New Haven, Conn.: Yale University Press, 1970.

Jacobs, Wilbur, et al. *Turner, Bolton, and Webb: Three Historians of the American Frontier.* Seattle: University of Washington Press, 1965.

Noble, David W. *Historians Against History: The Frontier Thesis and the National Covenant in American Historical Writing Since 1830.* Minneapolis: University of Minnesota Press, 1965.

Pierson, George Wilson. "The Frontier and American Institutions." *New England Quarterly* 15 (June 1942).

Potter, David M. *People of Plenty: Economic Abundance and the American Character.* Chicago: University of Chicago Press, 1954.

Richmond, Robert W., and Mardock, Robert W., eds. *A Nation Moving West: Readings in the History of the American Frontier.* Lincoln: University of Nebraska Press, 1966.

Riegel, Robert E., and Athearn, R. G. *America Moves West.* 4th ed. New York: Holt, Rinehart & Winston, 1964.

Taylor, George R., ed. *The Turner Thesis Concerning the Role of the Frontier in American History.* Boston: D. C. Heath, 1956.

Turner, Frederick Jackson. *Frederick Jackson Turner's Legacy: Unpublished Writings in American History.* Edited by Wilbur Jacobs. San Marino, Calif.: Huntington Library, 1966.

Turner, Frederick Jackson. *Frontier and Section: Selected Essays.* Edited by Ray Allen Billington. Englewood Cliffs, N. J.: Prentice-Hall, 1961.

Turner, Frederick Jackson. "Sections and Nation." *The Yale Review* 12 (October 1922): 1–21.

Wayman, Walker D., and Kroeber, Clifton B. *The Frontier in Perspective.* Milwaukee: University of Wisconsin Press, 1957.

Wish, Harvey. *The American Historian.* New York: Oxford University Press, 1960.

Wright, Benjamin F. "Political Institutions and the Frontier." In *Sources of Culture in the Middle West,* edited by Dixon Ryan Fox. New York: Appleton-Century-Crofts, 1934.

## Chapter Two

*The American Heritage Book of Indians.* New York: American Heritage, 1961.

Andrist, Ralph K. *The Long Death.* New York: Macmillan Co., 1964.

*Black Elk Speaks, Being the Life Story of a Holy Man of the Oglala Sioux.* As told through John G. Neihardt (Flaming Rainbow). Lincoln: University of Nebraska Press, 1961.

Brown, Dee. *Bury My Heart at Wounded Knee: An Indian History of the American West.* New York: Bantam Books, 1972.

Custer, George Armstrong. *My Life on the Plains.* Edited by Milo Milton Quaife. Lincoln: University of Nebraska Press, 1971.

Dodge, Richard. *Our Wild Indians: Thirty-Three Years' Personal Experience Among the Red Men of the Great West.* New York: Archer House, 1956.

Gibson, Arrell M. *The Chickasaws.* Norman: University of Oklahoma Press, 1971.

Guinn, Jack. "The Red Man's Last Struggle." *Empire* Magazine. *The Denver Post*, 1966.

Haines, Francis. "Horses for Western Indians." *The American West* 2, no. 2 (1966).

Hassrick, Royal B., et al. *The Sioux: Life and Customs of a Warrior Society.* Norman: University of Oklahoma Press, 1964.

Hyde, George E. *Red Cloud's Folk: A History of the Oglala Sioux.* Rev. ed. Norman: University of Oklahoma Press, 1957.

Hyde, George E. *Spotted Tail's Folk: A History of the Brulé Sioux.* Norman: University of Oklahoma Press, 1961.

*Indians of the Americas.* Washington, D.C.: National Geographic Society, 1955.

Josephy, Alvin M., Jr. *The Indian Heritage of America.* New York: Bantam Books, 1969.

La Farge, Oliver. *A Pictorial History of the American Indian.* New York: Crown, 1956.

Lowie, Robert H. *Indians of the Plains.* New York: Natural History Press, 1963.

Mayer, Frank H., and Roth, Charles B. *The Last of the Buffalo Hunters.* Chicago: The Swallow Press, 1972.

Miller, David H. *The Ghost Dance.* New York: Duell, Sloan & Pearce, 1959.

Prucha, Francis Paul. *Americanizing the American Indians: Writings by the Friends of the Indian, 1880–1900.* Cambridge: Harvard University Press, 1973.

Underhill, Ruth M. *The Red Man's America: A History of the Indians in the United States.* Chicago: University of Chicago Press, 1953.

Underhill, Ruth M. *The Red Man's Religion: Beliefs and Practices of the Indians North of Mexico.* Chicago: University of Chicago Press, 1965.

Utley, Robert M. *The Last of the Sioux Nation.* New Haven, Conn.: Yale University Press, 1963.

Ware, Eugene F. *The Indian War of 1894.* Lincoln: University of Nebraska Press, 1963.

Webb, Walter Prescott. *The Great Plains.* Waltham, Mass.: Blaisdell, 1959.

Weltfish, Gene. *The Lost Universe.* New York: Ballantine Books, 1971.

## Chapter Three

Beckwourth, James P. *The Life and Adventures of James P. Beckwourth.* New York: Harper, 1856.

Billington, Ray Allen. *The Far Western Frontier: 1830–1860.* New York: Harper & Row, 1956.

Bingham, Edwin R. *The Fur Trade in the West.* Boston: D. C. Heath, 1960.

Chittenden, Hiram. *The Fur Trade of the Far West.* San Francisco: Academic Reprints, 1954.

Cleland, Robert. *This Reckless Breed of Men: The Trappers and Fur Traders of the Southwest.* New York: Alfred A. Knopf, 1950.

De Voto, Bernard. *Across the Wide Missouri.* Boston: Houghton Mifflin, 1947.

De Voto, Bernard, ed. *The Journals of Lewis and Clark.* Boston: Houghton Mifflin, 1953.

Favour, Alpheus Hoyt. *Old Bill Williams, Mountain Man.* Norman: University of Oklahoma Press, 1962.

Field, Matthew C. *Matt Field on the Santa Fe Trail.* Norman: University of Oklahoma Press, 1960.

Garrard, Lewis H. *Wah-To-Yah and the Taos Trail.* Norman: University of Oklahoma Press, 1955.

Garst, Doris. *Jim Bridger: Greatest of the Mountain Men.* Boston: Houghton Mifflin, 1952.

Gregg, Josiah. *Commerce of the Prairies.* Edited by Milo Milton Quaife. Lincoln: University of Nebraska Press, 1967.

Hafen, LeRoy. *The Mountain Men and the Fur Trade.* 8 vols. Glendale, Calif.: Arthur H. Clark, 1965–1969.

Lavender, David. *Bent's Fort.* Garden City, N. Y.: Doubleday, 1954.

Lavender, David. *The Fist in the Wilderness.* Garden City, N. Y.: Doubleday, 1964.

Lavender, David. *The Trail to Santa Fe.* Boston: Houghton Mifflin, 1958.

Lent, Geneva D. *West of the Mountains.* Seattle: University of Washington Press, 1963.

Leonard, Zenas. *The Adventures of Zenas Leonard, Fur Trader.* Edited by John C. Ewers. Norman: University of Oklahoma Press, 1959.

Mayer, Frank H., and Roth, Charles B. *The Buffalo Harvest.* Chicago: Swallow Press, Sage Books, 1958.

Morgan, Dale L. *Jedediah Smith and the Opening of the West.* Lincoln: University of Nebraska Press, 1953.

Oglesby, Richard. *Manuel Lisa and the Opening of the Missouri Fur Trade.* Norman: University of Oklahoma Press, 1963.

Phillips, Paul C., and Smurr, J. W. *The Fur Trade.* 2 vols. Norman: University of Oklahoma Press, 1961.

Porter, Mae Reed, and Davenport, Odessa. *Scotsman in Buckskin.* New York: Hastings House, 1963.

Rawling, Gerald. *The Pathfinders.* New York: Macmillan Co., 1964.

Ross, Alexander. *The Fur Hunters of the Far West.* Norman: University of Oklahoma Press, 1956.

Russell, Osborne. *Journal of a Trapper.* Portland: Oregon Historical Society.

Ruxton, George F. *Life in the Far West.* Norman: University of Oklahoma Press, 1959.

Sandoz, Mari. *The Beaver Men.* New York: Hastings House, 1964.

Vestal, Stanley. *Kit Carson, the Happy Warrior of the Old West.* Boston: Houghton Mifflin, 1928.

**Chapter Four**

Angle, Paul, ed. *The American Reader.* Chicago: Rand McNally, 1958.

Billington, Ray Allen. *The Far Western Frontier: 1830–1860.* New York: Harper & Row, 1956.

Bingham, Edwin R., ed. *California Gold.* Boston: D. C. Heath, 1959.

Borah, Woodrow W. "The California Mission." In *Ethnic Conflict in California History,* edited by Charles Wollenberg. Los Angeles: Tinnon-Brown, 1970.

Cook, Sherburne F. "The California Indian and Anglo-American Culture." In *Ethnic Conflict in California History,* edited by Charles Wollenberg. Los Angeles: Tinnon-Brown, 1970.

Fritz, Percy S. *Colorado, the Centennial State.* New York: Prentice-Hall, 1941.

Greever, William S. *Bonanza West, the Story of the Western Mining Rushes, 1848–1900.* Norman: University of Oklahoma Press, 1968.

Hafen, LeRoy R. and Ann W., eds. *Journals of Forty-Niners.* Glendale, Calif.: Arthur H. Clark, 1954.

Hine, Robert V., and Bingham, Edwin R. *The Frontier Experience.* Belmont, Calif.: Wadsworth, 1963.

Kroeber, Theodora. *Ishi in Two Worlds: A Biography of the Last Wild Indian in North America.* Berkeley: University of California Press, 1970.

Lingenfelter, Richard E. *The Hardrock Miners: A History of the Mining Movement in the American West, 1863–1893.* Berkeley: University of California Press, 1974.

Lotchin, Roger. *San Francisco, 1846–1856: From Hamlet to City.* New York: Oxford University Press, 1974.

Marryat, Frank. *Mountains and Molehills.* Philadelphia: J. B. Lippincott, 1962.

Paul, Rodman W. *Mining Frontiers of the Far West, 1848–1880.* New York: Holt, Rinehart & Winston, 1963.

Perkin, Robert L. *The First Hundred Years.* Garden City, N. Y.: Doubleday, 1959.

Peters, Harry T. *California on Stone.* Garden City, N. Y.: Doubleday, 1935.

Pitt, Leonard. *The Decline of the Californios: A Social History of the Spanish-Speaking Californians, 1846–1890.* Berkeley: University of California Press, 1970.

Potter, David M., ed. *The Trail to California: The Overland Journal of Vincent Geiger and Wakeman Bryarly.* New Haven, Conn.: Yale University Press, 1962.

Shinn, Charles Howard. *Mining Camps, a Study in American Frontier Government.* New York: Harper & Row, 1965.

Smith, Duane A. *Rocky Mountain Mining Camps: The Urban Frontier.* Bloomington: Indiana University Press, 1967.

Stone, Irving. *Men to Match My Mountains: The Story of the Opening of the Far West, 1840–1900.* Garden City, N. Y.: Doubleday, 1956.

## Chapter Five

Adams, Andy. *The Log of a Cowboy: A Narrative of the Old Trail Days.* Lincoln: University of Nebraska Press, 1964.

Adams, Ramon F. "A Cowman's Philosophy." *The American West* 2, no. 4 (1965).

Adams, Ramon F. *Western Words: A Dictionary of the American West.* Norman: University of Oklahoma Press, 1944.

Atherton, Lewis. *The Cattle Kings.* Bloomington: Indiana University Press, 1961.

Bronson, Edgar B. *Reminiscences of a Ranchman.* Lincoln: University of Nebraska Press, 1962.

Clay, John. *My Life on the Range.* Norman: University of Oklahoma Press, 1962.

Collinson, Frank. *Life in the Saddle.* Edited by Mary Wheatley Clark. Norman: University of Oklahoma Press, 1963.

Dale, Edward Everett. *The Range Cattle Industry: Ranching on the Great Plains from 1865 to 1925.* Norman: University of Oklahoma Press, 1960.

Dick, Everett. *Vanguards of the Frontier: A Social History of the Northern Plains and Rocky Mountains from the Fur Traders to the Sod Busters.* Lincoln: University of Nebraska Press, 1965.

Dobie, J. Frank. *Cow People.* Boston: Little, Brown, 1964.

Dobie, J. Frank. *The Longhorns.* New York: Grosset & Dunlap, 1941.

Drago, Harry Sinclair. *Great American Cattle Trails.* New York: Dodd, Mead, 1965.

Durham, Philip, and Jones, Everett L. *The Negro Cowboys.* New York: Dodd, Mead, 1965.

Dykstra, Robert. *The Cattle Towns.* New York: Alfred A. Knopf, 1968.

Frantz, Joe B., and Choate, Julian E., Jr. *The American Cowboy: The Myth and the Reality.* Norman: University of Oklahoma Press, 1955.

Gressley, Gene M. *Bankers and Cattlemen.* New York: Alfred A. Knopf, 1966.

Haley, J. Evetts. *The XIT Ranch of Texas and the Early Days of the Llano Estacado.* Norman: University of Oklahoma Press, 1967.

Lambert, Neal. "A Cowboy Writes to Owen Wister." *The American West* 2, no. 4 (1965).

Lea, Tom. *The King Ranch.* 2 vols. Boston: Little, Brown, 1957.

Mothershead, Harmon. *The Swan Land & Cattle Company, Ltd.* Norman: University of Oklahoma Press, 1971.

Osgood, Ernest Staples. *The Day of the Cattleman.* Chicago: University of Chicago Press, 1957.

Rojas, Arnold R. "The Vaquero." *The American West* 1, no. 2 (1964).

Russell, Charles M. *Trails Plowed Under.* Garden City, N. Y.: Doubleday, 1953.

Sandoz, Mari. *The Cattlemen.* New York: Hastings House, 1958.

Streeter, Floyd Benjamin. *Prairie Trails and Cow Towns.* New York: Devin-Adair, 1963.

Tinker, Edward Larocque. *The Horsemen of the Americas and the Literature They Inspired.* New York: Hastings House, 1953.

Ulph, Owen C. "Cowhands, Cow Horses, and Cows." *The American West* 3, no. 1 (1966).

Ulph, Owen C. "Literature and the American West." *The American West* 1, no. 1 (1964).

Webb, Walter Prescott. *The Great Plains.* Waltham, Mass.: Blaisdell, 1959.

**Chapter Six**

*The American Heritage History of the Great West.* New York: American Heritage, 1965.

Barry, Louise. *The Beginning of the West.* Topeka: Kansas State Historical Society, 1972.

Billington, Ray Allen. *Westward Expansion: A History of the American Frontier.* New York: Macmillan Co., 1960.

Buley, R. C. *The Old Northwest.* 2 vols. Bloomington: Indiana University Press, 1950.

Carstensen, Vernon. *Farmer Discontent: 1865–1900.* New York: John Wiley & Sons, 1974.

Caruso, John. *The Great Lakes Frontier.* Indianapolis: Bobbs-Merrill, 1961.

*Chimney Rock.* Washington, D. C.: National Park Service, U. S. Department of the Interior, 1966.

Chittenden, Hiram, and Richardson, Alfred. *The Life, Letters and Travels of Father Pierre-Jean De Smet.* New York: F. P. Harper, 1905.

Clark, Thomas D. *Frontier America: The Story of the Westward Movement.* 2nd ed. New York: Charles Scribner's Sons, 1969.

Coons, Frederica, *The Trail to Oregon.* Portland, Ore.: Binfords & Mort, 1954.

Danker, Donald. "Nebraska's Homemade Windmills." *The American West* 3, no. 1 (1966).

De Voto, Bernard. *The Year of Decision: 1846.* Boston: Houghton Mifflin, 1942.

Dick, Everett, *The Sod-House Frontier, 1854–1890.* Lincoln, Neb.: Johnsen Publishing Co., 1954.

Eaton, Herbert. *The Overland Trail to California in 1852.* New York: G. P. Putnam's Sons, 1974.

Ellis, William D. *The Cuyahoga.* Rivers of America Series. New York: Holt, Rinehart & Winston, 1967.

Erdman, Loula. "The Devil's Hatband." *The American West* 2, no. 1 (1965).

Fite, Gilbert. *The Farmer's Frontier, 1865–1900.* New York: Holt, Rinehart & Winston, 1966.

Gates, Paul W. *The Farmer's Age.* New York: Harper & Row, 1960.

Ghent, William. *The Road to Oregon, a Chronicle of the Great Emigrant Trail.* New York: Longmans, Green, 1929.

Gregg, J. R. *A History of the Oregon Trail.* Portland, Ore.: Binfords & Mort, 1955.

Gudde, Erwin G., and Elizabeth K., eds. *From St. Louis to Sutter's Fort, 1846: The Journal of Heinrich Lienhard.* Norman: University of Oklahoma Press, 1961.

Havighurst, Walter. *The Heartland: Ohio, Indiana, Illinois.* New York: Harper & Row, 1962.

Hayter, Earl. *The Troubled Farmer.* DeKalb: Northern Illinois University Press, 1968.

Hine, Robert V., and Bingham, Edwin R. *The Frontier Experience.* Belmont, Calif.: Wadsworth, 1963.

James, Alfred. *The Ohio Company.* Pittsburgh: University of Pittsburgh Press, 1959.

Jones, Evan. *Citadel in the Wilderness.* New York: Coward-McCann, 1966.

Keller, George. *A Trip Across the Plains.* Oakland, Calif.: Biobooks, 1955.

Kraenzel, Carl F. *The Great Plains in Transition.* Norman: University of Oklahoma Press, 1955.

Lamar, Howard R. *The Far Southwest, 1846–1912: A Territorial History.* New Haven: Yale University Press, 1966.

Lavender, David. *Westward Vision: The Story of the Oregon Trail.* New York: McGraw-Hill, 1963.

McCallum, Henry D. and Frances T. *The Wire That Fenced the West.* Norman: University of Oklahoma Press, 1965.

McGlashan, Charles F. *The History of the Donner Party: A Tragedy of the Sierra.* Rev. ed. Stanford, Calif.: Stanford University Press, 1947.

McKee, Russell. *Great Lakes Country.* New York: Thomas Y. Crowell, 1966.

Paden, Irene. *The Wake of the Prairie Schooner.* New York: Macmillan Co., 1943.

Parkman, Francis. *The Oregon Trail.* New York: New American Library, 1964.

Richmond, Robert W., and Mardock, Robert W., eds. *A Nation Moving West: Readings in the History of the American Frontier.* Lincoln: University of Nebraska Press, 1966.

Ridge, Martin. "Why They Went West." *The American West* 1, no. 3 (1964).

Robertson, Frank. *Fort Hall: Gateway to Oregon Country.* New York: Hastings House, 1963.

Ruede, Howard. *Sod-House Days, 1877-1878.* New York: Cooper Square, 1966.

Schmitt, Martin F., and Brown, Dee. *The Settler's West.* New York: Charles Scribner's Sons, 1955.

Shannon, Fred A. *The Farmer's Last Frontier, 1860-1897.* New York: Harper & Row, 1968.

Smith, Henry Nash. *Virgin Land.* Cambridge: Harvard University Press, 1970.

Spaulding, Kenneth A., ed. *On the Oregon Trail: The Diary of Robert Stuart.* Norman: University of Oklahoma Press, 1953.

Stewart, Elinore P. *Letters of a Woman Homesteader.* Lincoln: University of Nebraska Press, 1961.

Udell, John. *The Journal of John Udell.* New Haven, Conn.: Yale University Press, 1952.

Walker, Henry. *The Wagonmasters: High Plains Freighting from the Earliest Days of the Santa Fe Trail to 1880.* Norman: University of Oklahoma Press, 1966.

Webb, Walter Prescott. *The Great Plains.* Waltham, Mass.: Blaisdell, 1959.

### Chapter Seven

Anderson, George. *Colorado Railroad Building, 1870-1880.* Colorado Springs: Colorado College, 1936.

Bancroft, Caroline. *Mile High Denver.* Lakewood, Colo.: Golden Press, 1952.

Barney, Libeus. *Letters of the Pikes Peak Gold Rush.* San Jose, Calif.: Talisman Press, 1959.

Brettell, Richard. *Historic Denver.* Denver: Historic Denver, Inc., 1973.

Bridenbaugh, Carl. *Cities in the Wilderness.* New York: Alfred A. Knopf, 1955.

Brown, Dee. *Bury My Heart at Wounded Knee: An Indian History of the American West.* New York: Bantam Books, 1972.

Fowler, Gene. *Timber Line.* Garden City, N. Y.: Doubleday, 1956.

Glaab, Charles N. *The American City: A Documentary History.* Homewood, Ill.: Dorsey Press, 1963.

Green, Constance M. *American Cities in the Growth of the Nation.* New York: Harper & Row, 1957.

Kohl, Edith. *Denver's Historic Mansions.* Chicago: Swallow Press, Sage Books, 1957.

McKelvey, Blake. *The Urbanization of America, 1860–1915.* New Brunswick, N. J.: Rutgers University Press, 1963.

Mumey, Nolie. *Clark, Gruber and Company: A Pioneer Denver Mint.* Denver: Artcraft Press, 1950.

Mumey, Nolie. *A History of the Early Settlement of Denver.* Glendale, Calif.: Arthur H. Clark, 1942.

Mumford, Lewis. *The City in History.* New York: Harcourt, Brace & World, 1961.

Perkin, Robert L. *The First Hundred Years.* Garden City, N. Y.: Doubleday, 1959.

Schlesinger, Arthur M. *The Rise of the City, 1878–1898.* New York: Macmillan Co., 1933.

Smiley, Jerome. *History of Denver.* Denver: Times and Sun Publishing Co., 1901.

Smith, Duane A. *Rocky Mountain Mining Camps: The Urban Frontier.* Bloomington: Indiana University Press, 1967.

Vickers, William. *History of Denver.* Chicago: Buskin, 1880.

Wade, Richard. *The Urban Frontier: The Rise of Western Cities, 1780–1830.* Cambridge: Harvard University Press, 1959.

Wharton, Junius. *History of the City of Denver.* Denver: Byers, 1866.

Zamonski, Stanley, and Keller, Teddy. *The Fifty-Niners.* Chicago: Swallow Press, Sage Books, 1961.

# INDEX